CAMBRIDGE LIBRARY COLLECTION

Books of enduring scholarly value

History

The books reissued in this series include accounts of historical events and movements by eye-witnesses and contemporaries, as well as landmark studies that assembled significant source materials or developed new historiographical methods. The series includes work in social, political and military history on a wide range of periods and regions, giving modern scholars ready access to influential publications of the past.

Founded Upon the Seas

Sir Walter Oakeshott was a British scholar who is best known as the discoverer of the Winchester Manuscript of Malory's *Morte d'Arthur* while he was an assistant master at Winchester College. He later became Rector of Lincoln College, and Vice-Chancellor of the University of Oxford from 1962 to 1964. Oakeshott had a scholarly interest in Elizabethan exploration, which he examines in this volume, first published in 1942. He describes the military and exploratory achievements of the Elizabethan and Stuart navy, including attempts to find the Northwest Passage, the settlement of Virginia and the defeat of the Spanish Armada. Oakeshott also discusses the role of Renaissance thought and contemporary politics in these achievements, through changes in naval tactics and advances in cartography. The personalities of leading explorers including Sir Francis Drake, Sir John Hawkins and Sir Walter Raleigh are also vividly described in this clear and concise historical account.

Cambridge University Press has long been a pioneer in the reissuing of out-of-print titles from its own backlist, producing digital reprints of books that are still sought after by scholars and students but could not be reprinted economically using traditional technology. The Cambridge Library Collection extends this activity to a wider range of books which are still of importance to researchers and professionals, either for the source material they contain, or as landmarks in the history of their academic discipline.

Drawing from the world-renowned collections in the Cambridge University Library, and guided by the advice of experts in each subject area, Cambridge University Press is using state-of-the-art scanning machines in its own Printing House to capture the content of each book selected for inclusion. The files are processed to give a consistently clear, crisp image, and the books finished to the high quality standard for which the Press is recognised around the world. The latest print-on-demand technology ensures that the books will remain available indefinitely, and that orders for single or multiple copies can quickly be supplied.

The Cambridge Library Collection will bring back to life books of enduring scholarly value (including out-of-copyright works originally issued by other publishers) across a wide range of disciplines in the humanities and social sciences and in science and technology.

Founded Upon the Seas

A Narrative of some English Maritime and Overseas Enterprises during the Period 1550 to 1616

WALTER OAKESHOTT

CAMBRIDGE
UNIVERSITY PRESS

CAMBRIDGE UNIVERSITY PRESS

Cambridge, New York, Melbourne, Madrid, Cape Town, Singapore,
São Paolo, Delhi, Dubai, Tokyo, Mexico City

Published in the United States of America by Cambridge University Press, New York

www.cambridge.org
Information on this title: www.cambridge.org/9781108013420

This edition first published 1942
This digitally printed version 2010

ISBN 978-1-108-01342-0 Paperback

FOUNDED UPON THE SEAS

CAMBRIDGE
UNIVERSITY PRESS
LONDON: BENTLEY HOUSE
NEW YORK TORONTO BOMBAY
CALCUTTA MADRAS: MACMILLAN

I. QUEEN ELIZABETH, aged 59

(The Ditchley portrait, now in the National Portrait Gallery)

FOUNDED UPON THE SEAS

A Narrative of
Some English Maritime and Overseas Enterprises
during the period
1550 to 1616

BY

WALTER OAKESHOTT

"Alwaies obedience to be used and practised by al persons in their degrees, not only for duetie and conscience sake towards God, under whose mercifull hand navigants above all other creatures naturally bee most nigh,..., but also for prudent and worldly pollicie, and publike weale."
Instructions for the intended voyage to Cathay, compiled by the most worshipful Sebastian Cabot Esquire; in Hakluyt.

CAMBRIDGE
AT THE UNIVERSITY PRESS
1942

PRINTED IN GREAT BRITAIN

Contents

IN MEMORIAM

P. M.

Preface

This book, which has no pretensions to original scholarship, was begun after the evacuation from Dunkirk, and was written mainly during the following winter. It was suggested by a speech made by the First Lord of the Admiralty on the work of the Royal Navy and of the Merchant Navy. When Mr Alexander spoke, the transfer of fifty American destroyers to the navy of the allied nations had just taken place. The maritime achievements of the Elizabethan and early Stuart period, part of the shared inheritance of the English-speaking peoples—an inheritance in very truth, to use the Psalmist's phrase, founded upon the seas—had for many years been an inspiration to me; and it seemed that the story of some of them might at this time be of interest to others, and that to write it was in any event the only tribute I could pay to the successors of Drake and Hawkins and Ralegh and of the crews who made their enterprises possible. Recent events were therefore never very far from my mind as I wrote the book, though I have tried to keep references to them from unduly obtruding into it.

To attempt to cover much of the same ground as is covered by Froude's brilliant *English Seamen in the Sixteenth Century* is a rash undertaking. But that book, if it is brilliant, is partisan. It contains some obvious misstatements, and in the background the lines of the Reformation are perhaps too prominent while those of the Renaissance hardly appear. I cannot hope to have avoided mistakes at a time when access to reference books has not been easy, and could wish that there was any likelihood of my narrative being as readable as his. But the work of scholars such as Sir Julian Corbett, Dr J. A. Williamson, Professor V. T. Harlow and Professor E. G. R. Taylor (to name four only of those whose books I have found invaluable) has made it possible in some respects at any rate to get nearer the truth than did Froude. I have generally written however with some of the original documents rather than the books of modern scholars at my hand, though often more than one of those which ought to have been consulted was not available. Where I had an original edition to work with or where the modern reprint gave the original spelling, that has been retained. But often I have had to use modern spelling because that was the spelling of the reprint used and because it was impossible to get at the books or letters themselves.

My thanks are due to the Warden and Fellows of Winchester for permission to reproduce the map of the Northern Regions from Mercator's great Atlas (Pl. III). It was access in Winchester College Library to the Renaissance and Elizabethan editions of the books and atlases concerned—to the 1600 edition of Hakluyt, for instance, to Hariot's *Virginia*, to the 1625 Purchas and the splendid Ulm Ptolemy of 1486—that first made this phase of history alive for me. Mrs Schwerdt has generously given leave for the reproduction of an illustration in a manuscript from her husband's library that has not before been published and is a contemporary sketch by someone who took part in Drake's expedition to the Caribbean (Pl. VI). I owe Pls. II and IV to the courtesy of Messrs Maggs, and to Mr Frank Maggs a very great debt for putting his wide knowledge of cartography unreservedly at my disposal and for finding early maps and charts by which in more than one instance difficulties have been explained. The Master and Fellows of Magdalene College, Cambridge, have given leave for the reproduction of what is probably a picture of the first 'Ark Royal' (Pl. XI), and Mr H. T. Pledge, Librarian of the Science Museum, kindly secured a print of the photograph for me, which I should not otherwise have obtained. Thanks are due also to the Trustees of the British Museum for Pl. VIII, to the Trustees of the National Portrait Gallery for Pls. I and VII, and to the National Maritime Museum for Pls. X and XII. Mr Charles Mitchell, of that Museum (at present of the Admiralty), has given me help in many details as regards both text and illustrations. And he has given me permission to dedicate my book to the memory of his wife Prudence Mitchell, with whom the plan of it was discussed, but who was killed in an air raid on London in 1940. If she had lived, her taste and judgment would have made the book a better one.

Many other people have helped me directly and indirectly, and it is not possible to name them all. Mr C. E. R. Clarabut read the whole book in typescript, and almost all the suggestions he made have been adopted. Dr Thomas Wood read the proofs and saved me from some at any rate of the pitfalls that beset a landsman's path in attempting this kind of narrative. Mr A. B. Cook also read the proofs, and he and others of my present and former colleagues and pupils have helped in many different ways. My thanks are due to all of those who have done so.

No attempt has been made in the notes to list fully the many modern books that have been used—such as Professor Neale's *Queen Elizabeth*, or Mr A. L. Rowse's *Sir Richard Grenville*—but it seemed desirable to give there some indication of the main sources used for each chapter, more especially the original accounts and the maps that have helped to throw light on them. A long-standing interest in the maps of the period may have made it possible here and there to give a clearer account of a particular incident than has been given before.

Any author's profits that the book may make during the war will be paid to the funds of the Training Ship 'Arethusa'. It is a privilege to be allowed to offer this token of gratitude to an institution that is doing fine work for the Navy.

WALTER OAKESHOTT

ST PAUL'S SCHOOL
MAY 1942

List of Illustrations

WITH NOTES

This portrait of the queen is an allegorical conceit painted to commemorate her visit to Sir Henry Lee at Ditchley in 1592. As the fragmentary and still incompletely interpreted sonnet on the right indicates, the sun on the one hand and the thunderous sky on the other are emblems of the queen's divine grace and power. The ocean encompassing the map of England on which she stands is identified with the queen to whom, as rivers their waters to the ocean, her subjects return their gratitude:

'Rivers of thanks still to that oc(ean flow)
Where grace is grace above, power p(ower below).'

National Portrait Gallery.

Part of the so-called 'Admiral's Map', which has been attributed to Columbus, and which is closely connected with a chart drawn by Juan de la Cosa about 1502 (reproduced in Dr Williamson's *Voyages of the Cabots*). Greenland is marked as a peninsula of Europe, and the coast line west of it is that discovered by Cabot. This had not yet been brought into relation with the other American discoveries, and in this map is shown considerably further east than it ought to be, almost certainly to favour the Portuguese claim to it (cf. pp. 19, 20; also p. 15 for the division between Portuguese and Spanish claims to the newly discovered lands). From an atlas in the possession of Messrs Maggs.

Mercator's map of the North Polar regions; to illustrate the sixteenth-century conceptions of the North-East and North-West Passages. The northern part of Scotland is at the very foot of the map, China in the upper right-hand corner, and Asia is shown divided from America by the Strait of Anian. Off North Cape 'Sir Hugo Willoughbie's land' (see p. 191) is marked, and south-west of Iceland the large (but entirely imaginary) island of Frisland (see p. 13), of which there is also an inset map. The magnetic pole is marked as an island off the coast of Northern China. The map marks Davis Strait, and must therefore be after 1585. Mercator died in 1594. From the copy of Mercator's Atlas in Winchester College Library.

Map of Russia, drawn by Antony Jenkinson in 1562. This map is one of the first-fruits of the Russian discoveries, and the detail shows how interest extended south-eastwards towards Persia and in the direction of the land routes to China. From a copy in the possession of Messrs Maggs.

An eighteenth-century manuscript chart of the approaches to Vera Cruz, opposite which is the island of St Juan de Ulua. This island is shown on the south-western side of a shoal (marked N on the chart) immediately opposite the city—not yet built in Hawkins' time. The chart shows that the normal approach to the anchorage was from the north-west, not by the south-east channel. Sacrifice Island, where Hawkins took shelter the night following the battle, lies towards the right-hand edge of the chart (marked H). Unfortunately there is a break in the chart over the actual island of St Juan, but it shows the lie of the coast and gives the soundings of the channels.

Plan of Nombre de Dios, from a manuscript book of pictures done at the time of Drake's attack. The picture is an imaginary one, since the three ships never lay off Nombre de Dios in this way. As compared with the Brueghel ship (Pl. X) these three show in the stern the characteristic horizontal lines that their English shipbuilders gave them, and even in a slight sketch of this kind their graceful character can be appreciated. In the background is shown the treasure road leading away towards Panama. Reproduced from the MS. in the possession of Mrs Schwerdt.

This engraving, made to commemorate Drake's circumnavigation, is a genuine likeness, done from the life. Through the window may be seen a prospect of the small port of Plymouth, from which Drake set out and to which he returned, contrasting with the vast spaces of the globe which hangs in the embrasure. The plate, left unfinished by the original engraver, was touched up in the eighteenth century by the patriotic engraver and antiquary George Vertue. National Portrait Gallery.

Plan of Carthagena, from the *Summarie and True Discourse of Sir Francis Drake's West Indian Voyage*. For a note on this plan, see p. 194. Reproduced from a copy in the British Museum.

An eighteenth-century manuscript plan of Cadiz harbour. Opposite Cadiz is St Mary Port (p. 114). The rocks known as Las Puercas (p. 115) lie immediately north of Cadiz and are marked R on the plan. Puerto Real, in the inner harbour, is marked G. The main force of galleys was drawn up under cover of the Cadiz forts off the north-eastern side of the promontory. The shoal on which the 'Edward Bonaventure' went aground is presumably that shown on the plan east of the Puercas rocks, and marked S (also ringed). On Borough's own plan (reproduced in the Navy Records Society's *Spanish War*, 1585–7) the point she went aground is shown considerably further in, perhaps because if it had been given its true position it would have been clear how far out Borough himself had moved.

Brueghel's design of a Flemish man of war with topsails set running before the wind, along with the galley standing away on her larboard bow, illustrates the contrast between Mediterranean and oceanic seamanship. In the Mediterranean, where ships could normally run into port to escape stormy seas, the lightly-built galley—sometimes assisted by the wind but never reliant upon it—could be manœuvred by oars to bear down on her adversary from any quarter and ram him. Atlantic conditions fashioned another kind of naval architecture and different tactics: square-rigged ships with a high freeboard and armed with great guns. Fifteenth-century ships had carried light guns to train down on the enemy and assist or repel boarding parties; but the broadside with heavy pieces of artillery did not become a decisive weapon of sea-warfare until early sixteenth-century shipwrights ventured to cut gun-ports in the hulls of ships. Gun-ports along the whole broadside appeared about 1540: twenty-five years later, when Brueghel made his drawing, the age of ramming and boarding (in northern waters) was past and that of the broadside had begun. In ships very like these, with heavy guns stowed low and formidable stern-chasers, Elizabethan seamen worked out the tactics of oceanic warfare. Engraving by Frans Huys after Pieter Brueghel the elder; in the National Maritime Museum.

Among the manuscripts left by Samuel Pepys to his college, Magdalene College, Cambridge, was a treatise on *Ancient English Shipwrightry* by the Elizabethan shipbuilder Matthew Baker, illustrated by coloured draughts of ships, of which this is one. It shows the way in which the superstructure of an Elizabethan galleon was painted with a geometrical decoration in red, yellow, green, blue and mauve. This drawing has an added importance because it includes a sail-plan similar to that known to have been possessed by the 'Ark Royal'—Lord Howard of Effingham's flagship at the Armada, built as the 'Ark Ralegh' by Richard Chapman at Deptford for Sir Walter Ralegh in 1587. The identification is not beyond dispute; but Baker's drawing gives a much truer idea of what the 'Ark' looked like than the well-known commemorative woodcut in the British Museum. Because we associate Elizabethan ships with more or less crude engravings of them, we are apt to think of them as clumsy, cranky ships. As this drawing shows they were not: they were fast ships, with a clean sheer, low freeboard, a regular gun-deck and fine lines which enabled them to ride over the waves. From *Ancient English Shipwrightry*, Pepysian MSS., Magdalene College, Cambridge.

This tapestry of Sir Richard Grenville's hopeless action in the 'Revenge'—an isolated episode in Lord Thomas Howard's expedition against the home-coming Spanish trade off the Azores—was woven only seven years after the event. It depicts the 'Revenge' with her foremast gone by the board, beset by three Spanish ships. On her larboard quarter is an English ship, probably intended for the 'Pilgrim', commanded by Jacob Whiddon who, according to Ralegh, 'hovered all night to see the success, but in the morning, bearing with the "Revenge", was hunted like a hare amongst many ravenous hounds', and escaped destruction. The island in the background is Pico. From the collection of M. Hypolite Worms. Photograph from the National Maritime Museum.

Chapter I

NEW WORLDS FOR OLD

THERE are few things more interesting than the documents in which the great navigators of the Renaissance record their achievements. The implications are so new, and so far-reaching, that even the most matter of fact cannot help stirring the imagination. 'If we consider all these regions,' says the preface to the account of Amerigo Vespucci's voyage to Brazil in 1501, 'we must conclude certainly that they make another world, and it is not out of keeping therefore if I have called them the New World. The Greeks and Romans believed that southward from the equinoctial line there was nothing but limitless sea with a few scorched and desert islands. This opinion is now refuted by this voyage, which has proved to all that such a view is false.' It was a discovery that went to the head; and there is no wonder that some of the explorers' narratives are embellished with exaggerated or invented stories. But the truth when it became known proved stranger even than these fictions. The discoveries of Mexico and Peru, highly civilised societies cut off completely from the outside world, were the climax; and for more than a century afterwards, first in the myth of Eldorado which attracted Ralegh to his death, then in the story of Prester John in Africa, the expectation of yet newer worlds persisted, and became at length one of the most powerful themes of romantic writers.

In that great age of discovery and the recovery of ancient knowledge, all things, as it must have seemed, were being made new. In almost every department of thought it was the same story. Leonardo da Vinci, artist, inventor and thinker, was puzzling out the problems of mechanical movement and even of flight. In his dissecting rooms at Louvain and Padua, Vesalius was explaining the mechanisms of the human body, revealing the muscles and bones and assigning their functions to them. Machiavelli was dissecting, with ruthless clarity, the organism of the state, and politicians were making a new world of Europe, destroying the old cosmopolitan institutions and dealing the death blow to that cosmopolitan society of the Renaissance to which they themselves owed so much. No one was more certainly a child of the Renaissance than our own Henry VIII. Yet his brave new world was an England no longer part of Christendom, but master of its own destiny, and in planning it he turned his back on the cosmopolitan tradition to which he belonged. Few men were wise enough to see that there was something good in the old as well as in the new, and their Utopias (unlike Machiavelli's states, which were reality itself) were unfortunately too good to be true. 'The land of nowhere' Sir Thomas More called his imagined world, but even it was placed in a real setting beyond the Atlantic, and the description of it was put in the mouth of an aged sailor, one of those twenty-four men left behind in America by Amerigo Vespucci in 1504. No one who reads Amerigo's account of his voyages can doubt that the writer of *Utopia* had read it too. Not only are those twenty-four men part of actual history, but the description of Utopia follows closely the form that Amerigo had adopted in his own story. More had perhaps even heard rumours of the civilisation of the Incas, not yet fully revealed, in Peru, and some of his ideas of the good society may have been based on scraps of information from that untroubled kingdom of the philosophers, doomed to be a tragic victim, not so long after, of Europe's imperialists. More's mariner is, incidentally, a pioneer in another way also. He may be claimed as the first to circumnavigate the globe, for he is stated to have come back to Europe by way of India and Ceylon.[1]

In no science was the revolution of ideas greater than in the science of geography, or cosmography as the explorers themselves preferred to call it. Medieval conceptions of the world took a variety of forms. In some accounts of the universe the tradition that the world was round persisted, for the idea that the earth was a sphere had been generally accepted by the Greek and Roman geographers. An Englishman, John Holywood, wrote, as early as the thirteenth century, a treatise on the earth's spherical nature (*de Sphaera Mundi*). But this roundness was often interpreted in medieval times as that of a plate or disc, and one of the commonest forms of diagrammatic representation of the world was a circle with a T set within it, the horizontal stroke being a diameter and the vertical a radius of the circle. In this figure the circle represented the stream of ocean flowing round the inhabited earth, the upright represented the Mediterranean, and the horizontal the Black Sea and the river Don on the one hand, the Nile or the Red Sea on the other. Thus the upper half of the diagram was the continent of Asia, with Europe and Africa below. The plan fitted in happily with the idea that

Jerusalem, as the scene of Christ's birth and death, must be in the centre of the world. Some maps drawn on this plan were very elaborate, and in the thirteenth-century world map in Hereford Cathedral, for instance, many details are included in something that approximates to the right position relative to one another. As we approach Paradise at the top or eastern end of these maps, the detail becomes appropriately vague and the degree of accuracy less and less. We should be wrong to regard these as maps, in the modern sense of the term. They are analogous rather to the map of a railway system in which the lines are represented as straight and the stations equidistant, and they are intended only to convey certain general notions about relative positions. There were very few who had any thought of producing a scientific map. Roger Bacon, who worked in Oxford in the thirteenth century, made a plea for the construction of a map on scientific principles, as the Greek geographers had constructed it, based on observations of the elevation of sun and stars and drawn over a framework of lines of longitude and latitude. This suggestion made no impression at the time, and well into the fifteenth century the old form of map was being repeated, modified sometimes into lozenge form to fit more conveniently into the page.

Yet while the theoretical geographers made little or no advance, the seamen had begun to build up a more accurate tradition about the coasts along which they sailed. Well before the Renaissance proper began, two inventions had been developed in Europe, each of which played a great part in the progress of maritime discovery. One was that of the mariner's compass, an invention which has been attributed to the Chinese but which was more probably made independently in Western Europe, where it is mentioned as early as the twelfth century. Another is the astrolabe, for measuring latitude by finding the altitude of the stars. This instrument dates back to classical antiquity, but it first began to be used extensively in the fifteenth century. Chaucer wrote for his young son a treatise on its use in 1391. With these inventions there comes gradually an improvement in the quality of charts produced, and the chart-makers of the Italian commercial republics, Venice and Genoa, were producing by the mid-fifteenth century elaborate 'portolans' or sailing maps in which the delineation of the Mediterranean coast line is remarkably accurate.

During this same period the incentive to undertake ocean voyages had grown. In the thirteenth century Western travellers, notably

Marco Polo, had visited China and other regions of the Far East, and brought back disturbing stories of their prosperity. It was a chapter in Marco Polo which later suggested *Kubla Khan* to Coleridge, and the account of that marvellous palace, which he turned into pure romance, was read as literal fact in Renaissance Europe. In Alexandria Italian merchants came into constant contact with Arabs who had sailed to India and beyond it, and the books of the Arab geographers, based originally largely on Greek authors, contained material drawn from the stories of merchants who had penetrated to regions far beyond those of which classical geographers had had any accurate knowledge. Early in the fifteenth century the great problem of cosmography, its central problem till the reign of James I, was already beginning to be formulated. Was there an ocean route from Europe to these fabled regions of the East? Were there, perhaps, several such routes, and to whom was going to fall the prize of opening them?

In due course these developments began to affect Western geographical theory as well as practical navigation. Among those classical texts which were eagerly read in the fifteenth century were texts of the geographers, and two in particular had immense influence on cosmography. One was Macrobius' commentary on a work by Cicero, the *Somnium Scipionis*, or 'Dream of Scipio'. In the 'Dream' there is imagined a vision of the universe seen by one standing outside it, with the sphere of the earth in the centre and the heavenly bodies moving round it—as all the sixteenth-century navigators still thought of them. The surface of the globe is described as divided into five zones, two zones of extreme cold, two temperate, and a torrid zone between them. In one of the two temperate zones was the known world of Europe and Asia, and the other was equally habitable, but unknown and unknowable, seeing that a belt of fire which could not be traversed lay between it and the known world. This idea of a fiery zone at the equator is thus one which was in the minds of many navigators when ocean voyages began to be planned. It was yet to be seen whether Cicero and those who followed him were right, and the notion of flames licking up from sea to sky was very present in the imagination of fourteenth-century sailors.

More important than the 'Dream', however, was the rediscovery of the great work of the Greek geographer and astronomer Ptolemy, who had written about A.D. 140 in Alexandria. Ptolemy had compiled the material for an atlas of the known world, including Eastern Asia, drawn on scientific principles, the maps planned on a framework of lines of longitude and latitude, and the places plotted on this either from recorded observations or from calculations based on the diaries of travellers. For the well-known world of the Roman Empire these maps were surprisingly accurate, though outside this region errors grew. Ptolemy knew nothing of the Indian peninsula, for example, though he knew of the Ganges and Indus—and his Ceylon was enormous, almost continental in size. He knew nothing of Africa south of Cape Guardafui, and in some versions of his world map the Indian Ocean was represented as a vast inland sea, with Africa and Asia joining in the far south. Moreover, his calculation for the circumference of the earth was too low by about a third, and for the length of the continental mass of Europe and Asia too high. The result of these two mistakes was to make Asia stretch much too far round his globe, so that its shores were within the distance of a reasonable voyage from Spain. The miscalculation had important results, and explains Columbus' belief when he reached the West Indies that he was in the region of Japan. Ptolemy was translated into Latin in 1420, and copies of this version, with the maps in woodcut or copperplate, were among the classical works printed, very soon after the invention of the art of printing, by the presses of Germany and Italy. By 1492, several such printed editions were available and to compare them with some of the medieval maps is to realise how great was the revolution which was worked in geographical thought by the revival of classical learning. Indeed the classical geographers began to be credited with an infallibility which some time later did some harm, for when the new discoveries contradicted their views, the cartographers tended to reject the discoveries and retain the classical tradition. Even the map-makers Mercator and Ortelius, working in the reign of Elizabeth, still quoted classical authorities such as Pliny for the shape of the coast of Northern Asia; of which it may safely be said that Pliny knew no more than he knew about many other things which he mentioned in his immense but inaccurate encyclopaedia.

To discover the real springs of the great movement of exploration with which this book is concerned would be to discover the sources of the Renaissance itself. And as the search for the sources of this would take us further and further back into the medieval age, to the founding of universities in the twelfth century, or the growth of the knowledge of Aristotelian thought which followed it, or even (in more material matters) to the increase in book production which was made possible by the increasing manufacture of paper in Western Europe from 1200 onwards, so with this movement of exploration too the ultimate origins lie far back beyond the fifteenth century. The stimulus which actually impelled the navigators was generally simple. Columbus was after honour, gold, and power; and the early voyages to the coast of Guinea had as their purpose the discovery of lands from which must come those caravans that reached the North African coast, bearing gold dust from across the Sahara desert. These voyages were repeated because they brought material success, supplies of gold and in particular of slaves, for which there was a ready market. But what made the planning of such undertakings possible was the new knowledge. Columbus was a map-maker who had corresponded with the geographical theorists and had found out what there was to be found out in the ancient geographers about the form of the world, and about the Far East and its approaches. It was Greek and Roman geography that made his ambitions fertile and Greek astronomy that made his instruments work. More than any other department of life, classical knowledge (and speculation) had affected geographical thought, giving information that purported to be exact about lands which were beyond the bounds of ordinary experience, but were waiting to be revisited and offering almost limitless riches to those who reached them. 'Why then, the world's mine oyster, which I with sword will open.' The exclamation of one of Shakespeare's swaggering characters might have come from Drake's lips. And how different it was from that blend of piety, superstition, and the holiday spirit in which the pilgrim set out for the shrine of St James at Compostella or the knight took the cross to fight for the freedom of the Holy City!

The recovery of Ptolemy's work, then, affected Western European thought profoundly. The movement of exploration which sprang up so largely as a result of it cannot be claimed for any single nation or city, but like most of the great achievements of Western civilisation is European in character. It was in Bruges, not in Bristol, that More set the scene of his mariner's discourse on the manners of the Utopians, and his book, written in Latin, was printed first at Louvain and later at Basle. The calendars and astronomical tables which English seamen used were printed mainly in Germany or in Italy. Columbus, a Genoese by birth, offered his services indifferently to the kings of Spain, Portugal and England. Even in Elizabeth's reign, when Ralegh tried to plant a colony in Virginia, the splendid 'prospectus' for it was printed in Frankfurt, and besides the English edition, there were editions in French, German and Latin. And Hakluyt himself, ardent patriot that he was, was a cosmopolitan also, corresponding in Latin with Mercator at Antwerp about the north-west passage and making arrangements in Paris for the publication of accounts of French voyages of discovery. In Elizabeth's reign we seem to be able to discover in the lives of the English navigators a brilliance that, for its generation, is outstanding. But the background of their skill is not a national but a super-national achievement. Three generations before it had been the Italians. Then it was the Spaniards, the Portuguese and the French—and the difference was simply that with the English the achievements of the seamen became part of the national tradition, part of the texture of English life, in a way that happened nowhere else, save perhaps among the Dutch.

It is not possible to do more than summarise here the exploits of those Italian, Spanish and Portuguese navigators who first opened up the oceans to European ships. Of the pioneers, the name of Prince Henry the Navigator, of Portugal, must be mentioned. Born towards the end of the fourteenth century, he was alone in that period deeply concerned both with the theory and what may be called the practice of cosmography. He gathered round him mathematicians and astronomers as well as pilots; and, aiming originally at discovering the sources of the gold which was brought by caravan across the Sahara to the known regions of North Africa, he equipped successive expeditions which penetrated further and further southwards down the west coast of Africa and made familiar the islands off its coast, the 'Isles of the Hesperides', or the 'Fortunate Islands', as the ancient geographers had called them. These successes were the result of the planning and patronage of Henry himself, who though he did not sail with any of the expeditions concerned, provided not merely the financial backing for them, but the impulse which started them forth. After his death the quest of the south continued, and the objective gradually became more closely defined as that which has been mentioned above. It was to discover whether, as some ancient traditions maintained, there was a route round Africa to the Indian Ocean by which Calicut and Taprobane (Ceylon) could be reached. If so, this would bring to the discoverers the fabulous wealth of India and the Spice Islands that lay beyond it; and the textiles and porcelains, silks and muslins, the precious stones, rubies and pearls and emeralds, and the cargoes of spices, cloves, cinnamon, nutmeg and pepper which came through the hands of Arab middlemen, might be brought direct to Europe. The riches of these regions lost nothing in the telling, and the Arab stories of Sinbad the Sailor and the narrative of Marco Polo served almost equally well to whet the imagination for what might thus be realised.[2]

The voyage round the Cape of Good Hope was accomplished some years after Henry's death. It was Diaz who in 1489 in attempting to push further down the west coast was blown far south by a storm, turned north-east when it subsided and found open ocean still before him when by his reckoning he ought to be back on the African coast. He turned north-westwards, therefore, and when he made landfall knew that at last the first part of the problem had been solved. Southern Africa was not one with Southern Asia, as many of the maps showed. The Indian Ocean was accessible from the Atlantic, and it was only a matter of time before ships would be sailing from Portugal to Ceylon. Diaz' return with his problem solved did not satisfy Columbus, who had for years been urging the Spanish King to allow him to attempt the Atlantic crossing westwards from Spain. It was true that India could be reached by way of South Africa. But the voyage was a long one, and Columbus had other fish to fry. For it seems that his aim in crossing the Atlantic, in so far as he had formulated that aim clearly to himself, was not only to reach the eastern coast of Asia, which he was confident he could do, but also to discover a great unknown land, the Terra Australis or southern continent. This imaginary continent was shown on the maps for nearly three centuries as a vast amorphous mass spreading over the southern hemisphere, and it remained on them until the facts were at length settled by Captain Cook in the eighteenth century. Columbus was a mystic and declared later that he was the 'messenger of the New Heaven and the New Earth, spoken of by St John the Divine'. Although convinced of the roundness of the earth, he did not (according to the view put forward by a recent historian) believe it to be a sphere, but reckoned that it was pear-shaped, and that the southern continent was uppermost, rising up as it were towards the stalk at the pole. Some of the ocean currents he encountered seemed to confirm this, and when he found himself moving more easily northwards than southwards, his explanation was that the water was flowing downhill. This uppermost southern continent he believed to be the most desirable of all lands, and it was in search of it, most probably, that he turned the course of his successive voyages further southwards. His errors seem not so outrageous when we remember that a hundred years later Dr John Dee, laying the plans in his house in Chiswick for Drake's voyage of circumnavigation, was preoccupied with the precise location in the southern seas of the biblical Ophir whence Solomon got his gold. In many respects the Renaissance persists in remaining incorrigibly medieval.

To himself and his contemporaries Columbus was a failure. Except for the brilliant months following his first return from the West Indian Islands, he was, as he considered, invariably misunderstood and invariably underrated. Half of him always hankered after commercial success. In the first hours after making contact with a new world he records his diligence in enquiring whether there was gold found in that region. He is a successor to the medieval alchemist, seeking that which will turn base metal into precious, and always baffled on the threshold of discovery. Yet there remains an almost unparalleled achievement of faith. He sailed into nothingness in faith that he would find something beyond; in faith that those strange corpses said to have oriental features which were washed ashore on the Azores were in truth the bodies of Asiatics; in faith that those curiously carved sticks came not from one of the islands, Antilia or Brasil, which the chart-makers placed out there northwards in the ocean, but from a continent beyond. In a sense he was wrong, but he was superbly justified by his discovery of a new world in place of the old one he set out to reach.

The plan of an Atlantic voyage was conceived many years before it was carried out, but the difficulty was to secure financial backing for it and to find a backer who would accept his conditions. When at length the King of Spain agreed to them, there were other obstacles in the way, for it was almost impossible to raise a crew for such a voyage. It is said that the crews finally were made up partly of released prisoners. Seamanship was a rough trade. Galleys were regularly manned by prisoners, and there is nothing improbable about the story. The expedition comprised three ships, the 'Santa Maria', the 'Pinta' and the 'Nina', the largest being by current reckoning some 120 tons, the others small caravels. Not less than eighty-seven men in all sailed. The numbers may have been rather greater.

Columbus sailed on 3 August 1492, setting a course for the Canary Islands. Two days later the rudder of the 'Pinta' was found to be damaged and sabotage was suspected. At Tenerife they repaired the 'Pinta', and set sail again on 6 September. For two days they were becalmed, then it began to blow from the north-east, and next day Columbus started his dual reckoning of the distance covered, one reckoning for himself, another for the crew, that they might not be discouraged if the voyage was long. It was on the 16th that they 'began to see many tufts of grass, very green, which as it appeared had not long been torn from the earth'. On the 25th Columbus talked with the captain of the 'Pinta', Martin Alonzo Pinzon, about a chart he had sent across to him three days before 'which had certain islands depicted as being in that sea'. At sunset that evening, Martin Alonzo mounted the high poop of his ship and in great joy talked to Columbus, claiming a reward because he had sighted land; and Columbus 'fell on his knees to give thanks to our Lord', and Martin Alonzo with his men said the 'Gloria in Excelsis Deo'. Until night all thought it was land. But next day there was nothing to be seen except the waste of water. Day after day they sailed on. On 7 October in the caravel 'Nina' they thought again that land was in sight, and when it turned out once again to be a mistake, the course was changed to a course west-south-west, the direction in which migratory birds had been seen flying. On 10 October there were signs of mutiny, but on the day following those in the 'Pinta' saw canes and a small stick carved as they thought with iron; and those in the 'Nina' saw a branch covered with dog roses, so that at last they knew land must not be far off. At ten o'clock that night, Columbus, standing on the castle of the poop, saw a light. He called another who thought that he, too, saw it. Columbus promised a silk doublet to the man who should first sight land, and two hours after midnight it was won. Land appeared at a distance of two leagues. When it was light they could see men moving about on shore. They brought out the royal standard and the two banners of the Green Cross (bearing also the initials of Ferdinand and Isabella of Spain), which Columbus had been flying, and so went ashore in an armed boat and took possession of the land for their sovereigns. Columbus called the island San Salvador.[3] He was in an ecstasy, charmed with everything he saw. One of the things he noticed was the gold ornaments the 'Indians' wore in their noses, 'and', he says, 'from signs I was able to understand that, going to the south or going round the island to the south there was a king who had great vessels of it, and who possessed very much.... So I

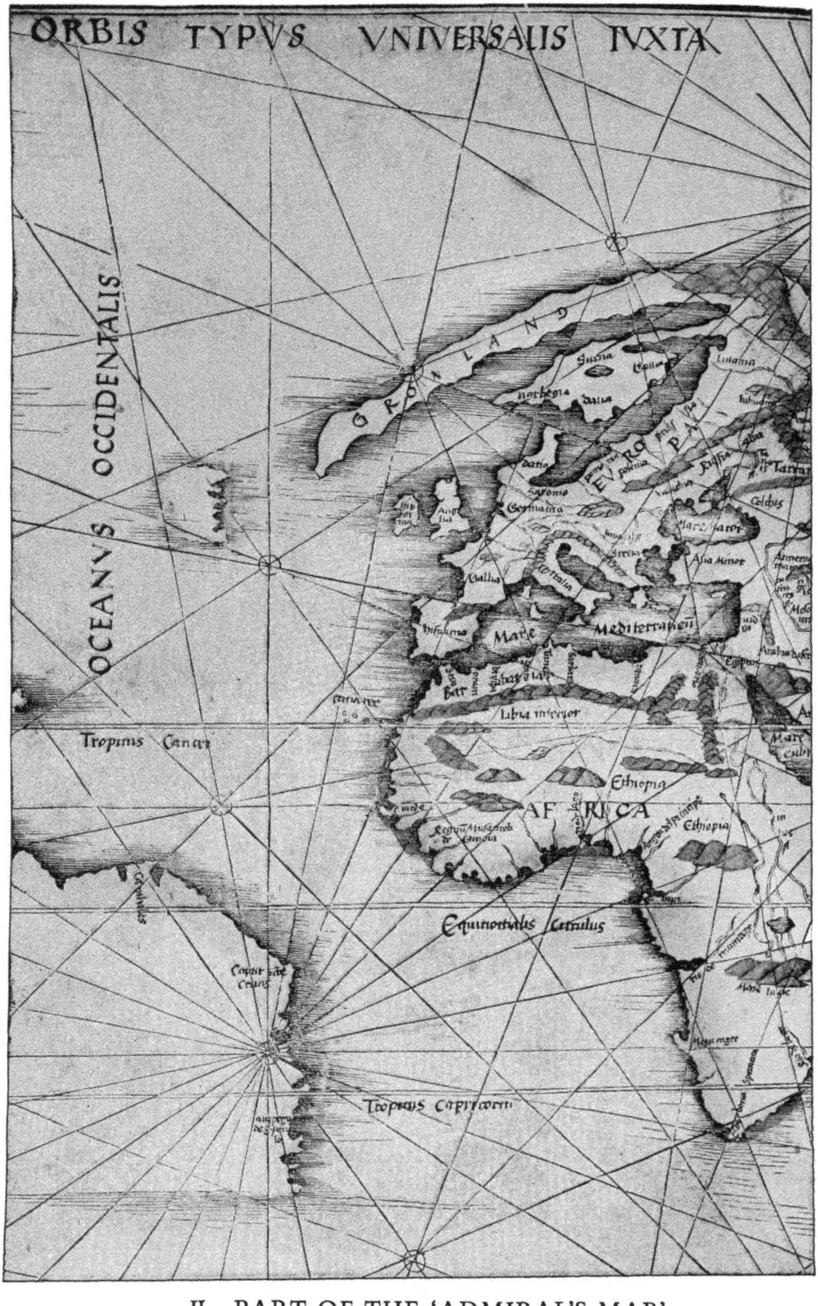

II. PART OF THE 'ADMIRAL'S MAP'

(Sometimes attributed to Columbus)

resolved to go to the south-west, to seek the gold and the precious stones.' The next three months were spent on this quest, and in the course of it Cuba and Haiti (called by Columbus Hispaniola, or 'little Spain') were discovered. But it was a voyage of promise rather than fulfilment. The quantity of gold actually discovered was small, though Columbus noted as he believed a large variety of spice-producing plants which were likely to prove profitable.

The voyage back to Spain began on 16 January. It was uneventful till its last stages. Then on 12 February a storm broke. There were heavy seas and lightning that night, throughout which the ship was running with bare poles. After a lull it blew again with redoubled fury, and so all through the next night, when the 'Pinta', with which they were keeping in touch with flares, disappeared from view. At last 'that their highnesses might know how our Lord had given him the victory in all that he desired in the matter of the Indies...and that if he were lost in that tempest his sovereigns might have news of his voyage, he took a parchment and wrote on it all that he could of all that he had found. This parchment he enclosed in a waxed cloth, very carefully fastened, and he commanded a large wooden barrel to be brought, and placed in it, without anyone knowing what it was, but they thought it was some act of devotion, and so he commanded that it should be thrown into the sea.' But that evening the storm began to subside, and next day land was sighted, the island of Santa Maria in the Azores. On 4 March they entered the Tagus for Lisbon.

We still have in the famous letter of Columbus to Ferdinand and Isabella, the publication of which announced the discovery to Europe, what must be the gist of the letter that was set adrift. For it is dated 'in the caravel, off the Canary Islands, on the Fifteenth of February in the Year one thousand four hundred and ninety three'. What Columbus wrote that day must be in substance what he had written the day before. The 'letter' is a lyrical account of the islands, emphasising the likelihood of great wealth in gold and spices being obtained from them. It has little precise detail, which is perhaps purposely omitted, and the only definite statement of latitude is inaccurate.[4] It gives some of that information for which the early Renaissance explorer was asked so eagerly of the strange customs and habits of the natives; and it makes clear Columbus' view that the islands were islands off the coast of Asia. He had actually sent a small party of men into the interior of Cuba (which he maintained till his death to be the mainland of Asia) to try to establish contact with the Great Khan. For the fourteen remaining years of his life he laboured under the same misapprehension, and died convinced that he had found the western route to Asia. What he had never found in that restless life was peace of mind, and more than anything else perhaps it was the phantom of the 'way through' to that southern continent which troubled him.

Before his death, however, as a result indeed of his own discovery of the mouth of the Orinoco with its great volume of water, it was suspected that there had been found not only islands but a new continent. The voyage of Amerigo Vespucci to South America put the matter beyond doubt, and he mapped a part of its north-eastern coast line. But this still remained unrelated to the discoveries that had been made in the north, by explorers setting out from England. We have been for a very long time, through thick and thin, a nation of shopkeepers, and it is characteristic that, whereas the accounts of Columbus' voyage exist in profuse detail drawn up by himself, the evidence for John Cabot's voyages comes largely from commercial entries in Bristol ledgers. Columbus found what he called a paradise, while the Bristol merchants who sailed with Cabot had an eye chiefly to the cod fisheries.

Several expeditions had sailed westwards from Bristol on voyages of Atlantic discovery before Cabot, like that of John Lloyd who went to look for the island of Brasil in 1480; and the voyage to Iceland was often being made. There were many likely objects for their search. It is indeed a mistake to think that that Atlantic was emptier in the days before Columbus than in the days after. It was thought to contain many islands of which detailed accounts were in some instances available. There was, for instance, besides this island of Brasil which the map-makers placed sometimes west of Ireland, sometimes further south, an island named Antilia, whither seven bishops had fled from Spain in the eighth century. They had found seven harbours (details of which the maps show) and established seven cities, and it was reported in the fifteenth century that a Portuguese ship had visited Antilia. There were the Fortunate Isles of Saint Brandan the Irish saint, perhaps actually the Hebrides and Iceland, though in the maps they appear further south; and there was the island of Frisland, on which two Venetians were said to have been shipwrecked in 1380. They were welcomed by a Prince who spoke to them courteously in Latin, as Hakluyt reports, and 'perceiving that they came from Italy...he was surprised with marvelous great joy'. These brothers were even provided with a posterity still living when the accounts were written, and it is astonishing to find the contemporaries of Frobisher and Davis, who knew so much about the North Atlantic, still putting Frisland on their maps or including the account of it in their books.[5]

It was the merchants of Bristol who put up the money for Cabot's voyage in 1497, and we may be sure that the project had some hard heads associated with it, interested in something other than the fate of Antilia's eighth-century bishops. Authority for it was granted by Henry VII, who perhaps felt that he had lost a good thing when he refused to assist Columbus. Cabot sailed in a ship named the 'Mathew', with probably eighteen men in all on board, on 2 May 1497. The course chosen was north-westerly and they made landfall at some point on the North American coast that cannot now be identified (possibly Nova Scotia) on Saint John Baptist's Day (24 June). A length of coast, later stated as 300 leagues, was explored, and traces of native life, notched trees, snares, and a tool of bone like a fisherman's netting needle, were found. The 'Mathew' arrived back in Bristol with her crew safe on 6 August, having made the homeward passage probably in twenty-six days. That is almost all that we know of the voyage, and some of these details are uncertain. But we know that four days later John Cabot was given £10 as a first instalment from the Privy Purse in recognition of his achievement; that he claimed that the new fisheries would make the Iceland voyage out of date; and that he believed he could penetrate further and reach Marco Polo's Japan and the region of spices and jewels. He thought that he had reached a wild north-eastern region of Asia, and many of the map-makers in the following decade followed this belief in drawing the coast he had discovered.

The first voyage had been a reconnaissance. It remained to realise the profits which the Bristol merchants associated with him believed, as he also believed, were to be realised. But about the expedition which set out the following year with this object we know even less for certain than about the first. There are the names of a few merchants who took part in it—Lancelot Thirkill, Thomas Bradley, John Carter and an Italian with the elegant names of Giovanni Antonio de Carbonariis. We know that five ships took part, that they sailed from Bristol, probably in May, and ran into a storm in which one was apparently disabled and put into an Irish port. But the rest is virtually silence, though we can guess, on the basis of later maps apparently using information derived from Cabot, that the ships made their way southwards as far as what is now the coast of Maine. They found no Asiatic cities, however, where they could dispose of their cargoes of cloth and obtain the spices they had hoped to carry back. It was a business failure. Losses were cut, and the return of the ships not thought worth even a bare record.

In the following year Vasco da Gama accomplished what Diaz had shown to be possible, and reached India by way of the Cape of Good Hope. But it was a costly achievement. Two-thirds of his crews were lost through disease by the time he returned to Portugal, so that though the feasibility of that particular route had been demonstrated, the question of a better route remained of first-rate importance. Certainly it remained in the minds of English merchants, and there is reason to believe that in 1508, or 1509, Sebastian Cabot, who had probably sailed as a lad with his father John Cabot on his two American voyages, explored the coast of Labrador northwards and perhaps actually penetrated through Hudson's Strait into Hudson's Bay, not reached again until a hundred years later. Meanwhile others were trying to consolidate the gains that had been made, and in a document of 1501 we hear first of the 'company adventurers into the new fownde ilondes'. They were to subdue, under sovereignty of the King, the lands they discovered, and were empowered to make laws for their government. For four years they were to be allowed the imports of one ship duty free and in all their ships masters and mariners were to be allowed small quantities of imports, duty free, on personal accounts. It is an anticipation of the charters on which imperial policy was to be based in the reigns of Elizabeth and the Stuarts. The material results were small, but the undertaking points towards a new conception of the objects of discovery planned to rival the growing achievements of Spain and Portugal.

Even in these English voyages from Bristol, foreigners often played a leading part. Cabot himself tried discreetly to pass himself off as an Englishman by putting an 'l' into the middle of his name, but the attempt failed lamentably, if we are to judge from the way in which the antiquary Stow, writing in 1580, speaks of him: 'Sebastian Gabato, a Genoa's sonne.' It was an almost impossible proposition to anglicise João Fernandez' name, who was largely concerned with the 'company adventurers' in the early years of the sixteenth century; and there was as yet little thought of the discoveries as an exclusively English perquisite. 'To Portyngales,' runs an entry for payment in one of Henry VII's household books, 'that brought Popyngais with catts of the mountaigne with other stuf to the king's grace, 100s.' There must have been many Bristol shipmasters sailing regularly to the Banks for cod, as the Goughs, Suttons and the rest had sailed twenty years before to Iceland, but they 'be of those that bare no record'. They did their jobs quietly and efficiently, so that their comings and goings were hardly noticed, and it was left to the Portugals to bring back the popinjays.

It was about this time that another Portuguese accomplished what must rank as one of the greatest achievements of seamanship of all time. Actually Magellan, though Portuguese by birth, had renounced his nationality, owing to a quarrel with the King of Portugal, before he set out on his voyage of circumnavigation, and sailed under the colours of the King of Spain. Like most other projects of this time, this was not intended simply as a voyage of exploration, but as a commercial venture. Magellan believed not only that a route to the Spice Islands by way of the south-western Atlantic was possible, but that it would prove shorter than the route opened by da Gama's voyage; and he said that he was prepared to sail, if need be, to latitude 75° to find the strait that he believed to exist between America and the southern continent. The rivalry between Spain and Portugal was growing. In 1494 there had been negotiated between the two countries the treaty of Tordeçillas, based on an award made by Pope Alexander VI the previous year. At that time Columbus' first voyage provided all the information available about the new lands. Portugal had already established a substantial claim to the African route, and the question was how the regions opening up for discovery were to be divided between the two countries. The treaty established a line 370 leagues west of the Cape Verde Islands as limiting Portugal's claims to the west, a line which ultimately gave her Brazil. But if the world was a globe the line must be carried all round it, and controversy was bound ultimately to arise (at a period when there were no satisfactory instruments for determining longitude) as to what regions in the Far East were in the sphere of Spain, what in the sphere of Portugal. Many of the maps of the period are faked in the interests of one or other claimant. Portuguese maps, for instance, show the new-found coast of North America well to the east of the line of demarcation (which is approximately the forty-fifth meridian). In fact it lay far to the west of it, but with the available instruments it was difficult to prove this, and there was everything to be said for staking one's claims generously. One of Magellan's objects was to prove that the Spice Islands lay in the Spanish sphere. This, in itself, shows that he did not realise the length of the voyage he had undertaken, and did not realise that the known distance from Brazil to the Spice Islands by way of Africa was less than half the circumference of the globe he was attempting to circumnavigate.

His five ships put to sea on 20 September 1519. At Port St Julian, in what is now the Argentinian province of Santa Cruz, there was a mutiny, and the gallows set up to hang the ringleaders were seen by Drake sixty years later on his own voyage round the world. In October 1520 Magellan found at last what he had been seeking—and what he told his crews he had already seen marked in certain charts—the entrance to the straits that now bear his name. The passage through, nearly 400 miles long, took more than a month. To the south, 'stark with eternal cold' lay the land which he called, from the fires sighted on it, Tierra del Fuego. He thought that it was part of the southern continent. The Great South Sea which lay beyond it had been discovered seven years before, by a Spanish adventurer, Balboa, who had crossed the mountains at the eastern end of the Panama isthmus and taken possession of the sea in the King of Spain's name. North-westwards across that ocean Magellan now boldly struck. It was ninety-eight days before he saw land that was inhabited. In those ninety-eight days he had sailed nearly half round the globe. There had been no fresh food, and scurvy, against which no antidote was known, took a frightful toll. It was probably at Guam that his crews were at last able to rest and refit. Less than two months later Magellan was dead, killed in a fight with islanders in the Philippines. One of the surviving three vessels was burnt, a second abandoned, and the other, laden with cloves, found her way back to Europe in the summer of 1522. There were on board her thirty-one men. The voyage was from one standpoint a failure. The route discovered was not a practicable one nor were the Spice Islands within that half of the globe that could be claimed by Spain. But Magellan had at last set a limit to the globe, and his feat is one of the most splendid in the splendid history of discovery.

To end this summary account of the events which preface the heroic age of English seamanship, there must be told briefly the stories of two Spanish adventurers in America. In 1504 a student of law from Salamanca University, Hernando Cortes, had gone out to San Domingo to seek his fortune. He found it. In 1518 he was given the task of conquering Mexico, about which a little, but only a little, was known as the result of discoveries made a few years previously. Cortes landed in Mexico early in 1519. By a curious irony, Western adventurers are often regarded as gods. Their strange equipment never seems to suggest (save to that highly civilised people, the Chinese) that they may be devils. Cortes was welcomed with munificent gifts by ambassadors from Montezuma, ruler of Mexico, founded Vera Cruz to use as a base of operations, and then taking as his allies chiefs hostile to Montezuma, he thus augmented his force and pressed forward over the mountains to Mexico city. It was situated on islets in a lake, and causeways joined these to the land. It might have been impregnable, but because he was believed to be a child of the sun, he was welcomed into the city, and succeeded in establishing himself in a fortified palace. Meanwhile, however, Spaniards had been killed in an attack on Vera Cruz, and this news dispelled the aura of deity. Realising that his position might become desperate, Cortes seized Montezuma, and forcing him to give up the men who had attacked Vera Cruz, he had them burnt alive in public in Mexico city. At this point he heard that another Spaniard had arrived to supersede him, so he withdrew from Mexico and defeated him. Returning, he was met by a revolt which forced him to leave the city again, but when a pitched battle was fought, his victory was decisive, and a year later he succeeded in retaking it. Mexico was the first of the Eldorados. Long afterwards Spaniards were staking their lives in search of seven other mythical cities to the north, which were said to rival it. But there was only one Mexico, and that, good and bad, with its magnificently developed civilisation and its barbaric human sacrifices, was obliterated by Cortes. Some years later he discovered the peninsula of California, which he believed to be an island, then returned to Europe and died in disfavour, in 1547. Like many another adventurer, he had not only found his fortune, but in the end lost it.

Before the discovery of Mexico, rumours had been heard of another empire to the south. Francisco Pizarro had crossed the isthmus with Balboa, and in 1522 was able to make his way some distance down the western coast of South America. There he heard more definite reports of the civilisation of the Incas, of which, as has been mentioned, vague accounts seem to have been received in Europe even before More wrote *Utopia*. He returned ten years later and, like Cortes, he was welcomed as a child of the sun. He belonged, in truth, to the same breed as Cortes, though he had luck where Cortes had skill, and his successes owed much more to treachery. He must have found the truth of Peru beyond his wildest dreams. It was a vast empire, immensely rich, organised, and highly organised, on a curiously paternal system, which was a sort of feudal state-socialism. One of the greatest of the Incas was only recently dead, and the succession was in dispute. In these troubled waters Pizarro set himself to fish. He was welcomed with friendliness, and then by treachery seized the victorious claimant to the throne. He offered to ransom the Inca, and when the fabulous ransom, a king's ransom indeed, had been paid, he murdered him and Peru thus came into his possession almost as easily as a ripe fruit is picked. His career as Governor was mercifully comparatively short, and in 1541 he was assassinated by his discontented followers.

The conquest of Peru is of outstanding importance in the history of the century. The supply of precious metals derived from it streamed eastwards, year after year, in the Spanish treasure fleets. Up the west coast it came to Panama, crossed the isthmus on the pack horses, and thence was shipped to Europe. This route became the lifeline of the Spanish Empire, and the lifeline was threatened, time after time in the second half of the century, by English and French privateers and fleets. There was no greater temptation in the world for the pirate.

For men of the time of Hawkins and Drake, therefore, there were two great objectives, and to each of them the way was closed. The Spice Islands in the Far East were the preserve of Portugal. The gold and silver of Peru were the prerogative of Spain. But these claims were not to go unchallenged.

Chapter II

NORTH-EAST PASSAGE

AMONG the prosperous merchant families of Bristol at the end of the fifteenth century and the beginning of the sixteenth were the Thornes. Robert Thorne's name appears in the Bristol records as early as 1479, when he was trading with Portugal. William, his brother, was also a merchant, and Robert Thorne had a son named after himself, who followed the same calling. Perhaps John Thorne, mentioned in the Bristol customs in 1522–3, was another son. Like other merchant families in London and Norwich also at this time, they were widely respected. The class they represented was playing an ever more important part in the public life of the country and in the determination of its destinies. Young Robert distinguished himself far outside his native city. In the course of business he settled in Seville, for Henry VIII had a Spanish wife and the associations of the two countries were close. He died in London and was buried in the Temple Church. He had been Mayor of Bristol, but as his epitaph implied, he had concerned himself not so much with the affairs of Bristol as with the affairs of England. While he was in Seville he wrote a remarkable pamphlet addressed to the English ambassador in Spain, with a preface addressed to Henry VIII himself. It is generally known as the *Declaration of the Indies*. He was not, perhaps, the first to advance the arguments it contains. But wherever they originated, they had so great an influence on the history of English seamanship at the time that they deserve examination.

It appears that the ambassador had consulted the 'worshipful Mr Thorne' about the matters in dispute between Spain and Portugal. Thorne describes the controversy over the ownership of the Spice Islands. 'These coastes', he says, 'and situations of the Islands, every of the cosmographers and Pilots of Portingal and Spayne do set after their purpose. The Spaniards more towards the Orient, because they should appeare to appertain to the Emperoure and the Portingals more toward the Occident, for that they should fal within their jurisdiction. So that the pilots and navigants thither, which in some cases should declare the truth, by their industrie do set them falsely every one to favour his prince.' The maps are, in other words, faked. It is impossible for the independent enquirer to discover from them what is the truth. But the author himself is not an altogether independent enquirer. He has an ulterior motive, which he demonstrates by means of a 'mappe or carde' attached to his book. The route of the King of Spain's ships to the Spice Islands is by way of the Straits of Magellan, to which he gives the Spanish name 'Estrecho de todos Santos', and which he puts correctly in latitude 53°. It is an immensely long route, as is also that of the King of Portugal, by way of the Cape of Good Hope. May there not be a shorter way? What of the route, he asks, to the north of the new-found land of Labrador, past the pole and then south down the other side of the globe; or the route past Iceland or Norway, and to the east of the pole? For the mariner who used these routes there would be various advantages. In the right season of the year the sun never sets in the far north. The region will be found (so he believes) temperate as the newly found lands are temperate. And in particular, the route would be short, shorter by more than two thousand leagues than the alternatives. If these passages by way of the north had existed, his estimate would have proved in no way to exaggerate the advantage of distance. It was the great circle course, or something near it, that he was suggesting. Like many of his contemporaries he regards the world, poised in space with the sun moving round it, as having the north pole uppermost. The countries 'under the equinoctial', or south of the equator as we should call them, are the richest and have the precious metals in as great abundance as the northern regions have the base metals. They are the great objective. It is true that in reaching them Englishmen would be entering the preserves of Spain and Portugal. But it will be a real advantage even if Englishmen content themselves only with the export of cloth to Tartary, or Northern China, so far not exploited either by Spain or by Portugal. And he is not unaware of the possibility of a struggle for the right of entry into the forbidden lands. His map must not be shown at the Spanish court, for though there is nothing in it to which objection ought to be taken, yet none may make maps except those appointed to do so, and it might not seem good to them that 'a stranger should know or discover their secretes'. There is the suggestion, surely, that the day may come when not only the secrets are known, but the door is unlocked, by others.

Yet what is impressive about the *Declaration of the Indies* is the new sense of the mastery of the world that lives in it. The old world that was passing had been peopled by evil spirits and demons. If a man passed safely through it was because his guardian angel guided him. But Thorne's world is a world to be conquered by a clear eye and a strong hand. 'I judge', he says, 'there is no land unhabitable, nor sea innavigable.' Man is, under God, his own master, and the oceans, no longer limitless, are fields of new conquests to be won. It is not a matter of Catholic or Protestant, for Thorne, like his sovereign, was doubtless Catholic. It is a matter rather of medieval and modern. The line has been crossed, and we are in a new age.

Many influences contributed to this new sense of mastery. One was the great improvement in the design of ships. England had a sailor king, who was not only building up a great navy, but designing ships himself. Thus we hear of him in a letter written fifteen years or so after the *Declaration of the Indies* as 'fetching from Italy three master shipwrights expert in making galleys' and causing to be built 'vessels with oars of which he is the designer and inventor'. After considerable experience he was beginning to work out the balance between sailing ships and oared ships for his navy, and the results can still be seen in that series of water-colour drawings some of which are in the British Museum, some in the Pepys Library at Magdalene College, Cambridge, in which Master Antony Antony depicted them. There they pass before us in notable pageant, some of them ships with whose great names, like the 'Jesus of Lubeck', we shall later become familiar. This attempt to work out a balance between the two, the oared 'ships of free movement' as Sir Julian Corbett called them, and the 'ships of large sea endurance', followed a period when Henry had gone too far ahead of his time and had pinned his faith solely on the ship of the future, the sailing ship. He had found in the war with France that oared galleys might still be necessary. But his instincts had been right and a time was coming when English fleets would depend on sails, and sails alone.

As so often in history, the requirements of war first brought about the improvements that were to be all important for commerce. In medieval times there had been a clear distinction between the ship of war and the merchant ship, a distinction that dated back to classical antiquity. In antiquity, the ship of war had been the long ship, as it was in the Venetian fleets of the fifteenth century; narrow in proportion to its length and of free movement, since it depended primarily on oars. The merchant ship of medieval times was a round ship, often no more than twice her own beam in length. The Venetian designers had evolved an intermediate type, the galleasse, to operate with the galleys; partly moving under sails, but oared also to secure some degree of free movement, and much narrower proportionately to her beam than the old merchant ships had been. The process that was worked out in Henry's fleets was the further adaptation of this type as an ocean-going vessel, relying entirely upon sails. Frenchmen had probably been the first to plan on these lines. Englishmen followed them, and introduced important modifications of their own. There is a chance mention in a letter of the time of a certain Mr Fletcher of Rye setting himself to solve the problem of building a ship that could sail closer to the wind; and in the Antony drawings we can see some of the first great examples of these inventions; like the galleasse 'Hart' with her long low lines and (if the impression given by the drawing is correct) her great length in proportion to her beam. The towering works, fore and aft, of the medieval ship are gone. The oars that were an auxiliary motive power in the Venetian galleasse are gone also; and whereas in the oared galley the armament would only be brought to bear ahead of her as a single point of fire, from the galleasse 'Hart' there stares out at us already the broadside that was to become so deadly a weapon, once men had learned to handle it.

It was a time when the line between the merchant ship and the ship of war was not easily drawn. Indeed, the merchant ship undertaking an ocean voyage needed a useful armament if she was to face successfully those dangers which might at any moment threaten her. Some of Henry VIII's own ships—the 'Jesus of Lubeck' is an example—started service as merchantmen, and Elizabeth used regularly to lease her ships to commercial expeditions when they were not actually engaged on a naval campaign. It is not surprising therefore that we find types designed originally as ships of war passing into general service, and the lines of the galleasse and galleon (terms which are often used interchangeably and which both imply a ship built on a much narrower plan than the old round ships) are the lines of most ocean-going vessels by the beginning of the seventeenth century.

Many of these things still lay in the future when Robert Thorne wrote his pamphlet. But the fishing fleets which sailed even at that time to the Newfoundland Banks must have been handy vessels

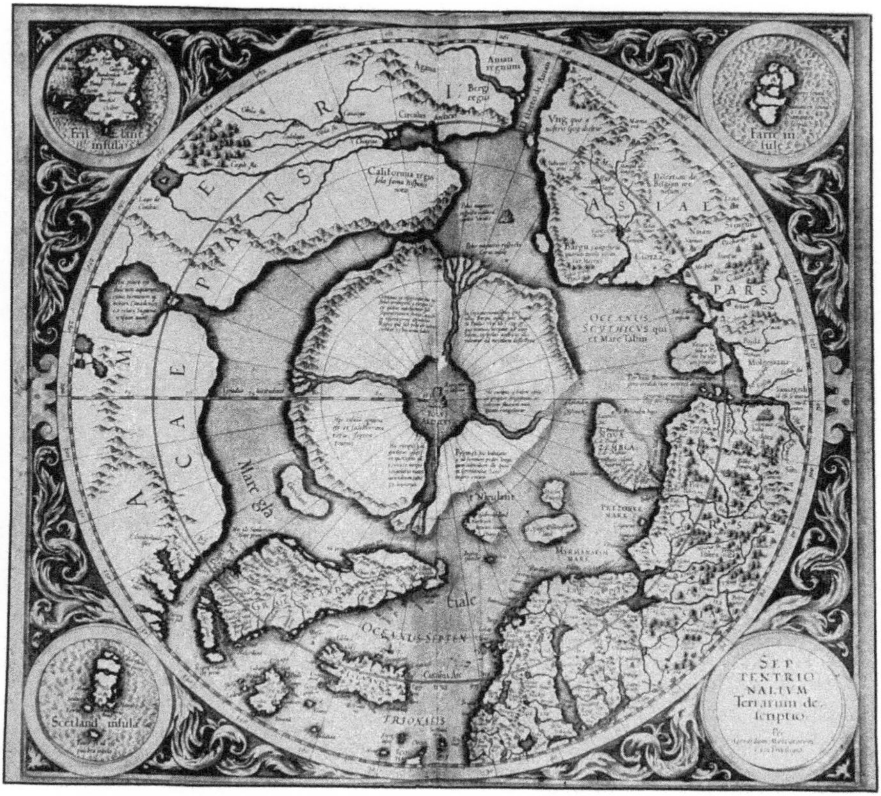

III. THE NORTH POLAR REGIONS

(*Mercator's map, drawn about 1585*)

compared with those of a hundred years before, and more must have been done by the time Sir Hugh Willoughby sailed in 1553 to attempt the discovery of the north-east passage. What the promoters of this voyage, of whom Sebastian Cabot was the chief, had in mind is clear. The results actually achieved led to the founding of the Muscovy company, but this was by no means the original objective. Even at the time of the second voyage when relations with Moscow had been established and it was known that a satisfactory trade might result, the further motive was always pressed forward. 'Item, it is to be had in mind', say the instructions issued by the promoters to the captains in 1555, 'that you use all wayes and meanes possible to learne howe men may passe from Russia, either by land or by sea to Cathaia' (i.e. to China). And the route according to the geographer, Mercator, writing twenty-five years later, when one expedition after another had shown that ice made travel in the far north almost impossible, was not difficult. 'I have often times marveiled', he said, 'that being so happily begun, it hath bene left of, and the course changed into the west, after that more than half of your voiage was discovered.' Dr Dee, the theorist, took the same view. From somewhere near the North Cape to the north-eastern promontory of China it was reckoned would take a matter of thirty-six days' sailing, and it might be done much quicker if the wind was favourable. The great Scandinavian explorer who finally accomplished the feat late in the nineteenth century took more than two years to do it.

The instructions issued for the guidance of those who took part are an interesting blend of sound common sense and shrewd business with a dash of the new Puritanism. The company was to have prayers morning and evening, with the other services appointed by the King's Majesty. 'Blasphemy of God' and 'detestable swearing' as well as ribaldry, dicing, carding and 'other devilish games' were strictly forbidden. At the same time, there was to be no proselytising. The effects of a policy of compulsory conversion had been demonstrated by the Spaniards, and the English, now or later, had none of it. It was forbidden, accordingly, even to 'disclose the state of our religion', and the crew were to seem to bear with such laws and rites as were used in the countries they visited. The instructions are big with the idea of wonderful new regions to be opened up on the way to that infinitely prosperous empire, the greatest in the world, of which Cambalu (Peking) was the capital, and it was with such hopes that the crews faced those desolate wastes of ice.

The first voyage was marked by tragedy. Its Captain-General was Sir Hugh Willoughby, who sailed in the 'Speranza' of 120 tons. There were two other ships, the 'Edward Bonaventure' of 60 tons, commanded by Richard Chancellor, chief pilot of the expedition, and the 'Bona Confidentia' of 90 tons. The ships had been specially fitted for the voyage with thin sheets of lead over the planking—an invention of which we hear now for the first time, to cheat the ravages of worm—and they were provisioned for eighteen months. They sailed from Deptford on 10 May 1553. Late in June and in early July there was bad weather, and they beat about the North Sea off the coasts of Scotland and Scandinavia. But they made successfully at last the Lofoten Islands off the Norwegian coast and made famous since by a dashing raid made on them at one of the darkest periods of this war. They were delayed there by the weather for a few days, but pressed onwards to the north as soon as it was possible, making for a Danish trading post east of North Cape, which was known to Englishmen as the 'Wardhouse'. Before they reached it, another gale struck them. Everywhere along the coast the cliffs were lofty, so that they had to make out to sea for comparative safety; and what with the high wind and thick mist, the ships could not keep together, and the 'Edward Bonaventure' became separated from her two consorts. The 'Speranza' and the 'Confidentia' made their way together, till the 'Confidentia' showed signs of having suffered dangerously in the bad weather and they began to look round for a harbour in which to refit. They were now off a low-lying uninhabited coast. The season was advancing and about 21 August, as far as can be told from Willoughby's own laconic account, they decided to turn back westwards.[1] Some three weeks later they made a harbour where they saw seals and many fish, and ashore great bears, deer and foxes, with other strange beasts unknown to them. The last few words of the account have an interest comparable, from the circumstances in which they were written, with Captain Scott's diaries. 'Thus remaining in this harbour with space of a weeke, seeing the yeare farre spent, and also very evill weather, as frost, snow and haile, as though it had been the deepe of winter, we thought best to winter there. Therefore we sent out three men South-South-West to search if they could find people, who went three dayes journey, which also returned without finding any people, or any similitude of habitation.' In that sombre harbour, known later as Arzina, in Lapland, the ships were found many months later. Willoughby and his crews had been frozen to death. There were found, besides his brief diary of the voyage, several notes—the names of the crews, and copies of the oaths administered to the captain and shipmasters; and there was found also a will, which showed that the commander and most of his company had still been living in January of that frightful northern winter. The mean temperature in the harbour that January—if it was a normal January for the region—was somewhere between 10° and 0° Fahrenheit.

So Willoughby died, 'a most valiant gentleman', as a contemporary called him.[2] Chancellor fared better. He might have turned back, but those in his ship evidently trusted him and it was decided to go forward as planned. They came at last, as Willoughby had done, to the region of the midnight sun, 'a continued lighte and brightnesse of the sunne shining clearely upon the huge and mightie sea'. They entered the White Sea, and on these shores at last they found signs of humanity, and succeeded by their restraint and kindness in winning the confidence of the fisherfolk who lived there. They found themselves to be in Russia, where perhaps no Englishman then living had been before them. Chancellor determined to make the journey himself to visit the Emperor in Moscow. He travelled by sled, a journey not much less than a thousand miles; was received in state by Ivan Vasilivitch 'the Terrible'; presented him with letters from Edward VI; marvelled at his gold and silver plate, but thought that the town of Moscow was a poor place compared with London. Meanwhile one of the merchants in his company was making a list of the commodities which offered likely profits; the furs, sable, mink, ermine, white foxes; seal oil, stockfish, salt and salmon, wax, hides and tallow, which were to make good money for many years for the Muscovy company. By the following winter they were back in London, and the provision that was made, when the second voyage set out in the spring of 1555, for establishing permanent agencies in Russia, shows that the newly opened region was thought to have distinct commercial possibilities. The voyage had been intended to short-circuit the monopoly of the Portuguese and Spaniards. In fact, it short-circuited a monopoly of much longer standing, though much less important, the monopoly of the Hanse towns which had for many years controlled Baltic trade.

The main problem, however, remained still to be solved. In 1556

Stephen Burrough, in the 'Searchthrift', made another gallant effort to solve it, only to come up against the almost impossible barrier of Nova Zemlya, from which Willoughby also had turned back. Burrough was able, however, to make a more detailed survey of its coast, to the island of Vaigatz at its southern end. He heard reports of the great river Ob, the estuary of which lay further east; and came into contact, for the first time, with the Samoyeds on that coast. On him and others with him one thing made a peculiarly vivid impression, the wooden idols, their mouths caked with blood, which the Samoyeds worshipped. One of Chancellor's servants, Richard Johnson, went with Stephen Burrough on that voyage, and his report of the Samoyeds loses nothing in the telling. Their religion appears to have been in the best Mumbo Jumbo tradition, and it went down well with Johnson and no doubt also with his public.

Burrough's own account of the voyage is matter of fact enough, save for one or two epic incidents:

> On St James' Day there was a monstrous whale aboord of us, so near to our side that we might have thrust a sworde or any other weapon in him, which we durst not doe, for fear that he should have overthrown our shippe; and then I called my company together and all of us shouted, and with the cry that we made he departed from us; there was as muche above water of his backe as the bredth of our pinesse, and at his falling downe, he made such a terrible noyse in the water that a man would greatly have marvelled, except hee had known the cause of it: but God be thanked, we were quietly delivered of him.

In those days the whale was still a problem for the mariner, but, like the walls of Jericho, he would fortunately succumb to shouting.

The last to attempt the passage were Jackman and Pet in 1580. They took discovery one stage further, threading their way through the ice which almost blocked the channel between Nova Zemlya and the mainland into the Kara Sea. There they found the trend of the coast to be south-eastwards, and this made it easy for the theorists to maintain that they had been within an ace of success. But their instinct was to come back, and they were right. The voyage was taking them towards the coldest region in the world, colder than the pole itself. It was by land from Russia that real advances were being made, thanks to the opening of the White Sea—Moscow route. In the 'sixties and 'seventies that amazing traveller, Antony Jenkinson, penetrated to the Caspian Sea, and beyond it to Persia and Bokhara.

He took the indefatigable Richard Johnson with him, who this time found the foreigners' ways less sensational and contented himself with collecting useful information from Persian merchants about the length of the land route to Cathay. The results of this journey were a magnificent map of Russia by Jenkinson, published in 1562, and the establishing of an important trade with Central Asia—and by that way with the Far East. Cathay had at last been reached, but no one could pretend that a short cut had been found thither.

Richard Hakluyt of immortal memory has already been mentioned more than once, and it is time that something was said about that remarkable group of men, or 'brains trust' as it might perhaps be called nowadays, which stood behind so many of the achievements of English seamanship, suggesting, calculating and planning. There are of course distinguished patrons associated with almost all the great seamen, men such as Walsingham, who backed some of Drake's voyages; Lord Lumley, in whose 'stately library' Hakluyt read Chancellor's own manuscript account of his Russian journey; and the Percys, one of whom was a close friend of Ralegh, and from whose library come many of the most interesting maps and plans of that date which have been preserved. But though these men played an important and practical part, it is the theorists whose work inspired both them and in many instances the mariners themselves. Richard Hakluyt the younger, whose great collection of the *Principal Navigations, Voyages, Traffiques and Discoveries of the English Nation* is much the most important single source of information about this aspect of the period, devoted his whole life to the pursuit of this one surpassing interest, sparing neither money nor labour where it was concerned, with the advancement of his country's greatness always before his eyes. He shared with his cousin not only his name but also his passion for navigation; and Richard Hakluyt the elder, of Middle Temple, plays no mean part among that distinguished company of thinkers. To have inspired the *Principal Navigations* would be in itself a high title to fame, and the younger Hakluyt has described how while he was still a boy the seed that was to be so fruitful was sown, and how listening to his cousin's discourse illustrated by 'certain bookes of cosmographie, an universall mappe, and the Bible', he made up his mind once for all 'to prosecute that kind of literature'. Perhaps it was from his cousin also, and from that same moment, that there came the devout faith which shines out in all his work and which is so splendid a mark of the men engaged on those enterprises which he recorded. It was Sebastian Cabot who wrote of 'God, under whose mercifull hand navigants above all other creatures naturally be most nigh'. Certainly these men, occupying their business in great waters, saw the Lord's works with keen eyes, and the man who chronicled their achievements was deeply aware of the master hand directing them.

A tiny detail sometimes gives a striking insight into character. I have seen recently a book that belonged to one of the two Hakluyts—it is hard to say which of them. The book is one of those collections of 'emblems' or illustrations, with poems generally of a moralising character attached to each. In this instance there are notes also. The language is French. The owner has in all marked four passages in the margin that caught his eye. One is a note on the fir tree, that 'because it is resinous and light, it is good for ship building'. Two are devotional, concerning contentment with the will of God and the inadequacy of man's wisdom without divine help. There is one, and only one, to which attention is drawn by an elaborate little design in the margin. 'The greatest things are accomplished', it reads, 'and greatest achievements won, by toil and by striving uninterrupted, toil as well of the body as of the spirit.' Not only the works of the mind, the work of the poet or the writer's prose, but the sheer physical mastery of the man who encompasses the world in his tiny ship, this too is to be reckoned among men's great achievements. Indeed the greatness of the age is that it was an age not only of thought, but also of action, and of this Hakluyt's work is an epitome.

His life was comparatively unadventurous. He went up to Christ Church, Oxford, from Westminster School, and soon after taking his degree began the first public lectures on geography at Oxford. As a result of his books he became acquainted with Lord Howard of Effingham, the Lord Admiral, and through him with the most notable English seamen of the time. When he was thirty he went to Paris and began there his association with some of the continental geographers and travellers. He returned in the year of the Armada, and devoted himself to his work of inspiring and recording maritime enterprise. His collection of voyages was first published in the following year. Ten years later a new and greatly enlarged edition appeared. It contains not only narratives of the voyages chronicled—narratives written sometimes by himself, but much more often by

IV. MAP OF RUSSIA

(Drawn by Antony Jenkinson in 1562)

the men who had taken part in them—but also documents concerned with them, instructions to shipmasters, descriptions of the regions visited, commercial notes on language, weights and measures of many different countries, charters, treaties, letters and geographical notes. It might have been made portentously dull—as his successor Purchas on the whole succeeded in making it. In Hakluyt's book even the lading bills for a cargo of English cloth become exciting, as if they were a symbol to him of the growth of the power of England and the spread of knowledge.

Among those who were in touch with Hakluyt were two great geographers of the Low Countries and Germany, Ortelius and Mercator. The former was born in Germany and did most of his work in Antwerp, while Mercator was professor at Duisberg. Ortelius produced the first great modern atlas, *Theatrum Orbis Terrarum*, as he called it, in 1570, and when Richard Hakluyt the elder drew up his instructions for Jackman and Pet's voyage he mentioned this book: 'If you take Ortelius' booke of Mappes with you to marke all these regions, it were not amisse; and if chance were, to present the same to the great Can, for it would be to a Prince of marveilous account.' The view of the north-east passage indicated in the map of Tartary is significant. Ortelius there suggests that just beyond the river Ob is a promontory (which may be regarded as the same as Nova Zemlya) running far to the north to latitude 81°; but when this had been rounded, the coast line, according to this map, tended sharply southwards, so that in a comparatively short time temperate regions would be reached and there was indeed thenceforward an almost direct route to Peking. Ortelius' ideas had a profound influence on the search for a north-east passage, and he was consulted on the north-west passage too by the elder Hakluyt. In an extant letter, Hakluyt asks him to send a map on rollers showing the famous Strait of the Three Brothers (the Fretum Trium Fratrum) north of Labrador, through which the route was believed to lie.

Mercator, the master from whom Ortelius had learnt, drew an interesting map of the polar regions to demonstrate his own theories of the possibilities. He did not believe in that direct southerly turn of the coast line of Northern Asia and imagined that the north-eastern promontory of Asia might be difficult to make because of the proximity of the magnetic pole; not by reason of the cold, but because it would damage the ship's compass. He believed, however, that there were great rivers flowing northwards into the ocean, and that these would offer likely routes for the opening up of trade with the interior of Asia. Mercator was asked directly his view of the prospects of the voyage, and his letter in reply to Hakluyt's question is extant, though it arrived after Jackman and Pet had sailed. Mercator never published a complete atlas, though his maps passed to his son, who added to their number and published them at length in atlas form—a book of surpassing interest. But he had during his lifetime produced a number of world maps and globes, modifying them as the work of the discoverers made them out of date; and these too influenced considerably, as we shall have often to notice, the planning of discovery.

One of the most interesting figures of the group, however, was Dr John Dee, part scholar, part perhaps charlatan. His portrait, done at the age of forty in 1562, shows him as in some respects already venerable. There is a depth about the eyes which suggests a mind slow moving but profound, and among his contemporaries, largely because of his deep interest in alchemy, he had an oracular reputation. Queen Elizabeth went to visit him, and Ivan the Terrible invited him to Russia, promising him a fee of a thousand roubles. Dee's ambition was to see his country as a great maritime power, and in the strange symbolical illustrations to his works, there are many allusions to this hope. His letters and notebooks show a great range of reading in the classics, but it was as a mathematician that he had a real claim to distinction. The navigators were beginning to feel the need for a better technical equipment in mathematics, at a time when great circle sailing was just coming into fashion and when ideas were being worked out for using the variation of the compass to determine longitude. In 1570 was published Dee's edition of Euclid in English, the first English translation, and it has a preface which surveys the mathematical basis of the sciences. It is a fascinating work, not only for its allusions to contemporary plans of discovery (such as that of Sir Humphrey Gilbert in 1567, to attempt the north-west or the north-east passage) but for the light it throws on Dee's own ideas and those of his contemporaries. It is strange to a modern mind to find a distinguished mathematician arguing the necessity for astrology to form a part of the technical equipment of the navigator, because 'man's body and all other Elementall bodies are altered, disposed, ordred, pleasured and displeasured by the Influentiall working of the Sunne, Mone, and other Starres and Planets'. Yet in this Dee is typical of his age, in which even so practical a seaman as

Drake once became convinced that his second-in-command was practising black magic against him. And in his insistence on the understanding of technical detail in navigation and on the use of exact instruments, Dee did the work of a pioneer.

Dee was constantly consulted on the likelihood of discoveries in unknown regions, and brought the weight of his immense learning to bear on problems such as that of locating the country from which Solomon's gold was brought. He himself lived in the hope that one day discoveries in the East would reveal the philosopher's stone which would turn base metal into precious, and he sometimes wrote of the East for that reason in almost mystical phrases. But like others who have sought that stone he died in poverty. 'Life is death and death is life' is the strange inscription that rings his portrait. He was always baffling, and almost as baffling to-day as he was to his own contemporaries, for that transparent faith and honesty in what we might be tempted to call his quackeries.

It is about the time of Chancellor's voyages that this brilliant group begins to bring its influence to bear. Some of the navigators had little to do with them, and there is no reason to think that Hawkins ever concerned his head about Dee's theories. But they were, nevertheless, of prime importance in many of the great enterprises of the time, such as Drake's voyage round the world. Romanticism and good sense always make, in combination, a powerfully explosive mixture. Such a mixture was working among the minds of these Elizabethans, and while the steady Hawkins was planning his slaving voyages, there were already men who foresaw the planting of the American colonies and a New England across two thousand miles of ocean.

Chapter III

JOHN HAWKINS IN THE WEST INDIES

THE motives which it is now fashionable to call ideologies are not new to history. Loyalty and heroism have always been shown in their finest forms when men thought they were fighting for intangible things—things like the liberty, equality and brotherhood of the French Revolution; and prospects of greater wealth, while they have been all powerful for individuals, have seldom meant very much to the ordinary fighting man. Leaders who are aware of this, like Napoleon, often use the knowledge for their own ends, but there comes in course of time a flagging of effort which cannot be counteracted altogether even by the growth of great personal loyalty. Thus the loyalty of Napoleon's armies was not enough to save him, once the ideals of liberty and brotherhood began to wear thin. With the religious ideologies of the sixteenth century there was this difference, that each had its own particular symbols, in the Catholic or in the reformed religious service. Men were directly aware whether the Latin Mass was being said or not in their own parish churches, and these symbols therefore kept living for years ideological differences that might otherwise have died down in a comparatively short time.

Even in the most practical of the Elizabethan seamen the religious inspiration is important. John Hawkins issued a famous order for keeping the ships together on his voyage of 1564. 'Serve God daily,' it ends, 'love one another, preserve your victuals, beware of fire, and keep good companie.'* 'Serve God daily.' Hawkins' own account of the third 'troublesome voyage' made to the West Indies in 1567 and 1568 is steeped in the idea of dependence on God. There has come down to us by chance a mention of the way in which young Francis Drake on the earlier of these two voyages strove to make converts for his Puritan ideas amongst the crews. No head was harder than Drake's; yet we find him in 1587, after his magnificently successful operations off the coast of Spain, writing to Walsingham of the 'enemies of the truth and upholders of Baal or Dagon's image which hath already fallen before the ark of our God

* I.e. keep ships together; do not stray from the flagship.

with his hands and arms and head stricken off'. At that same time, in writing to a famous divine, John Foxe, author of the *Book of Martyrs*, which was a second Bible for the Puritans, he signs himself 'your loving friend and faithful son in Christ Jesus'. The tone in which these words were written is not open to doubt. In Drake, as among the crews of the ships that sailed under his leadership, the flame of Puritanism burned fiercely, as fiercely as there glowed in Philip of Spain the conviction that Protestantism was frightful heresy, and that to exterminate it was to do God's work.

As has been said, once begun, these ideologies were partly a matter of symbols. They were symbols of the faith in which men had been brought up; for in the last third of the sixteenth century the reformation was already a generation old. There were other things, too, adding to their strength, ideas which in some respects might seem to nullify the religious conflict; above all the idea of nationality. There is before me, as I write, a Latin missal printed in the mid-sixteenth century for the use of the Carthusian order, and this copy belonged to a Carthusian monastery in Antwerp. On the fly-leaf someone has written in majestic script five Latin verses, commemorating and lamenting over that nightmare of 4 November 1576, the Spanish Fury, when Antwerp was handed over to the cruelty of Spanish armies, stifled and murdered, as the writer puts it, by fire and sword. The monk who wrote these words was a good Catholic. But what he saw was a savage attack on the citizens of his beloved city by Spanish foreigners, and in such a moment there are no doubts as to the side which holds his allegiance. So in England, too, there were Catholics who followed with breathless anxiety the schemes of Father Parsons and those other intrepid Jesuits who plotted against Elizabeth's life. But there were certainly others who, Catholics though they were, hated treason more than they hated heresy. Their loyalty to England was as strong as their loyalty to the Mass, and they were beginning to feel that the two were not incompatible.

Men certainly saw the conflict between England and Spain, according to the side which they took, as a conflict between what was old and rotten and what was new and vigorous, or between a revered tradition and an uncritical and destructive passion for novelty for the sake of its newness. There is on the one hand the power long established in unquestioned possession of its West Indian empire, and on the other the power struggling for more 'living room', as it might be called in the phrases of to-day; between the 'haves' and the 'have nots', between those who abide by 'law' and those who break it. And pressed into the service of the ideologies there is a degree of intrigue for parallels to which we must turn to the last ten years. One of the things which make Hawkins' voyages so hard to interpret is the uncertainty whether he is saying what he means; whether he is playing a double game and waiting to make up his mind until events show him what is the wise course to take, or whether he is deceiving Philip and his ambassador with consummate skill, to do what he likes with them later. And Cecil with his ubiquitous system of espionage, kidnapping in Antwerp a man whom he wishes to torture for evidence, or quietly opening and reading Philip's letters to the Queen of Scots before he seals them up again and forwards them innocently by her secret post, has his modern counterparts. Intriguer that he was, the intrigue was not all on Philip's part, and almost every movement that he made as he dabbled in English affairs was watched, silently, by the cautious enigmatic figure who stood at Elizabeth's side for so much of that great reign. It seems to some of us a strange mixture nowadays, this mixture of the methods of deceit with absolute personal loyalty. Perhaps for that too modern counterparts can be found. Yet he would be a cynic who did not feel that, with all its contradictions, the Elizabethan age in England, in historical retrospect, has not only a brilliance, but also a rightness about it, that is not to be discovered in Philip's Spain; though it is high time nowadays that we eliminated such contradictions, and relegated such treacherous and unscrupulous methods to the past.

In the slaving voyages of Hawkins we first begin to be aware of these conflicting ideologies. Hitherto England and Spain had been allies. Not many years before Elizabeth's accession Philip had sat at Mary's side in Winchester Cathedral, reckoning himself King of England; and one of the men who had welcomed him at Plymouth, and according to a Spanish account had been knighted by him, was John Hawkins, 'Juan de Aquines' as the Spaniards called him.

The insecurity of the Spaniards in the West Indies had been demonstrated by the French. French privateers were active, preying on the Spanish treasure ships, long before any Englishman had ventured into the business. In the north, Cartier's voyages had produced more permanent results in Canada than had those of English ships, and French settlements in Florida anticipated by many years the English settlements farther north. In the West Indies French corsairs held cities to ransom, as Drake was later to do, already during the mid-sixteenth century, and it is against this background of insecurity in the West Indies that Hawkins' voyages have to be seen.

As has been said, the interpretation of the motives which lay behind Hawkins' voyages is still a matter for controversy. There are some facts, however, which must be fitted in with any explanation that is given. One is the participation of the authorities in these voyages from the start. Hawkins was son-in-law to the Treasurer of the Navy, Benjamin Gonson, and the Surveyor of the Navy, William Wynter, was another member of the syndicate which found the money for the first venture. These two names make it virtually certain that even the first voyage had official sanction. In the later voyages this becomes explicit. Prior to his second voyage Hawkins had an audience of the Queen in which his plans were discussed. She had lent him a ship of her navy, the 'Jesus of Lubeck', and he flew the Queen's own standard in her. He was in 'one of the Queene's armadas of England', he told the Spanish authorities in the town of Burboroata, and he maintained during the negotiations that the 'thing pertained to our Queene's highnesse'. It is not easy to square with these facts, or with the show of force which Hawkins undoubtedly from the first was ready to make, Hawkins' constant references (in his dealings with Spaniards) to the King of Spain as 'the King my master', or to the services which he alleges he can do for the King. In an account of the voyage discovered and published by Dr Williamson, Hawkins goes yet further and speaks of himself as 'commanded by the Queen my mistress to serve [the King of Spain] with my navy as need requireth'. Was Hawkins actually suggesting, then, that in exchange for services he might render Spam, by patrolling West Indian waters, he might be allowed a privileged position in the West Indian slave trade, hitherto kept as a strict monopoly for certain Spanish firms? Or does it seem more likely that most of this about serving the King of Spain is what might be called diplomacy, and (in so far as it is anything else) implies no more than a vague suggestion that permission for Hawkins to trade would, in the long run, be an advantage to Spain as well as to John Hawkins? It looks as if the Queen, who in the first flush of that marvellous reign showed few signs of the indecision which later marked her methods, had seen the desirability of opening the West Indian trade to her subjects. She had been told, by Hawkins himself perhaps, that, in view of the desire of the colonists to trade, no real opposition would be encountered; and that once the trade became firmly established, the mutual advantages would be so great that nothing could stop it. She reckoned rightly, that whatever might happen in the West Indies, matters would not be pushed to war in Europe. She may have told Hawkins to go just as far as he could go; to sail as near the wind as he could sail. And if things should miscarry, Hawkins might be disowned, as others who served the Queen were publicly disowned, and praised only in private. The 'Jesus of Lubeck' was already long past her prime. She had been condemned as rotten years before, and it was no great loss to the Queen when she was at last abandoned in St Juan de Ulua. More than almost any other, then, of the enterprises with which we are concerned, this pertained to the Queen's majesty of England. It was not Hawkins fishing for an opportunity to make a good business connexion for himself, but England herself reaching out for the first time into American waters.

The accounts of the first voyage are meagre. Hakluyt's story is probably derived from Hawkins himself, but it was written long after, when the political situation had changed and it had become injudicious to say many of the things that might have been said. Hawkins had already made as a young man voyages to the Canaries where he had formed close business associations 'by his good and upright dealing'. He had learned there that there was a demand for negro slaves in Hispaniola, and that it would not be difficult to collect a supply of them from the Guinea coast. Three ships were equipped to take part in the expedition, the 'Solomon' of 120 tons, the 'Swallow' of 100 tons, and the 'Jonas', a bark of 40 tons. The crews numbered less than a hundred, all told, for Hawkins realised that the dangers from disease due to overcrowding were greater than that of having ships that were, according to the standards of the day, undermanned. They sailed in October 1562, and touching at Tenerife, went on to the African coast. There, partly by the sword and partly by other means (as he says), they obtained more than three hundred negroes. Portuguese accounts suggest that the 'other means' involved the exertion of considerable pressure on Portuguese slavers to sell their stocks; and allege that Hawkins used violence to get what he wanted. It is probable that these Portuguese accounts are exaggerated. The bare threat of force Hawkins was to find effective for most purposes. His first port of call in the West Indies was Isabella, in Hispaniola, where he sold part of his cargoes. When official opposition was encountered from the authorities in San Domingo, a demonstration was enough to convince the Governor (who seems to have been not unwilling to be convinced) that he had no option but to submit to Hawkins' demands, and the Englishman left without paying the full duty which the Spanish company had to pay the crown for the sale of slaves. A duty of $7\frac{1}{2}$ per cent, said Hawkins, was enough. That was the duty which an Englishman had to pay in dealing with European Spanish possessions. Hawkins was by nature law-abiding, but he tended to make for himself the laws by which he chose to abide, pointing out how reasonable they were. And, with Spanish planters eager for his slaves, he had no real difficulty. Spanish occupation of the Indies had acted like a blight on the native populations. Labour was urgently needed, and at various towns in Hispaniola he disposed of his wares to such profit that he chartered two other ships to carry to Europe the hides, spices and sugar which he had bought with the proceeds. He evidently did not expect the Spanish authorities would take any further action in the matter, for he consigned the cargoes of the two ships he had chartered to an English agent in Spain. There they were seized by representatives of the company that had monopoly rights of the slave trade with the Indies, and his efforts to secure redress failed. But what he had himself brought to England was enough to assure the commercial success of the venture, and another voyage was soon being planned on a larger scale.

The second voyage is represented in Hakluyt by a much fuller account, written by one of the gentlemen adventurers taking part. He observed keenly and wrote entertainingly, but he was not in the inner counsels of the promoters, and once again we are left in the dark as to the real motives of Hawkins and his backers. It was for this expedition that the Queen's ship, the 'Jesus of Lubeck', was lent, or rather hired, and as has been mentioned, Hawkins evidently had in a direct sense royal authority for the voyage. The 'Jesus' was a ship of 700 tons, far bigger than anything that had sailed on the previous voyage, and her picture in Antony's roll shows her with lofty upper works fore and aft such as were reckoned more and more out of date by the leading seamen of the time. In a later voyage her unseaworthiness was to prove disastrous, but in this voyage she was never tried by really bad weather, and Hawkins may have thought that the prestige she added to the expedition was important. The other three ships were much smaller, so that even on that expedition the total complement, gentlemen adventurers and all, was not above one hundred and seventy men. They sailed late in October 1564, from Plymouth to Tenerife, where Hawkins evidently talked business with his friends, while John Sparke (who wrote the account in Hakluyt) admired the volcano; then they passed on to the African coast and tried to acquire their cargo. Rumours of their intentions had preceded them, however, and there were no negroes at first to be had. A fight near the Rio Grande brought no result, but thereafter they gradually began to accumulate slaves, once again it appears partly at the expense of the Portuguese. In the course of subsequent affrays with the natives they lost heavily, and the accounts suggest that Hawkins had not that genius for operations on land which his pupil Drake was to develop. His men are described as being out of hand in the search for plunder, and in one case, at any rate, rash behaviour which led to disaster was due to drunkenness. But there were ultimately collected all the negroes that they wanted, and John Sparke had ample opportunity for observing native methods of warfare. The negroes used, he tells us, 'a marveilous crying in their fight, with leaping and turning their tayles, that it was most strange to see, and gave us great pleasure to behold them'. Few Elizabethan observers suffered from ennui, and John Sparke was certainly not one of them.

Hawkins, as plainly appears from the latter part of the narrative, had no adequate map of the Caribbean Sea, and once he left Hispaniola he was working in the dark. He had decided to turn southwards to the Spanish Main, the northern shore of South America, and his first objective was the town of Burboroata. But the official view was that trade with Englishmen in slaves was illicit, as he must, now at any rate after what had happened to his cargo in Seville, have fully realised; and when he arrived off Burboroata he was told that trade had been explicitly forbidden. Yet there were planters itching to buy from him, and so he began by saying that he had some negroes on his hands who had hardly been able to stand the voyage and must be put ashore at once, implying that it was these only that he wanted to sell and that his arrival in the Spanish Main at all was only due to the weather. When license to trade was granted, there was a further difficulty, as in the last voyage, over the customs dues on the slaves, and once again Hawkins refused to pay the 30 per cent, and offered 7½ per cent only. A landing in force was enough to convince the local authorities that this too was a concession that could reasonably be made. The whole story, with Hawkins' transparent excuses and the show of force designed to hurt nobody, is a curious commentary on the relations between the Spanish authorities in the colonies and the Government at home. It was repeated at Rio de la Hacha, and after a mock battle, staged apparently to make it clear that the Spaniards were acting under duress in allowing the trade, Hawkins actually left with a testimonial of good conduct from the Governor in his pocket. As before, the profits were invested in cargoes which would sell well in England, hides, spices, pearls and the precious metals. The voyage might have been even more profitable if Hawkins had found his way to Havana, which he hoped to do; but the lack of adequate charts prevented him and there was still space unoccupied in his holds when he reached home. On the way back he had visited the French settlement in Florida, which he found to be in difficulties. The reports that Florida was another Mexico had proved ill-founded, and many of the settlers were clamouring to return. The offer which Hawkins made to take them was refused, but he agreed to lend a ship and supplies to make escape possible. The accounts suggest rather that he had a warm fellow-feeling with the French than that he was trying to do his own and the Spanish Government a good service by moving them, though it might have been a useful card to play with the Spanish ambassador when he reached home, for there was no love lost between French and Spanish in the Indies. It was not long, indeed, before the Spanish Government themselves took the problem in hand. That summer, in accordance with the new policy of a strong hand in the Caribbean, a Spanish admiral swooped down on Florida. Every Frenchman caught there, save those who claimed to be Catholics, was killed.

The third 'troublesome voyage' of Hawkins to the Indies was planned in an atmosphere of intrigue. The Spanish ambassador was keeping a close eye on Hawkins, and had protested to the Queen against permission being allowed him to visit the Indies. But Queen Elizabeth was a master at dissembling, and never so happy as when she was planning secretly, with a man she could trust absolutely, to help him on some great enterprise. She kept the ambassadors of foreign princes guessing, almost as a matter of policy, making allusions that suggested to them that she knew (as she invariably did) more than she chose to say, and greeting them with that innocent charm which some of them at last began to suspect. And for all the changing moods of her later life, blowing hot and cold, giving orders and countermanding them, she always succeeded in winning the trust of the greatest of those Englishmen who worked with her. Her seamen had more cause, perhaps, than any of her subjects to blame her hesitation. Yet there is never a suggestion of disloyalty from one of them. 'Though you have had and may have many mightier and wiser Princes sitting in this Seat, yet you never had nor shall have any that will love you better.' These words, used to her last Parliament in 1601, expressed something which they all knew to be true; and they were ready to bear the storms of that raging temper for the sunshine which they knew would follow. Elizabeth flirted with many men. She lost her heart to none of them, for she had lost it to her people. If any woman was constant, it was she. And England's heart was lost, too, from that January Sunday in 1559 when, as she went to her coronation, she noticed an old man turning his back and weeping: 'I warrant you it is for gladness', she said—till those days a generation later when the golden bowl was broken and the silver cord loosed; when old age had come to her also, and men, looking askance at the dyed red hair and the painted face, were nevertheless still aware of that undying spirit, and still felt its inspiration.

John Hawkins was not without experience of the Queen's diplomacy even before the third voyage began to be planned. When the Spanish ambassador had made his protest to the Queen, an official enquiry had been held, ostensibly that the Queen might be informed whether the expedition then on the stocks (in which she was interested financially and with the details of which she was certainly familiar) could conceivably have the West Indies as its objective. As a result, Hawkins had been directed by her Council to provide a guarantee of £500 that he would not sail to the West Indies. The expedition had, therefore, to be led by a deputy, who bungled it. This time there must be no bungling, and an opportunity arose of throwing dust in the ambassador's eyes while the foundations were being well and truly laid. It consisted in the story of two Portuguese adventurers who said that they would lead the way to a mysterious but enormously rich gold mine in Africa. The expedition was nominally equipped to find it. At the same time, stocks of provisions such as would be needed if negroes had to be transported across to the Spanish Main were loaded, and a short time before the expedition sailed the two Portuguese disappeared. At a time when plot and counterplot were so thick and when documents were as often as not written for the eyes of the spy as well as the recipient it is hardly possible to distinguish what part the gold story really played; whether Elizabeth and Hawkins half believed it themselves or whether they used it simply as a blind.[1] The Spanish ambassador was suspicious. 'A daughter of the devil' one Spanish ambassador called Elizabeth, writing to his sovereign about her. And there was no doubt a touch of the cloven hoof somewhere in the pedigree. However that may be, in September 1567 Hawkins was ready in Plymouth harbour to sail on the most momentous of all the expeditions he commanded.

On 2 October 1567 the gallant old 'Jesus of Lubeck' sailed out of Plymouth on her last voyage, with five consorts, all much smaller than their flagship, and four hundred and eight men all told. Their start was ominous. Forty leagues north of Cape Finisterre there was an 'extreme storm'. It blew for four days; 'seven days and seven nights', that excellent man Job Hartop, powder maker, called it in the book he wrote twenty-three years later about his 'travels, miseries and dangers'. But even the four days were in truth bad enough. The long boats and a pinnace were lost, and some lives too, and Hawkins says that he had it in mind to turn back. But in time the weather mended and they pushed on southwards. Capturing negroes was becoming progressively a more difficult business. Near Cape Verde they landed and captured a few, but Hawkins himself and some others were wounded with arrows that proved to be poisoned. The hurts seemed to be slight, but some days later eight men died of them and Hawkins regarded his own escape as providential. In eight weeks they procured only one hundred and fifty negroes, and Hawkins half thought of crossing to the West Indies at once to sell them with such merchandise as he had, for the season was getting late and he would have to reckon, if he delayed too long, with the 'Furicanos' as he calls them, of the Caribbean; it was these storms in the 'still vex'd Bermoothes' (Bermudas) that were going to father the Tempest in Shakespeare's play nearly fifty years later. Time was of vital importance. But negroes were important too, and when an offer came along from a negro potentate of prisoners of war, provided he first helped to capture them, he decided to stay. They were cheated, but secured nevertheless some prisoners and had between four and five hundred negroes when they made at last the middle passage to the Indies. It was a difficult and long crossing, of a piece with the misfortunes of the voyage. When they reached Dominica they found that Spanish officials had strict orders not to allow trade with Hawkins. 'Notwithstanding', he says, 'we had reasonable trade and courteous entertainement'; till they came to Rio de la Hacha. Hitherto they had traded on the whole satisfactorily, if 'somewhat hardly' as Hawkins remarks. But here it was necessary to make a demonstration. A strong force, two hundred men, was thrown ashore. The town was taken but its Governor still refused license to trade. Hawkins replied that, if no license was granted, he would burn the town, and in the excitement some houses were actually burned. The Governor sent a number of the citizens to say that, even if the town were burned, the license would be withheld, but some of those he sent were less unwilling to listen to the Englishman's proposals, and indeed he was, as the Governor afterwards said, 'such a man that any man talking to him hath no power to deny him anything he doth request'. A few days later came Hawkins' chance, and with it an incident that throws a grim light on these slaving voyages. A negro slave belonging to the Governor escaped, and came to Hawkins to tell him, in return for his freedom, where the treasure of the town had been hidden. The prospect of losing that was too much for the townspeople. An agreement was reached and Hawkins secured his license, albeit a secret license, to trade. As part of the agreement the slave was returned to his master.[2] Slaves were the chattels in which Hawkins dealt. John Hawkins 'coveted no man's goods wrongfully, but would pay for anything he did take', as one of his associates in the 'Jesus' wrote at this time. Fair dealing did not extend to that negro slave; and in his treatment of him Hawkins is no different from his generation. It was left for Drake to show another way, and to extort a terrible revenge from the Spaniards for a murdered negro slave boy.

At Rio de la Hacha they thus sold one hundred and fifty slaves and other wares. The next port of call was Santa Marta. Hawkins paid a visit in secret to the Governor, and a plan of campaign was concocted between them. Hawkins was to return to his ship, then land in force with one hundred and fifty men, shooting half a score shot over the town to lend colour to the proceeding. The shots were fired, the men landed with Hawkins at their head in armour. In the market-place he was met by a flag of truce to say that the Governor was waiting to parley with him. Hawkins stated that he was anxious about his men, seeing that if he did not sell his negroes he would have no money to pay them. Apart from that he had no ill designs upon the town whatever. So they had 'very friendly traffic', including banquets on shore and aboard the ships, and another hundred negroes were sold. Carthagena, the next port of call, was a tougher nut. It was heavily defended and Hawkins contented himself with letting off a salvo of half a dozen cannon in its direction, writing his usual polite letter to the Governor asking for license to trade (to which request he received a peremptory negative), and watering at a nearby island. This was one of the pleasure resorts of Carthagena. He found there a supply of excellent wines which he removed, and left good English cloth in payment for them. It is a Gilbertian story, and it might almost be the captain of H.M.S. 'Pinafore' dealing with a whole series of Dukes of Plaza Toro. The interest lies in the explanation it surely gives of Hawkins' persistence, in the face of continuous opposition from the Spanish authorities in Europe. He could hardly have continued as he did if there had not been a strong feeling among the Spanish colonists that he had something good to offer them.

The slaves were not yet all sold. But those furicanos might break out at any moment, and Hawkins decided that he must make his way home. They left Carthagena on 24 July and ran northwards, west of Cuba. It was too late. On 12 August a storm burst on them and raged for four days. The upper works of the 'Jesus' were cut down to relieve the strain on her hull, which was leaking so badly that they contemplated abandoning her. It was perhaps Hawkins' sense of obligation to the Queen, the 'Jesus' being a Queen's ship, that decided him against this. They searched along the coast of Florida for a harbour in which to refit, but found nothing. One extraordinary feature of these expeditions is indeed that Hawkins seems always to have been working in the dark without any real information, except hearsay, of the seas he was sailing. He knew only of a port or roadstead, used by goods bound for Mexico, in the south-western corner of the Caribbean—the island of St Juan de Ulua. Years later the city of Vera Cruz, which at that time was some miles away, was moved to the coast opposite this island. But in 1568 there seems to have been no settlement on the mainland.[3] What few huts there were, for the negroes who worked as labourers in the port and for the small garrison, were presumably on the island.

The danger on this coast is the north-westerly gales against which the roadstead of St Juan offered some shelter. What protection there is is given by a number of reefs or sandbanks, three of which may be dignified with the name of island, two standing somewhat further out than St Juan, and St Juan which itself lies rather more than half a mile from the mainland.[4] It had been little more than a heap of shingle, eight hundred yards or so at its greatest length, when the Spaniards came. But they had built a wall or quay along the landward side of the island with buttresses at each end, between which ships could ride so close in that the projecting bows might overhang the wall and a man leap ashore. The lie of the island is roughly south-east and north-west, and the main entrance to the roadstead is at the north-western end, where a ship is protected as she approaches by the shoal that stretches northward from the island of St Juan de Ulua. The entrance to the roadstead at its south-eastern end is more difficult, but not impassable.

Hawkins made this port on 16 September. As he approached, his ships were mistaken for a Spanish fleet that was daily expected, and a small boat was sent out to meet him. He told them that he had been driven out of his course by the weather and needed to refit and to revictual, but that he had no desire for anything that he had not already been allowed at other Spanish ports; and he asked for two Spaniards of estimation immediately to be sent to Mexico to explain his needs, for he realised that a Spanish force was expected and that unless definite instructions had been received from Mexico, their arrival might cause some trouble. The message, as he believed, was despatched that same night, though the Governor did not in fact allow it to be sent. Next morning, 17 September, thirteen great ships were sighted. Hawkins instantly sent out a boat to inform the Spanish admiral of the position, and to say that he could not permit the fleet to enter until terms had been agreed which safeguarded the English ships. It so happened that there was on board the new Viceroy of Mexico, who was evidently displeased at being shut out of his own haven. There was some bluster, in the course of which the Spaniard said that he was Viceroy, had a thousand men and would certainly come in whoever tried to stop him. Hawkins replied that he too represented his Queen's person, and that he was not afraid of a thousand men. He was in a difficult dilemma. He might have defended the harbour, and indeed had apparently reinforced his own armament with guns taken from the Spanish ships. But that meant war, for if the north wind got up, the Spanish ships would inevitably have been wrecked. He might let the Spaniard in. But he knew well enough his own record in the books of Spain, and he did not trust the new

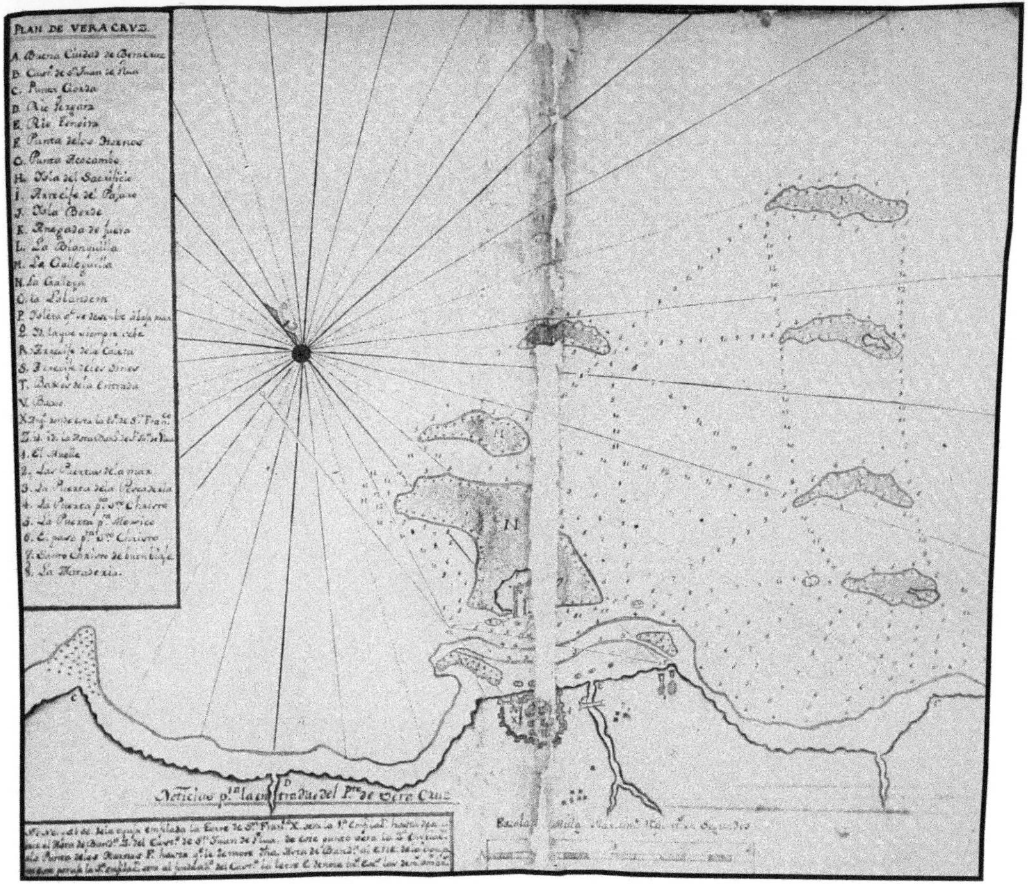

V. ST JUAN DE ULUA (VERA CRUZ)

(From a manuscript chart of about 1780)

Viceroy, Don Martin Enriquez, an inch. It was finally agreed that the Spaniards should enter. Hawkins was to be allowed to buy what he needed, and to sell enough to pay for it. He was to be allowed to repair his ships. During his stay, the island, on which he had already mounted eleven guns, was to remain in English hands. It seems that Hawkins had first asked that no Spaniard should land on it, but the terms were modified, no Spaniard being allowed to land armed. Ten hostages were exchanged, and the agreement was signed and sealed by the Viceroy's hand. It had been on Friday that the Spanish ships were first sighted. On the Monday they entered, and the fleets saluted one another. Meanwhile the Spanish commander had secretly sent to Vera Cruz for reinforcements. In dealing with a well-known corsair there was no need to be punctilious.

All the next two days they laboured dividing the English and Spanish ships, in order to remove an obvious chance for friction, and there was great amity on all sides. It was impossible to leave much space between the two fleets, for the room was not there. On the Thursday morning it was noticed that there were frequent goings and comings between the Spanish ships. A huge Spanish hulk of 900 tons was moored next the 'Minion', and new ports were obviously being cut in the sides of some Spanish ships, while the cannon were being shifted. It looked as if the object was to command the island. Hawkins was uneasy, and complained to the Viceroy, who at once gave orders that any cause for suspicion should be removed. Still Hawkins did not like the look of things. It was said that there were three hundred men in the hulk next the 'Minion', while there were large numbers of Spaniards ashore fraternising with the English sailors, some of whom it appears were the worse for drink by dinner time. Just before dinner, Hawkins determined to send the master of the 'Jesus', who could talk Spanish, to make further enquiries. On his arrival the Spanish Viceroy realised that further concealment was impossible. The signal was given and the Spaniards ashore set on the Englishmen there, who were apparently taken completely by surprise, and fearing that they might be cut off, instead of manning the batteries, rushed for the ships. The 'Minion' had been warned of Hawkins' suspicions half an hour before. She instantly loosed the headfasts* which held her bows to the shore and was drawn out by the sternfasts.* In the initial surprise, a few Spaniards had boarded her from the hulk. Hawkins in the 'Jesus'

* Hawkins' own terms.

was sitting at dinner when the alarm was given, and the Spaniard waiting on him had a dagger hidden in his sleeve to kill him, but it was noticed and he was prevented. Hawkins ran on deck, shouting 'God and Saint George upon those traiterous villaines, and rescue the "Minion"! I trust in God the day shalbe ours.' Some of his men leaped into the 'Minion'[5] and dislodged the few Spaniards who had obtained a footing on her. At the same time she opened fire even before the enemy could begin. The first shot killed a Spanish gunner and soon two of the nearer Spanish ships, the Capitana and Almirante of the fleet, had been severely handled. Then a shot fired a barrel of powder in the Almirante, and she was burnt to the waterline with almost everything in her. The crew began to abandon the other ship also, in which the Viceroy was left almost alone, with the royal standard still flying.

The 'Minion' had escaped the brunt of the attack from the Spanish hulk by moving out from shore. It fell on the 'Jesus', on which they were struggling to let go the headfasts, as had been done in the 'Minion'. She was attacked by the hulk and two other Spanish ships simultaneously, but she also drove the Spaniards off her deck. Their comrades had by now seized the shore batteries which from the start of the engagement had been deserted by the English gunners, and the Spanish admiral in command of one, the Governor of the port at the other, directed a heavy fire on the 'Jesus' and the smaller ships. Nevertheless, she was able to throw off her headfasts and move out by hauling in the hawsers at the stern. Of the smaller ships, the 'Angel' was sunk and the 'Swallow' taken. Only three of the Englishmen ashore escaped, one of whom is said to have been Drake, who swarmed aboard the 'Judith' by the hawser. The others saved themselves by swimming to the 'Jesus'. The 'Judith' may have been the easternmost of the English ships. Her armament was small, and she made her way, probably out of the eastern channel, and stood by till she was told to come in and help the 'Minion' by taking men and stores aboard, which she did.

The 'Jesus' and the 'Minion' were now about two ships' lengths from the Spanish fleet, and the 'Jesus' had been heavily punished. She had five shot through her mainmast and her foremast broken in two by a chain shot, while her hull had been pierced in many places. Hawkins was constantly cheering soldiers and gunners. A cup of beer was shot from his hand, but he called to his men not to fear; 'for God who hath preserved me from this shot, will also deliver us from these traitours and villaines'. He was giving as good, or better, than he got. Besides the two ships already mentioned as sunk or burnt, four others had been sunk, and a Spanish report sent to Mexico gave the number of Spaniards killed as five hundred and forty. It was the possession of the land batteries that turned the battle from a Spanish defeat into a Spanish victory. Hawkins was a great leader, but once again his failure to see to the vital details of land operations is noteworthy. It was Drake's mastery in both, his eye for combined attack by sea and by land, that put him in a different class from his contemporaries.

One reason why the 'Jesus' had suffered so heavily was that in the later stages of the fight she had been shielding the 'Minion'. The two ships apparently lay alongside, the 'Jesus' between the 'Minion' and the shore batteries; and stores, including apparently some remaining slaves, were transferred from the 'Jesus', probably also most of the proceeds of the voyage. It may have been at this stage that the 'Judith' stood in to help. The fight, which had apparently begun before noon,[6] went on till the evening. Then the Spaniards sent down two great fire-ships on to the 'Jesus'.[7] There was no means of grappling them. The moral effect of this device was almost always enough. Some shouted that they should wait to see where the fire-ships drifted, but others that they should set sail at once. There were men in the 'Minion' waiting to cut sail at any moment, and when they heard these shouts, to make sure work, they started at once, without waiting for definite orders. The 'Minion' began to move away. There was a rush from the 'Jesus'. Hawkins leaped into the 'Minion' just in time and was 'very hardly received into her'. Some who had not jumped escaped in a boat. But some, including the injured men, must have been left behind as the 'Minion' moved away from the abandoned ship and stood out towards the open sea.

During the night the 'Minion' and the 'Judith' parted company. Hawkins thought that Drake had deserted him, though there is a fine reticence about the phrase he uses. 'So with the "Minion" only and "Judith" (a small barke of 50 tunne)', he says, 'we escaped, which barke the same night forsooke us in our great miserie.' There may have been two sides to the story. A north wind was getting up, from which Hawkins sheltered next day under Sacrifice Island, between two and three miles away from St Juan. That may have been the cause of the mishap, and there is no reason to think that any rendezvous had been arranged. But Hawkins' own condemnation is difficult to explain away. However that may be, he was unmolested by the Spaniards. They had had enough.

The battle, a magnificent fight against overwhelming odds, is also a turning point in English history. The end of Camden's brief account, written some years later, shows how Hawkins was regarded as the champion of English sea-borne commerce, not as fighting simply his own battle:

> The Spaniards being let in, who scorned to have conditions given them within their own dominions, watched their opportunity, set upon the English, slew many, tooke three ships, and pillaged the goods. Yet got they not the victory without blood. Hereat the many sea faring men all over England fretted, and demanded warre against the Spaniards, exclaiming that they were league breakers, inasmuch as it was agreed by the League between the Emperor Charles the Fifth and the King Henry the eight, that there should be free commerce between the subjects of both Princes, in all and singuler their Kingdomes, Dominions, and Iles, not excepting America, which then belonged to the said Charles. But the Queene shut her eares against them, being called away by Scottish matter.

This 'Scottish matter' we shall have to examine later. The end of the voyage must first be briefly told. Very little revictualling had been done when the fight took place. The 'Minion' was crowded with men and there were no provisions for them. Some actually suggested surrendering to the Spaniards. They wandered about the Caribbean for two weeks, starving, eating rats, parrots, monkeys, anything. Then they found a place where in fair weather a boat could be got ashore. A hundred and fourteen men, half of those who remained, asked to be set ashore. They were each given six yards of cloth to barter, and money if they wished. They found their way at length into Spanish service, and one or two, Job Hartop the gunner among them, got back at long last to England. The 'Minion' took in fresh water and sailed on 15 October. On the homeward voyage many men died of hunger. When they reached Portugal at last, forty-six died from the effects of eating fresh meat after a long period of starvation. On 25 January 1569 the 'Minion' reached Mount's Bay in Cornwall. William Hawkins, Hawkins' brother, had to send a fresh crew from Plymouth to bring her back to her home port. Only five days before the 'Minion' reached Mount's Bay, the 'Judith' had sailed into Plymouth Sound.

They found that during the few weeks preceding, a change had come about in the relations between England and Spain. The ideologies were becoming more clearly defined; the Catholics and the Protestants in Europe were finding their way into opposite camps. England's traditional policy had been to stand aside at such a moment. Henry VIII himself had stood aside, making it clear that he had no further use for Papal supremacy in England, but making it abundantly clear also that no one must be so mistaken as to suppose him to be in favour of any kind of democracy in religious affairs. So Elizabeth also tried for a long time to stand aside, and refused to accept the leadership of Protestant Europe when it was offered to her. In Europe the conflict had by now begun, and though England had not definitely entered it she had at least adopted what would now be called a policy of non-intervention. This meant that a great many Englishmen had accepted service under French Protestant leaders, and a privateer fleet, which was in fact largely English, was making havoc with the Catholic shipping in the Channel.

In the Spanish provinces in Flanders, Protestantism was causing serious anxiety to the authorities, and the Duke of Alva had been sent by Philip with orders to stamp it out. Later, in 1568, Philip had succeeded in obtaining a large loan from Italian financiers for the payment of Alva's armies, and the money was sent from Spain by sea, in an unarmed merchantman and several smaller craft. How this mistake came to be made it is difficult to imagine. The privateers were quick to see the opportunity. The new Spanish ambassador, de Espes, appealed to Elizabeth to help, and she sent urgent orders to William Wynter, who was at sea with a small naval force, to protect the treasure. It was probably only this that saved it from falling into the privateers' hands, and reserved it for a more interesting fate.

For protection, the Spanish ships had taken refuge some in Plymouth, Fowey and Falmouth, the largest in Southampton. Off Southampton waited three French and English privateers to pounce when a chance should offer. Meanwhile de Espes had asked Elizabeth for a safe conduct for the treasure overland to ports from which it could be shipped direct to Antwerp, and negotiations to this end proceeded. On 2 December a safe conduct was signed by the Queen, and shortly afterwards it was taken down to Southampton and Plymouth by de Espes' representatives, who were to make the necessary arrangements for conveyance.

It happened, however, that the representative in London of the Italian bankers with whom the loan had been negotiated, one Benedict Spinola, had been interested financially in one of Hawkins' voyages, and may possibly have invested money in that which has just been described also. About this time he had a letter from a correspondent in Spain which brought disquieting news. Hawkins, it said, had been ambushed, while marching inland to carry through his trading ventures, and with all his men he had been killed. This news of disaster followed hard on the heels of rumours of brilliant success, and Spinola at once sent information of it to Wynter, who passed it on in his turn to William Hawkins at Plymouth. The elder Hawkins was deeply disturbed about his brother. He wrote immediately to Cecil, Elizabeth's great Secretary of State, telling him of his forebodings, urging that Spinola should be questioned as to the news that had been received, and that if it should turn out to be true, the King of Spain's money should be detained by way of reprisal. It was probably while Spinola was being examined that a further material point came to light. The treasure, he said, did not actually belong to King Philip, and would not technically be his until it was handed over in Antwerp. Why should not Elizabeth borrow it herself?

The safe conduct for the treasure had been signed and was now in Spanish hands, and arrangements for transport were being made. But another letter was soon on its way to Southampton. When it reached him, Horsey, Governor of the Wight, acted quickly. He represented to the captain of the ship that had taken refuge that it was not safe for such a sum of money to be kept on board ship. At any moment privateers by some daring stroke might capture it, for Wynter had business elsewhere, and could not remain indefinitely on guard. Fifty-nine chests of money were unloaded at Southampton, and similar orders were given for the unloading of ships that had taken refuge in other ports.

Philip's ambassador, de Espes, a blustering fool, had only recently been appointed to replace de Silva, who was a diplomat. The new ambassador believed that swift action would bring Elizabeth to her senses, and wrote post-haste to Alva in the Netherlands saying that he believed the Queen intended to convert the treasure to her own use. Instant reprisals must be taken against the goods of English merchants in Antwerp and the Low Countries. Alva took his advice immediately, and on 29 December an embargo was declared, and a general arrest of English goods carried out, not only in the Netherlands, but ultimately in Spain also. Elizabeth held all the cards and played them rapidly. Once again there is no sign of that distracting indecision which often marked her actions later. English ships in Spain were recalled before the embargo there was declared, and by a proclamation issued on 6 January it was enacted that trade with Spain and the Spanish provinces should cease. Alva had arrested English goods without troubling to make himself conversant with the facts, at a time when de Espes was still negotiating for the safe conduct of the treasure. The Spaniards had not only put themselves in the wrong and justified what must be regarded as a piece of somewhat sharp practice on Elizabeth's part; they had also made a false step, for the value of Spanish property seized in England far exceeded that of English property arrested abroad. The loss of the money was a dangerous blow to Philip's tottering finances, which bolstered though they were by bags of gold from the Indies, never seemed to get any less shaky. It was not long before Alva, realising his mistake, sent to open negotiations with Cecil. His envoy received short shrift at Cecil's hands.

It may have been a piece of sharp practice on the part of Elizabeth to seize this treasure after a safe conduct had been given. But the circumstances must be remembered. There is no evidence that when the negotiations for the safe conduct were taking place, she had any ulterior motive in view. Hard on its signature had come news that suggested an act of war by the Spaniards against an English fleet, her fleet, in the West Indies. On these rumours she evidently decided to take measures that would at least lead to some delay in the transit of the money. If there was to be a quarrel between herself and Philip, it would have been madness to let that out of her reach before it began. The measures taken in no way committed her till her hand was forced by the action of de Espes and Alva. On the 20th Drake arrived in Plymouth with the full story. On the 25th Hawkins reached Mount's Bay. When he travelled up from Plymouth the proceeds of his voyage that he had been able to salvage went with him on four pack-horses. But King Philip's fifty-nine money chests went with him too, and the days when he could talk of 'serving his master, the King of Spain', without his tongue in his cheek, now, at any rate, were over.

Chapter IV

KING PHILIP, JOHN HAWKINS, AND THE SCOTTISH MATTER

ANALOGIES between past and present are notoriously misleading. We observe them and fail to observe the subtle differences of background that are all-important; those differences of moral preconceptions, for instance, which mark off one age unmistakably from another. But the analogy between Elizabethan days and our own time, already implied by the use of the word 'ideology', is striking for the way in which national unity was then undermined by religious fanaticism, as it was in Belgium or France in 1940 by devotion to political creeds. It was a time when many men were ready to betray their nation in the belief, often held in all honesty, that something else for which they took up arms was of prime importance. Yet then, as now, when we look deeper into their conduct, we may well wonder whether it was religion, or ambition, that was the light they followed. Did the Duke of Norfolk believe so passionately in the Mass—or did he believe rather in his own star, and see it guiding him to the throne of Scotland?

In one of the conspiracies against Elizabeth's life that were bred so freely in that atmosphere of violent religious feeling, Hawkins now found himself involved. Like the other two leading actors, Cecil, who about this time became Lord Burghley, and Elizabeth herself, he played his part with consummate coolness and skill. Elizabeth was never more completely at her ease than when she was herself in danger. She was one of those who are steadied, not flustered, by it. She would fly into a passion when she thought her dignity had been slighted, but when her life was threatened she played with conspiracy as if it were a game of skill at which she was a master. As for Burghley, holding the threads in those deft fingers, no knot was so complicated that he had not the patience to unravel it. Commanding the most elaborate secret service in Europe, his right hand seemed hardly to know what his left was doing, and not a flicker betrayed his intention till he was ready for action.

The woman who was the central figure in this conspiracy, Mary

Queen of Scots, had lived through adventures enough for many lives by the time that Hawkins' emissary came to visit her at Sheffield in 1571. She had been married when little more than a child to a French prince, had been left a widow, had returned to Scotland and been again married to a husband who not long after was murdered. She had been kidnapped by the murderer, and against her will, so she said, forced into yet another marriage, with him; and when this proved too much for her people to stomach, she had fled to England, while he fled elsewhere. But this 'seeming-virtuous Queen' was far from being a mere adventuress, nor was it merely that men who saw her always admired her. Her own passionate nature aroused in others devotion of a quality that it has been given to few to enjoy. She showed a loyalty to her friends which Elizabeth, with her changing moods, certainly cannot claim, and a courage in disaster which compelled the admiration even of her detractors. If Elizabeth had not been a Queen, she would have been a comparative nonentity. Her brilliance lay in the way in which she realised to the full the possibilities of her position and used her remarkable intellect in its service. Mary was a great human being with a vivid and generous kindliness that made her friends even among her enemies. Her letters show her as master of an incomparable eloquence and pathos, and very few who met her failed to fall under the spell of that irresistible personality. Moreover, she was a Catholic by deep conviction, and heir presumptive to the throne of England. If Elizabeth should die without a child no title to the throne would be as good as that of Mary, great-granddaughter of Henry VII. It made her an awkward guest at a time when the rift between Catholics and Protestants was widening, when Elizabeth's enemies were bound to appeal to Catholic sympathies in England and might reckon on a body of support uncertain in its extent though doubtless considerable. She brought into Elizabeth's policy the first traces of that indecision which was going to be so marked a failing later. Elizabeth had originally supported Mary and offered her a refuge, from which Mary was confident the Queen of England would help to restore her to the throne of Scotland. She once sent Elizabeth a ring, with lines written for it by George Buchanan:

O si fors mihi faxit, utriusque
Nectam ut corda adamantina catena,
Quam nec suspicio, aemulatiove
Livore, aut odium, aut senecta solvat!

'If it might be my fate', the ring was supposed to say, 'to bind together the hearts of those twain with a chain of adamant, which neither suspicion nor envious jealousy nor hatred nor age should ever loose!' That chain was never forged. To restore a Catholic sovereign to a Protestant Scotland would never have been easy, even if it had been good politics. And as Mary's exile gradually became a captivity, she turned naturally to those foreign powers which might help her, as Elizabeth had not done, to recover her throne. Her choice of friends and counsellors was impulsive and ill-judged and under their direction her fortunes became involved in the almost endless conspiracy that ultimately and inevitably brought her to the scaffold. A Catholic rising in England, in support of Mary, was always central to the plan, which in its later forms involved also the intervention of some foreign power in its support and the assassination of Elizabeth.

In the latter part of 1569, Hawkins almost certainly hoped to lead a naval attack on the Spanish colonies and rescue the prisoners who had been left behind after the battle of St Juan. The French ambassador reported in that year that Hawkins was pressing on with the armament of seven men-of-war which were said to be bound for the Indies. He was doubtful about this report, and thought that they might be intended to help the French Protestants. Events in Europe were too serious for the Government to allow Hawkins to go when the time came. For they never realised the rightness of the seamen's intuition that attack was the surest form of defence, and year after year they paralysed their action for that very reason. It meant, however, that another way of achieving his hopes must be found. Hawkins found it in a direct approach to the Spanish ambassador.

When this approach was made, the conspiracy had lately raised its head again, after one failure, through the energy of an Italian merchant named Ridolfi. This man had been in touch with Mary's ambassador in London, the Bishop of Ross, and also with the Duke of Norfolk, to whom Mary was by now beginning to regard herself as secretly affianced. It was probably the Bishop of Ross and the Spanish ambassador who laid the detailed plans and Ridolfi who supplied the energy. Between them they drew up a letter of instruction for Ridolfi, nominally dictated by the Duke of Norfolk, in which the authors point out that the English Catholics are more numerous and powerful than the Protestants; that Norfolk, though professing Protestantism, is ready to declare himself a Catholic as soon as the project shall be on the way to success; but that he must have an auxiliary force of eight thousand infantry, a quantity of guns, and a supply of other military stores. These were to be landed at Harwich or Portsmouth, and if possible, small forces were to be sent to Ireland and Scotland also to distract Elizabeth's attention from the main effort. The letter was addressed to the Pope and the King of Spain, and armed with it, Ridolfi went to see the Duke of Alva, Philip's general in the Netherlands, in the hope of winning his support. Meanwhile, Mary's part was to feign resignation, and she wrote a friendly letter to Elizabeth, saying that she had placed her cause entirely in her hands. Three days before it was written, Ridolfi had left for the Netherlands, and it was only seven days before that Mary had herself written and given to John Hamilton to take to the Duke of Alva a note of her own hopes and plans concerning the projected invasion.

While Ridolfi was in Brussels, he met one of the Bishop of Ross' servants, Bailly by name, who had been working there on the bishop's behalf. Together they coded despatches containing the story of Ridolfi's interviews with Alva so that they should be safe from prying eyes when Bailly took them back to England. In fact these interviews had been anything but a success. Alva described Ridolfi to Philip as a 'great babbler'. But Ridolfi was nothing daunted, and hurried off to Rome to solicit the help of the Pope. Meanwhile Bailly returned to England. As he landed at Dover he was arrested by Burghley's orders. As it happened, however, the Warden of the Cinque Ports, Lord Cobham, was favourably affected towards Mary. The Bishop of Ross persuaded him to hand over secretly for a short time the packet of papers seized on Bailly. He abstracted all those documents which specifically related to any of the English nobility, forwarding to Norfolk and to Lord Lumley those addressed to them. In their place he substituted some vaguely incriminating documents, suspicious enough to let Burghley feel that he had not drawn a blank, but too vague for him to obtain from them any useful information. He then wrote to Burghley, asking if the letters seized by Lord Cobham might be returned to him, and protesting with an air of injured innocence that no letters should be forwarded till Burghley had satisfied himself of their harmlessness. Burghley complied. But he took the precaution of keeping Bailly under lock and key. The suspect was finally removed to the Tower, where he was racked, and under torture gave away the secret of the code that had been used. Burghley was thus able to read letters that Bailly himself had written in prison, revealing something of the bishop's real intentions. But what he could not discover was the identity of the English noblemen who had evidently been implicated. '30' and '40' the letters called them. The prelate maintained that they were the Spanish ambassador and the Queen of Scots herself. But that would not work. '30' and '40' were to march with their power towards London. Neither Mary nor the Spanish ambassador had any power, and the Spanish ambassador was in London already. How were '30' and '40' to be identified?

Burghley found unexpectedly another means of approach. For Hawkins' mind was made up to do something for those of his men whom he knew to be captives in Spanish prisons and some of whom, as he now learnt, were in Seville. One of those captives left it on record later how, after the battle of St Juan, when Hawkins set them ashore, 'he counselled us to serve God, and to love one another, and thus courteously he gave us a sorowful fare well, and promised if God sent him safe home he would do what he could, that so many of us as lived should by some means be brought into England, and so he did'. This promise remained on Hawkins' conscience. Now there came news from an English merchant in Spain of some of them suffering ill-treatment and hardship. It was followed by the arrival of one in person, George Fitzwilliam.[1] He had been one of the gentlemen adventurers on the voyage. A kinswoman of his had married a Spanish nobleman, the Duke of Feria, and it was through this that the order for his release had been obtained. Hawkins always kept his own counsel. This makes the facts about his actions often very difficult to unravel. It has even been suggested that he never revealed to Fitzwilliam, his own confidential agent, his plans for outwitting Philip, and that Fitzwilliam acted in good faith as a go-between in what followed. The documents make this most improbable, but, however it may be, Hawkins sent him back to Spain to secure an audience with Philip, and managed to arm him with a recommendation from the Spanish ambassador. For Hawkins had been seeing the ambassador lately, and representing to him that he was tired of the Queen's service. There were other sailors dissatisfied too; in fact he could transfer the allegiance of a great fleet of English ships to King Philip. At a time when the armed merchantmen formed so powerful an element in the strength of the navy, the plan was not on the face of it an unlikely one, and the Western

Squadron, which Hawkins commanded, might well have secured control of the Channel. One thing only he wanted in return. Men who had served under him were eating their hearts out in a Spanish dungeon. Let them be released, and Hawkins would be King Philip's man.

The ambassador was enthusiastic. Here was precisely what was lacking in the Bishop of Ross' plan. Alva had an excellent army across the Channel. The only problem was how to transfer it across that strip of water. With Hawkins and his friends in the Spanish service, that problem would cease to exist. Fitzwilliam crossed to Spain and tried out the story. Philip hesitated. It looked too good to be true; and he decided at last that the leopard could not have changed its spots—or that at any rate further proof of it was necessary. He told Fitzwilliam that if Hawkins could produce credentials from Mary Queen of Scots herself he might be interested, but that meanwhile he could go no further in the matter.

The Ferias were much more helpful. They gave Fitzwilliam presents and letters for Mary which he brought back to London. Mary Queen of Scots was kept under close surveillance. She could not be visited unless official instructions were given. But in this instance there were good reasons why permission should be given, and he visited her at Sheffield. She became as enthusiastic as the Ferias had been. 'Being somewhat doubtful at first to write, yet she said she must pity prisoners, for that she was used as one herself, having all intelligence taken from her; yet she said she would do any pleasure she could to relieve any Englishman out of prison.' It was not the first time that her generous impulses betrayed her. Back went Fitzwilliam to Spain with the precious recommendation, and a book for the Ferias, 'the old service written in Latin', and in the end of it she wrote in her own great sprawling hand:

> Absit nobis gloriari nisi in cruce
> Domini nostri Jesu Christi.
>
> MARIA R.

'Let it be far from me to boast save in the cross of our Lord Christ Jesus....' Philip was convinced. The menace of Hawkins, who had done him such damage in the Indies, was at last removed for ever. In his pleasure he not only released his captives—or at least those of whose existence Hawkins was aware—but gave them each money to return to England. Hawkins was granted a pardon for all his piracies. In September or October the coup could be attempted. For the equipment of Hawkins' ships, King Philip arranged for the transfer of 40,000 ducats[2] to him, and as a mark of special favour created him a grandee of Spain.

Fitzwilliam's mission had been from Hawkins' standpoint brilliantly successful. He returned to England and Hawkins sat down to let Burghley know that all had gone according to plan.

My very good Lord,

It may please your honour to be advertised that Fitzwilliams is returned from the court of Spain, where his message was acceptably received, both by the King himself, the Duke of Feria, and others of his privy council. His despatch and answer was with great expedition and with great countenance and favour of the king.

The articles are sent to the ambassador, with order also for the money to be paid to me by him for the enterprise to proceed with all diligence.

The pretence is that my power should join with the Duke of Alva's power which he doth shortly provide in Flanders, as well as with the power which cometh with the Duke of Medina out of Spain, and so all together to invade this realm and set up the Queen of Scots.

They have practised with us for the burning of Her Majesty's ships, therefore there would be some good care had of them, but not as it may appear that anything is discovered, as your lordship's consideration can well provide.

The King hath sent a ruby of good price to the Queen of Scots, with letters also, which in my judgment were good to be delivered. The letters be of no importance, but his message by word is to comfort her and say that he now hath none other care than to place her in her own. It were good also that the Ambassador did make request unto your Lordship that Fitzwilliams may have access to the Queen of Scots, to render thanks for the delivery of our prisoners which are now at liberty; it will be a very good colour for your lordship to confer with him [Fitzwilliam] more largely.

I have sent your lordship the copy of my pardon from the King of Spain in the very order and manner I have it. Also the Duke of Medina and the Duke of Alva have every of them one of the same pardons, more amplified, to present unto me (although this be large enough) with very great titles and honours from the King, from which God deliver me.

I send your lordship also the copy of my letter from the Duke of Feria in the very manner as it was written, with his wife and son's hand in the end.

Their practices be very mischievous, and they be never idle, but God, I hope, will confound them and turn their devices upon their own necks.

I will put my business in some order and give mine attendance upon Her Majesty, to do her that service that by your lordship shall be thought most convenient in this case.

I am not tedious with your lordship because Fitzwilliams cometh himself, and I mind not to be long after him, and thus I trouble your good lordship no further.

From Plymouth the 4th day of September, 1571
Your good lordship's most faithfully in my power,
JOHN HAWKYNS.

As he read this letter, Burghley might have been disappointed, for he had originally hoped that the names of those two noblemen might perhaps have become known at last. But another chance had just given him what he wanted. He knew now that '30' was the Duke of Norfolk; and the day after Hawkins' letter was written, Norfolk was conveyed to the Tower, and in due course executed.

It might appear that this was nothing more or less than an affair of a 'fifth column' and secret police. But the implication is unwarranted. Elizabethan England was not a totalitarian state, and perhaps the best answer to such a suggestion is in a remarkable document drawn up by one of Elizabeth's enemies, intercepted on its travels, and published in England just after the defeat of the Armada, in 1588. It is a letter written to the Spanish ambassador in France by Richard Leigh, a seminary priest who was executed for high treason committed at the time that the Spanish Armada was on the seas. Leigh's theme is the real state of opinion in England and the mistakes and misconceptions of Spanish propaganda and Spanish policy; and he is faced with the conclusion that the militant Roman Catholics in England 'put their trust wholly in worldly strength' and that that was the reason why, for their good, 'Christ showed himself to be a Lutheran'. It is not true, he says, that men were hanged and burnt for being Catholics. They died indeed protesting the Catholic faith. But they died because they were traitors, inciting men to rebellion against the Queen and her Government, publishing the bull of deposition which in the very year of the events just narrated had been nailed to the gates of Lambeth Palace. He describes how those who argue with him on these matters point out that 'the great number of gentlemen and gentlewomen, yea some of honourable calling and of other meaner degrees are knowne manifestly to be of a contrary religion to the lawes of the Realme both neere the Court and farre of, and yet they are never pursued by any fourme of law to put their lives in danger, or questioned, or imprisoned, for their opinions in religion, whereby to bring them in any danger.' While he cannot wholly allow such arguments 'yet surely', he says, 'they do move me'. He has described already the impressive unity of Protestants and Catholics in the face of the common danger, and described how even those Roman Catholics who were interned in the Isle of Ely while the campaign was in progress (suffering no restraint but the bare restriction of movement) had loyally offered to fight for the Queen 'whom they named their undoubted soveraigne lady and Queene, against all foreign forces, though the same were sent from the Pope or by his commandement'. Nationalism, patriotism rather, had brought with it in England grace, the grace of tolerance—while in France Huguenots were hunted from place to place, and while the Inquisition reached out to discover even those Englishmen who were working as slaves to Spanish masters in Mexico. And that generation which in its youth pored over Foxe's *Book of Martyrs*, and which in its mellow maturity produced the Authorised Version of the Bible, was not indifferent to religion. They were not unprepared if need be to die for it. But they had some glimmering of a notion that the sacrifices that God demanded, whatever else they might be, were not the lives of Catholics, burnt at the stake in Smithfield. And what Burghley's spies were doing in saving England from the plots of Ridolfi and his friends was to spare her the terrible experience of civil war which at this time began to destroy the vitality of France. Burghley did not seek aggrandisement or gain. And if he served his Queen with complete devotion, it was because he knew that for all her mistakes she too was after one thing, and one thing alone; and that was not her own personal glory.

Chapter V

DRAKE IN THE CARIBBEAN AND PACIFIC

WHATEVER may have been the facts about Drake's desertion of Hawkins after the battle of St Juan, there was thereafter no mistaking his leadership. He exerted a spell over the men who served with him such as is without parallel in the period. If he was planning an expedition, men flocked to join it. If he called on them to perform some extraordinary feat of endurance, they responded without hesitation. And the planning of the voyage of 1572 and 1573 shows that his success was based not merely on personal ascendancy over his followers, but also on the quality of his judgment and the brilliance of its execution. This expedition is, indeed, a little masterpiece. We know virtually nothing of the two visits to the West Indies, one with a single ship, the 'Swan', one with two ships, the 'Swan' and the 'Dragon', in 1570 and 1571, save that they were reconnaissances designed to discover what had to be known before the real attempt was made. They were to 'gain such intelligences as might further him', says the narrative authorised later by Drake himself. His familiarity with the coast along which he was working—with the difficult Boca Chica of Carthagena harbour, for example, which a Spanish pilot of the time described as so dangerous that a ship entering it must take soundings constantly and employ a local pilot—shows how thorough this preparation had been. The organisation of his supply depots along the Darien coast is of a piece with this. And there is already that insistence on the maintenance of the sailing qualities of the ships used, which becomes an integral part of Drake's methods. We cannot imagine him going to sea in the 'Jesus of Lubeck', for instance, since to him a ship was a delicate instrument to be handled with a deft touch and an accurate apprehension of the results to be achieved. It seems to have been prestige which weighed with Hawkins in his choice of his flagship. Drake cared greatly about his reputation as a seaman and greatly about his reputation as a gentleman (one might almost say a hidalgo), but the prestige conferred by a large ship that leaked was not likely to affect him.

For Drake like Hawkins was planning to recover his losses from

King Philip with substantial interest. Their methods contrast characteristically. Hawkins sailed always on the weather side of the law, so that King Philip never knew whether he had been in earnest or not. Drake took the law into his own hands. His plan was to attack the treasure route, not in the Caribbean Sea or the Atlantic, a task which was to prove later to present very difficult problems and to depend largely on luck for success, but rather by land. And when he set out from Plymouth on the Saturday before Whit Sunday, he knew precisely the spot which he intended to make his base and what form his first endeavour was to take. He intended to make a direct attack on Nombre de Dios, the port at the Caribbean end of the isthmus road, by which the vast treasure from Peru was brought across from Panama. His acquaintance with the plan of Nombre de Dios suggests that he had visited it in 1571. We are told that 'by sundry intelligences the year before' Drake had learnt of a project to establish a battery on the hill to the east of the town. It is difficult to believe that he could have heard this anywhere other than in Nombre de Dios itself.

The base for operations was a port in the Gulf of Darien which he had seen on a previous visit, Port Pheasant. Its entrance was half a cable's length only across, though the harbour within opened out to eight or ten cables in breadth, with good, deep anchorage and excellent supplies of food, pheasants and fish. Six or seven weeks after leaving Plymouth they were there. And then the first hitch occurred. Someone had been there before them. He had left but recently. For fires he had lighted were still burning; and there was found nailed to the trunk of a huge tree a piece of lead with a message for Drake scratched on it:

CAPTAIN DRAKE

If you fortune to come to this port, make haste away! For the Spaniard which you had with you here the last year have bewrayed this place and taken away all that you left here. I depart from hence this present 7th of July, 1572.

Your very loving friend,
JOHN GARRET.

Garret, himself from Plymouth, had been led to Port Pheasant by someone who had been there the previous year with Drake.

His advice was not taken. Drake's plan of campaign included the setting up in West Indian waters of 'three dainty pinnaces', Plymouth built, which he had stowed in pieces and brought with him, and he considered Port Pheasant the right place to do this. After a fort, pentagonal in shape according to the regular military practice of the times, had been built out of the great trees which grew near the shore, this work was carried out and was completed seven days after their arrival at Port Pheasant. There had been no interruptions except the arrival of an Englishman, Captain Ranse, who asked to be taken into partnership.

Their plan was for an immediate attack on Nombre de Dios, and the little fleet slipped unnoticed along the coast towards its objective. On the way lay the Isles of Pines, where they fell in with two frigates from Nombre de Dios which were taking timber on board. These were stopped, to prevent news reaching Nombre de Dios before Drake himself should arrive, and the negroes from them were put ashore on the coast. Travel overland was so difficult that there was no fear of their reaching the town before him. And they were accordingly given the chance of their liberty, and encouraged, if they wished, to join the Cimaroons (or Maroons, as contemporary accounts sometimes call them), the descendants of escaped negro prisoners who had succeeded in building up independent 'nations' which constituted a severe threat to the Spaniards. Drake's policy, no doubt laid down already on previous expeditions and thereafter regularly followed, was to conciliate these negro peoples. He had learnt from those now captured that, owing to the threat from the Cimaroons, preparations for defence at Nombre de Dios were being made, and reinforcements of soldiers expected.

The Isles of Pines were used as an advanced base. There went on towards the town only the three pinnaces and a shallop of Captain Ranse, with no more than seventy-four men in all. But it was a carefully selected force, nicely balanced according to the military ideas then prevailing, with musketeers, bowmen, pikemen, firepikes and others. Nombre de Dios was five days' sailing for the pinnaces, and when they were within striking distance of the town they rode at anchor out of sight of the watch house till nightfall. When it was dark they rowed on silently to the harbour, and there rested, planning to make the attempt at dawn. For a time they waited. But the night dragged on, and the men were uneasy, talking of the strength of the opposition they would have to face. Drake did not like this and quickly made up his mind what to do. Three hours after midnight the moon would rise. It would grow lighter, and in that pale gleam the attempt could be made. As they rowed forward they were seen from a ship in the harbour, which sent a ship's boat towards the shore with the news. But she was intercepted. They landed near an emplacement for artillery, which was dismantled immediately. But the gunner escaped and presently they heard the great bell in the church clanging the alarm. They heard too the rattle of drums, as drummers ran about rousing the people. The Cimaroons must be attacking. In a few moments the moonlight was alive with movement.

They had first to discover whether the new battery said to command the town from the west had yet been installed. It had not, and they proceeded therefore to the occupation of the market-place. The English firepikes and drums gave the impression that the tiny force was much larger than it was. Nevertheless, the townspeople and garrison mustered at the corner of the market-place which was nearest the gate of the town, and as the Englishmen advanced towards it from two directions, Drake in command of one force, his brother of another, they were met with a 'jolly hot volley of shot' as Nichols' account calls it. The reply was a volley of the arrows which Drake had had specially made in England and which throughout the campaign did valuable service. This was followed by the pikemen, and the sudden appearance of the second column of Englishmen was too much for the Spaniards, who fled out through the gate. A few who were captured were forced to show where the treasure was kept—the silver lying in bars in the Governor's house, and the really precious stuff, pearls and gold, in a strongly built house of stone nearby. By the light of a candle in the Governor's house they could see the silver stacked twelve feet high, so they reckoned, and in a pile seventy feet long. But silver was too bulky to be worth taking. It was the gold and pearls which was their object. In spite of their success, however, there were doubts spreading. A rumour went round that there were troops in the town and that if re-embarkation were not effected before dawn, when their numbers would be known, it would certainly be prevented. The men left with the pinnaces were nervy, seeing the lights darting to and fro, and hearing the cries of the bewildered Spaniards; and to make matters worse there suddenly burst a tropical shower of rain in the darkness, obscuring the moonlight and wetting bowstrings and powder. Drake shouted to them that he had brought them to the mouth of the treasure house of all the world. They rallied, and as the rain stopped, Drake's brother moved off to try to break into the house where the gold was stored. But it was too late. As Drake himself stepped forward, he

VI. NOMBRE DE DIOS

(From a sketch made at the time of Drake's attack)

staggered and fell. He had fainted. In the first attack he had been wounded, but had concealed the hurt. Now it had shown itself, and though he was revived with a flask of wine, his followers were appalled at what they saw of his hurt, and refused to risk his life by any further endeavour. In vain he pressed them on. They carried him back to the pinnaces, and, embarking, stopped only to capture a ship carrying wines that lay in the harbour, for besides Drake himself, there were many other wounded. Thence they proceeded to an island a short way from the city, where they stopped two days for refreshment. The Governor sent there under a flag of truce a 'proper gentleman' to pay his respects. And though it was obvious that his compliments were an excuse for a very good look at the Englishmen's position, Drake was as usual much too pleased with the compliment to grudge him his information. Drake said that he wanted no medical supplies. But what he did want was 'some of their harvest which they got out of the earth and send into Spain to trouble all the earth'. And he meant to have it.

So the plan failed. It had been worked out, with consummate skill, over a period of nearly three years. It had come within an ace of success, and then a chance Spanish bullet had frustrated it. All was to do again, and it is little wonder if in the next few months Drake's mind seems uncertain and his plans indefinite. Captain Ranse indeed now left Drake's company, evidently seeing little further hope for the expedition.

On the way back to the Isles of Pines a reconnaissance was made to the river Chagres. This river opened west of Nombre de Dios and was sometimes used for the transport of treasure, which came down from the town of Venta Cruz by water. An attack on that route must be considered. Some weeks were spent in a demonstration along the coast to Carthagena, during which prizes were taken. But the immediate need was for new bases to be taken, and provisioned from Spanish shipping. This meant action by sea. For this to be effective, it was essential that the pinnaces should be fully manned, and this entailed abandoning one of the larger ships. It was to be the 'Swan', which his brother commanded. But she was neat and fast and to abandon her would break hearts. So he called her carpenter, his trusted friend, Tom Moone, to him. At midnight Moone was to go down into the well of the ship and bore three holes near the keel, with a spike gimlet. Something must be put against them to stifle the noise. If the ship was found to be leaking irreparably, perhaps his brother's crew could be persuaded to leave her. Next day he invited his brother to come fishing with him, and as they met, casually remarked that the 'Swan' was very low in the water. Immediately his brother realised that something was wrong. A man was sent down to investigate and stepped into water up to his waist. The pumps were manned, but all efforts were of no avail and the 'Swan' was abandoned. Drake handed over to his brother the command of the 'Pasha', saying that he would find a command for himself later among the prizes he captured. Thus he secured the right distribution of personnel for his pinnaces.

The next few months were spent in selecting the new base and in provisioning it. John Drake established touch with the Cimaroons, and a friendly relationship grew up. It developed in time into that devotion which most men felt who served Drake. Drake meanwhile was still moving constantly up and down the coast, in the hope, so he says, of gaining intelligence of the Spanish fleets' movements. Somehow the voyage must be 'made', and action by sea still remained a possibility if opportunity should offer. On one such occasion Drake was away for nearly two months. He left his brother in charge of building operations on the fort at the new base. One day John Drake was out in a pinnace, when a Spanish frigate was sighted. His men urged him to attack it. Though they were almost completely unarmed, Spanish prizes had been falling to them so easily that the attempt seemed worth making. Against his better judgment John Drake was persuaded. But when they boarded they were met with deadly fire. They struggled back to the pinnace, but John Drake had been mortally wounded and died an hour later. Nor was this all. Six weeks after Francis Drake's return, another brother, Joseph, was taken ill of a disease that had struck down others and killed many of them. He died in Francis Drake's arms. Drake asked that the surgeon should hold a post-mortem on the body to try to discover the reason for the malady, and there, under those tropical skies, the task was done. It was in that age a desperate step to take, and might have had a disastrous moral effect on the superstitious crew if their captain's ascendancy over them had not been so great. As it was, they felt that at least he was taking every action possible to him. But when they finally set out on the land expedition in February 1573, twenty-eight men, something like a third of their number, had died.

Their way led through dense woods and over hills, but there was an escort of Cimaroons with them, who built them huts of wood and leaves to sleep in at nights, and showed them what animals and fruits to eat. Drake's purpose was to cross to the Pacific coast, and on a memorable day, 28 February 1573, they came to the top of the ridge that lay between the two seas. There was a great tree with a ladder up it, and towards the top a sort of bower had been made. Trees had been felled around to open the view. It was a day of brilliant clearness, and there at last lay that other great ocean before them. So Drake prayed that he might be granted life and leave to sail it.

After two days' more marching through the forest they reached open country, whence it was possible for them from time to time to catch sight of Panama city from the hills, and as they approached, they saw ships riding in the road. During the last miles of the route their movements were made with all possible secrecy, for they wished to reach a grove of trees on the Nombre de Dios road a league or thereabouts from Panama; perhaps near where eighteenth-century maps show the village of Maria Enrique, or perhaps further east on the Venta Cruz road. The early part of the journey towards Nombre de Dios was made by the mule trains at night because of the intense heat. They did not move by day until they reached the forest region.

The Englishmen reached their post in the grove during the afternoon, and sent out a spy to discover the situation in the town. He returned safely with splendid news. The Treasurer of Lima himself was on his way to Spain, with his family. There was a mule train of fourteen mules, eight laden with gold and one with jewels. This train would pass over the road first, and following it would come two others, much larger but carrying only food, except for a little silver.

When this intelligence had been obtained, they moved back along the road towards Venta Cruz, so as to remain unobserved. Then they set an ambush on either side of the road, half the force on one side with John Oxnam, the other half with Drake, but further back, so that the mule train would be caught between them and completely cut off from possible escape. The night was very still, and long before the mule train arrived they heard in the distance the deep sound of the mule bells.

The men had been primed with spirits, and they waited with intense eagerness. They had been ordered to wear their white shirts outside their body armour, in order to be easily distinguishable from the enemy. Before the train arrived, there came from the other direction a horseman to meet them. As he passed the second post, one of the men, too well primed, it seems, started up, but was pulled down again by the Cimaroon with him. Drake, who was in the post nearest Venta Cruz, heard the horse's hooves clattering down the road at a gallop. Then all was still for a time till the booming of the bells started again. When the mule train was safely in the trap, the jaws closed and the men leaped up from their ambush. Without a blow being struck, the mules and the men guarding them were taken. But as they began to look through the loads, it suddenly became apparent that fate had cheated them. There were two loads of silver. Apart from that nothing—only food and stores. The horseman, catching sight of the figure in white and guessing that something was wrong, had given the alarm. The treasure train had been stopped, and another had been sent ahead to test the ambush instead. By the indiscretion of one man, everything had been lost.

There was nothing for it but to return to the ships, unless perhaps treasure should be found in Venta Cruz. Though Drake had only a handful of men, it seemed worth trying, and try they did. A heavy volley of hail shot greeted their attack, and mortally wounded one of the Englishmen and hurt others, but the reply was as usual a volley of arrows, encouraged by which the Cimaroons, who had been taken aback at first by the shot, leaped forward with a war cry on the Spaniards among the trees. The Spaniards were armed with pikes. But the attack was too much for them and they broke and fled. So Drake entered the town. But there was no treasure inside it. They waited a few hours for refreshment, and long enough characteristically for Drake politely to reassure the ladies in the hospital. Then back, disconsolately, by the rough forest route to the ships. For the captain was anxious about those who had been left behind, since many had been weak from sickness, and he refused to wait, as the Cimaroons tried to persuade him to do, to rest in one of their towns.

Still there was no thought of leaving till something more should have been accomplished. That meant securing further supplies by preying on shipping, and working out yet another plan of attack. On one of these foraging expeditions they fell in with the ship of a Frenchman, Têtu, from Havre, who had been looking for Drake for some time and hoped for his help. His first need was a supply of water, which was given him. Then the two captains exchanged presents, and an arrangement was made whereby the seventy Frenchmen should share, equally with the thirty-one English, any profits which the expedition should now realise.

Once again the plan adopted was to waylay the mule trains as they travelled between Panama and Nombre de Dios, for the season was now in full swing when this route was in constant use. So a party landed at Rio Francisco, five leagues to the east of Nombre de Dios, and struck through the forest. Once again secrecy was of vital importance, and as they approached Nombre de Dios, the scene of the expedition's first brilliant failure, they could hear through the stillness of the night the noise of work going on in the shipyards of the town; for because of the heat by day, the shipwrights worked through the night. Once again the plan was to hold up the mule train between two parties ambushed by the road. Once again they heard in the distance the sound of the bells as the mules approached. But this time no horseman came out to meet the train. This time no one gave away their hiding place. The mules were carrying thirty tons of silver. But there was gold as well in bars and quoits. The whole of the booty could not possibly be taken away, and fifteen tons of silver was roughly buried in the holes made by land crabs, under the roots of trees, or in the bed of a nearby stream. Two hours were thus spent, after which they made off through the forest. But Têtu had been left behind. He had been severely wounded in the first encounter, and he stayed to rest with two of his company. When the Rio Francisco was reached, John Oxnam was sent back with another to try to secure news of the French captain. It was discovered that he had been captured, with one of the two men with him, half an hour after the English had left.

So the voyage was 'made'—to use Drake's own word—at last. As they sailed by Carthagena, the cross of St George was flying from the frigate's main top, and she was dressed with silk streamers and flags down to the water. They were after one more batch of provisions, which fell to them without difficulty. Then back to one of their island refuges, where the ships were scraped and tallowed, fresh trimmed and rigged, and the pinnaces pulled to pieces that the Cimaroons might have the iron work. The voyage home was prosperous. On Sunday, 7 August, they arrived in Plymouth, about sermon time. A whisper went around the congregation, and 'very few or none' remained to hear the preacher. For, after all, here was living evidence of God's gracious love and blessing towards the Queen and towards England; and that was better than many a sermon.

Drake was by this time becoming a figure of international reputation, and his movements were henceforward affected by questions of high policy. His own ambitions become involved in the attitude of the authorities towards Spain, and in Queen Elizabeth's Council there was the cleavage between those who advocated open war with Spain, as did Leicester and Walsingham, and those who advised caution, as did Burghley. John Oxnam, who had been with Drake at the isthmus and like him had prayed to be allowed to sail the Pacific, was subject to no such restraint as Drake. He had seen how easy the game looked played by a master hand. Why not return to the isthmus, build pinnaces on a river leading down to the western ocean, and there prey on Spanish shipping on the journey between Peru and Central America? If the scheme had been executed by someone with Drake's capacity for planning, for waiting and then striking with a quickness that took his enemies completely off their guard, it would have succeeded. As it was, it came near to success but ended in catastrophe. Oxnam captured his treasure in the Pacific. But his rash words and rash actions off Panama were not the end of the story. Things went wrong. Concealment proved impossible, and once the tiny force he had with him failed to keep its whereabouts secret, it was at the mercy of any Spanish punitive expedition. Thus Oxnam's adventures ended on the gallows, and if a new attack was to be made, new plans would have to be made too. It was this that was in Drake's mind, and as he worked at it, he came into contact with other minds which were preoccupied with the problems of the Pacific.

These were problems of theory, on which speculation had been fostered by the recently received reports of an Englishman, Roger Bodenham, who had been in the Indies some ten years before and is mentioned as one of the leaders of a Spanish expedition to the Philippines—though it is uncertain whether he actually travelled there or not. It is certain, however, that he knew something of the voyage across the Pacific made by Urdaneta in 1565, which had shown the possibilities of Pacific exploration. News of this achievement had sent the theorists, and in particular Dr John Dee, back to their books. They found that Marco Polo had described a region which he called Locach, or as some versions read it, Beach, as being rich in gold. Mercator had located this region, in a world map recently published, in the great southern continent, or Terra Australis, at a place somewhere near the latitude and longitude of New Guinea. Between this and the Straits of Magellan were the 'Islands of Solomon' of which Englishmen were hearing reports already. They got their name from the idea that in this part of the world was to be sought the Ophir from which King Solomon's gold had come. The maps of the Pacific in Drake's day, with their extraordinary diversity, gave their sanction to the wildest flights of fancy. Was there a navigable strait towards Asia, running north of America, but with its western opening in latitude 40° N., as was supposed? Urdaneta, who had crossed the Pacific, was believed in England at some time actually to have passed through this strait from west to east, and there were men who claimed to have seen charts of it. Was Locach to be found somewhere on that unknown stretch of coast of which the southern side of Magellan's strait was supposed to be part, and which was believed to run from there as far as the Spice Islands? Did the mainland of Asia extend far to the north-east across the northern end of America, like the 'new moon, with the old moon in her arms', and was that the reason why the Eskimos of Greenland appeared to be similar to the people of Tartary? Above all, might not a venture in the Pacific reveal the secret of the philosopher's stone? 'The consequence of this exploit', wrote Dr Dee of such a project, with Drake's own venture in his mind, 'is greater than is yet to any Christian state credible.' And that is what he meant; the stone that would turn base metal to gold, the source of life itself perhaps. Early in 1577, when the voyage of circumnavigation was being planned, Drake's friends and patrons were in close touch with Dee. One of them who knew Dee well was Hatton, whose crest was a Golden Hind and in whose honour Drake was later going to rename his ship the 'Pelican'. Dee wrote that year:

> Of how great importance...is that attempt which is by a British subject presently intended to God's glory, the benefit of all Christendom, and the honour and profit of this realm chiefly, and contentment of many a noble mind which delighteth to hear how 'Domini est terra et Plenitudo eius, orbis Terrarum et universi qui habitant in eo'; who (God sparing life and health) hath secretly offered up to God and his natural Sovereign and country the employing of all his skill and talent, and the patient enduring of the great toil of his body, to that place being the very ends of the world

from us to be reckoned, to accomplish that discovery which of so many and so valiant captains, By Land and Sea hath been so often attempted in vain.[1]

It may be taken that Dee knew of Drake's intention and was actually referring to it in this passage.

There was something more to it, however, than the theories of the armchair navigators and that elusive quest of a magic key to riches and to life. Drake knew that there was gold to be had in the Pacific. In those secure seas, French and English pirates had not yet strayed—save for Oxnam who had met the fate he deserved. The great galleons which carried gold and silver from Peru to Panama plied along the coast without heed of danger, for the dangers of foreign attack did not yet exist. Drake's seamen were enrolled for a voyage to Alexandria. But perhaps some of them had some suspicion that the voyage was hitched to another star, and that that star was no other than one of the Southern Cross. Whatever argument there might be about the gold-bearing region of Beach or Urdaneta's supposed straits, there were more solid arguments in favour of a Pacific voyage. Drake was deaf neither to the one nor to the others.

One man in the fleet at least besides Drake himself knew of his plans. There sailed with the expedition a number of gentlemen, among whom were brothers named Doughty. One of these had acted as Hatton's secretary, and, perhaps from him, had obtained an inkling of Drake's plans. The Queen knew of these plans, but those of her advisers who favoured an understanding with Spain did not. Burghley was kept in the dark, by the Queen's express orders, until Doughty, who had a great idea of his own importance, told him what was afoot. Burghley kept his own counsel. In the autumn of 1577 opinion had swung round again, and whereas Drake on his arrival had been in disgrace at court because of his attacks on Spanish possessions, now the cry was for such attacks to be pressed harder.

Burghley could not, therefore, act if he had wished to do so, and Drake weighed anchor unhindered in November with a sizable fleet: the 'Pelican' of 100 tons; the 'Elizabeth' of 80 tons—master, John Wynter; a store ship named the 'Swan' of 50 tons; the 'Marigold' of 30; and a pinnace, the 'Benedict' of 15 tons, of which Tom Moone, the ship's carpenter of that other 'Swan' that had been sunk in the West Indies, was in command. The crews of these ships were a hundred and sixty-four men, including, as we find on the later voyages, a small number of 'gentlemen' seeking excitement, distinction and money as well as an apprenticeship at sea. In comparison with the family affair the last expedition had been, this was on a large scale. From the first difficulties began to appear of the kind which the great captain was always to encounter in his dealings with highly placed subordinates. Doughty, for example, seems to have thought that his position was equal in some respects with that of Drake, and here were the seeds of trouble. It was the bad old tradition that the soldiers were the men who counted in a fleet, and the sailors only there to bring them to grips with the enemy. Drake and the other great captains of the time were showing brilliantly that a fleet was something different from that; that a sailing ship might be a magnificent weapon of offence though she had not a single soldier on board. But the change took time, and the senior service was still often regarded as being in an inferior position.

The start of the voyage was not propitious. A gale struck the fleet off the Lizard. The 'Pelican's' mast had to be cut down, and the 'Marigold' was driven ashore, so that they had to put back to Plymouth to refit. When they set out again they had lost nearly a month. Then at Santiago, where a Portuguese pilot, Nuno da Silva, was taken on a prize and agreed to come with the expedition, the trouble with Doughty began. It is said that Drake had been warned, before the expedition sailed, not to trust Doughty. More probably, if we had letters of his written at that time, they would prove as enthusiastic about him as those written about Borough before the start of the expedition to Cadiz. Rumour began saying, however, that Doughty was pilfering the cargoes of prizes, and though the fault was eventually overlooked, Drake's suspicions were thoroughly aroused. Moreover, there were reports of remarks made by Doughty which suggested the usurpation of Drake's authority and almost incitement to mutiny. Later these accusations were brought out explicitly when Doughty was tried. For the time nothing more than whispers came to Drake's ears, but he was prone to suspicion and became anxious.

For everything seemed to be going wrong. After leaving the Cape Verde Islands it was fifty-four days before they sighted land again. For three weeks, as they were crossing the line, they were becalmed. Then, when they made landfall in 33° S. (not far that is from Rio Grande), they were off a coast that one of their number, the chaplain, Fletcher, describes on his chart as 'terra demonum', the 'land of devils'. 'Being discovered at sea by the inhabitants of the countrey', says the writer of Hakluyt's account, 'they made upon the coast great fires for a sacrifice (as we learned) to the devils, about which they use conjurations, making heapes of sande and other ceremonies, that when any ship shall goe about to stay upon their coast, not onely sands may be gathered together in shoalds in every place, but also that stormes and tempests may arise, to the casting away of ships and men....' Drake and his crews were not, we may suppose, more sophisticated than Shakespeare's audiences, for whom the witches in *Macbeth* provided an authentic shiver down the spine, and for whom Prospero's magic was part of the ordinary apparatus of mystery. Those glowing fires and the strange figures moving about them added to the general uneasiness. The crews needed rest and refreshment, however, and when a suitable harbour was found, they stood in to the shore. Then a thick blanket of fog descended, followed by a sudden storm, with lightning, rain and thunder. It cleared equally suddenly, but the 'Christopher', one of the prizes they had brought with them fully manned, had disappeared.

For some days they looked for her, then entered the river Plate, which was to be the rendezvous in the event of the ships becoming separated; and here, to the great delight of Drake, the 'Christopher' came back into company. 'Cape Joy' Drake called the place. They put out to sea again on their way southwards, and then the 'Swan', with Doughty on board her, somehow disappeared. It was at this point that Drake's suspicions broke out into open expression, and he avowed that Doughty was a 'conjuror and a witch'. Apparently Doughty's brother had actually claimed that they could 'call spirits from the vasty deep', and raise the devil in the form of a bear, a lion, or a man in armour. Strange as it must now seem, this claim had been taken seriously and, passed on to Drake, confirmed his worst fears. South of the Gulf of St George a likely harbour was discovered for the reorganising of the fleet. Drake himself went ashore and was caught again in fog and storm, during which his brother's ship was lost. Two ships gone. The harbour was not good enough for Drake's purpose, so they moved onwards towards the next appointed meeting place, Port St Julian. Drake knew well enough the accounts of Magellan's voyage. At Port St Julian he had wintered, and had rid himself of some of his 'disobedient and rebellious company'. When they reached it they found what they thought to be the gibbet still standing by the shore, where that sixty-year-old tragedy had been enacted. Drake, by this time, was well-nigh distracted, and that story of mutiny was working on his mind. During the whole time he was inveighing against Doughty. Before they entered Port St Julian, Wynter, whose own faith in the expedition was already wavering, was sent southwards in the 'Elizabeth' to look for the missing ships, while Drake, in the 'Pelican', turned back northwards. Almost immediately the 'Swan' was found.

We can hardly doubt that the captain's mind had been made up as to what was to be done. There had been, first, suspicions of Doughty's integrity when he had been found in possession of objects from the prizes that belonged to the common stock. There was the feeling that he had fostered discontent among the gentlemen against the seamen, and an unreasonable notion of superiority. Then there were suggestions of actual mutiny against Drake, and then this long tale of misfortunes that seemed to be due to the working of the black arts. A short time before, they had gone ashore to burn one of the pinnaces. They had seen the natives 'naked, saving only about their waste the skinne of some beast with the furre or haire on, and something also wreathed on their heads; their faces were painted with divers colours, and some of them had on their heads the similitude of hornes'. This was where Fletcher notes on his map 'our first acquaintance of giants'. That Drake was getting to the end of his tether is surely not surprising. Doughty was the cause of all these troubles, pilfering, mutiny, and then magic. Like Magellan's disaffected officers, he must die for it.

How much there was in Drake's suspicions, it is not easy from the documents to discover. It looks as if Doughty had done unwise things, some of which might be reckoned as seditious. From what Drake said to Zarate afterwards it seems certain that Doughty was urging him to turn back, and that, with this and the wavering of others, the captain's own massive faith was beginning to be undermined. On one of the islands in the harbour a form of trial was held. A jury was chosen. Doughty questioned the validity of Drake's commission. 'I warrant you', said Drake, 'my commission is good enough', and indeed Doughty himself, when it suited his purposes, had earlier stated that Drake had power of life and death. The ground of the several accusations was traversed, and then there came out a detail that drove Drake to fury. Doughty suggested that consent for the expedition had been obtained from the Council, and from the

Queen herself, only by bribery; and he remarked that Burghley was opposed to the voyage. Drake said that Burghley knew nothing about it. 'My Lord Treasurer', said Doughty, 'had a plot [map] of the voyage. He had it from me.'

Drake was incensed. The Queen had given instructions that the matter was to be kept from Burghley. Doughty had betrayed it. What further need was there of witnesses? Doughty was found guilty, though the jury expressed doubts about the veracity of one of the witnesses against him. Drake may have imagined, as he did before the Cadiz voyage—and as Froude's narrative implies—that there was organised, if secret, opposition to him in high places. There was a suggestion that the death penalty might be avoided if Doughty was set ashore, as two of Magellan's captains had been. Wynter offered to be responsible for him. Drake refused. He had made up his mind. Doughty was the 'child of death'.

Two days later sentence was carried out. In the morning Drake and Doughty together received the communion at the hand of Mr Fletcher; 'which being done and the place of execution made ready, hee having embraced our generall and taken his leave of all the companie, with prayer for the Queenes majestie and our realme, in quiet sort laid his head to the blocke, where he ended his life'. It is indeed difficult to withhold all sympathy from him. Nothing in his life became him like the leaving of it.

Even that was not enough, and, some days later, Drake addressed the whole company ashore. This controversy between sailors and gentlemen must end. Above all, every man there must be ready to do his share of work, rough work, as well as the work of thinking and planning and leading. Great achievements are won by toil unremitting, as well of body as of mind. Drake himself had ever set a magnificent example. And so he told them: 'I must have the gentleman to hayle and draw with the mariner, and the maryner with the gentleman. What! Let us show owr selvs all to be of a company, and let us not gyve occasyon to the enemye to rejoyce at owr decaye and overthrowe. I would know hym that would refuse to set his hand to a roape, but I know there is not any suche heare.'

So blood was let and the trouble was cured. Some historians have seen in Drake, from this moment, an added seriousness and a new sense of responsibility. For the remainder of this voyage it is rather as if a load has been shifted from his shoulders, as if for a moment he were back in that carefree, reckless mood in which he sailed up and down 'on a bravado' before the batteries of Carthagena on the expedition to Nombre de Dios, or made archery butts and a bowling green at Port Pheasant. His troubles were not yet over. When he had passed through the straits into the Pacific, the gales struck him again, scattered his ships, and carried him far off his course. But in the extant accounts, there is nothing to suggest that his mind was still clouded with a doubt, as it had been before Port St Julian. The doubts had gone now, sunk deep in the waters of that bleak harbour; and as he scudded southwards[2] in the rechristened 'Golden Hind', careened and able to show a clean pair of heels to almost any ship afloat, his faith returned.

It was needed as they drove through the straits that Magellan had found. After they returned to England, a chart, illustrated with sketches of the mountains, was drawn which suggests vividly the difficulties they encountered. The prevailing wind is westerly, and they were sailing in the teeth of it. The coasts are 'very huge and mountainous', towering cliffs capped with snow, and blanketed with heavy cloud. There was continual frost and snow, and the evergreen trees of the forests seemed 'to stoope with the burden of the weather'. It looked as if there were good harbours, with fresh water, but the water was so deep that there was no anchorage, and indeed, shifting gusts of wind, sweeping down from the snows, made anchoring anyhow impossible.

The straits were entered on 21 August. On 6 September the 'Golden Hind' and her consorts reached the Pacific and turned northwards, only to be met almost immediately by a howling gale, the like of which few of them had ever encountered before, which drove them south-westwards. The details of Drake's movements from 6 September to 29 November, when the 'Golden Hind' was alone and had reached the island of la Mocha in 38° up the west coast of South America, are obscure. But there is good reason for that obscurity, and something can be done to throw light on it if the objects of the voyage are recalled.

One of these, as we have seen, was the discovery of the great southern continent, the 'terra australis nondum cognita' as the maps called it, the coast of which was believed to run north-west from the region of Tierra del Fuego to the Spice Islands. Turned south-westwards by the storm, Drake was content to drive before the wind in the confident expectation that this problem could now be solved. All the maps showed land in this region. Unanimity on this point was well-nigh complete, and he must have believed that at any moment landfall might be made, and land never visited by a European navigator be discovered. And so, in the words of the Portuguese pilot who was now on board the 'Golden Hind'—the Portuguese prize having been broken up and burnt at Port St Julian—they held this course south-westerly 'for the space of ten or twelve days with few sails up; and because the wind began to be very great they took in all their sails, and lay driving till the last of September'. Until 20 September or thereabouts, Drake believed that he was making towards the Terra Australis. He was not being carried out of his course, but was doing one of the things he set out to do. It is possible to fix the point he reached, as there was an eclipse of the moon at six o'clock on 15 September. In England this eclipse was at twelve. They were approximately in longitude 90° therefore, and reckoned that they were 'two hundred leagues and odd' westwards of the mouth of the straits, and one degree to the south. A few days after the 15th, Drake began to doubt the existence of land in that quarter. They took in sail, therefore, and as soon as it was possible to do so, turned back towards America. The mystery of the southern continent in that region had been solved, though the complete solution had to wait for Cook's great voyages. Terra Australis, the land south of the straits, did not stretch out almost limitlessly into the Pacific. In Fletcher's chart of the straits, the islands to the south of them are called 'terra australis nunc bene cognita'. In the published accounts, Drake's purpose in this voyage to the south-west is not made explicit, but there is enough evidence to show what it was, and to show that it was fulfilled.

They recovered the coast of America apparently about the end of September. Almost immediately another gale struck and scattered them, and this time they were carried southwards. Drake had thought, so we are told, even when he was passing through the straits, that the broken nature of the coast to the south suggested islands rather than a continent. Now the storm was going to confirm his suspicions. Fletcher describes how he landed on one of the group of islands and found it to be 'more Southerly three partes of a degree than anny of the Rest'. Drake himself also went ashore, so he told Sir Richard Hawkins later, and carrying 'a compass with him, and seeking out the southernmost part of the island cast himself down on the uttermost point, grovelling and so reached out his body over it'. He made observations which gave the latitude of Cape Horn with remarkable exactness; and then, the weather having as we may suppose once more mended, he turned northwards again.

The discovery of Cape Horn was one of great geographical and also strategic importance; and this is doubtless the reason why the details are shrouded in so much doubt. Drake was not in the habit of elaborating for publication the brief records that he kept of his movements. The details of some of his voyages are almost entirely obscure for that reason. But there was an obvious motive for keeping such a discovery concealed, and from Drake's arrival home till the present, his claim to have discovered Cape Horn, and to have sailed the strait that bears his name, has been doubted. It was vindicated, however, triumphantly by Sir Julian Corbett. Fletcher's charts are still extant with their overwhelming proof, and those details in the evidence which appear to conflict with the claim in fact in some ways support it. Why should the account, corrected from Drake's own records and published forty years later, when there was no longer motive for concealment, give the precisely correct latitude, as does also Fletcher's account drawn up at the time but not published, whereas the accounts published just after the voyage was over give an incorrect latitude? Why should Hakluyt's main narrative show signs of excisions at this point,[3] and the other two he published be obscure or incorrect? After what has been seen of the methods of the time, the answer surely cannot be in doubt. Concealment and falsification were necessary. But Dr John Dee was no doubt told that his southern continent, at any rate at this extremity, had vanished into thin air. Wherever else Locach might be, its coast line did not reach far down towards the Horn.

During the former of these two movements southwards, the three ships had kept company, another detail which suggests that, however strong the wind may have been, they were well under control and fulfilling some definite purpose, even if most of the crews were unaware what it was. After recovering the coast, however, they were scattered. Cliffe's account says that the 'Marigold' disappeared on 30 September at night in very foul weather, and that it was eight days later that Drake lost touch with the 'Elizabeth'. The 'Marigold' was never again seen. The 'Elizabeth' made her way back alone to the mouth of the straits, anchored for two days, and lit fires in the hope that Drake would see them. Then Wynter decided, against the wishes of his crew, to go home, although he had been given a rendezvous on the coast by Drake. It was now spring. He waited for three weeks for refitting and refreshment and then sailed home. We know, from his examination before the Admiralty court, that his relationship with his commander had not been altogether happy, though a touching letter written by Drake and given to the captain of one of his Spanish prizes (in case he should fall into Wynter's hands) bears no trace of this animosity:

> Master Winter, if it pleaseth God that you should chance to meete with this ship of Sant John de Anton, I pray you use him well, according to my word and promise given unto them, and if you want anything that is in this ship,...I pray you pay them double the value for it which I will satisfie againe, and command your men not to doe her any hurt,... although I am in doubt that this letter will never come to your hands,... desiring you for the Passion of Christ if you fall into any danger that you will not despaire of God's mercy for hee will defend you and preserve you from all danger, and bring us to our desired haven, to whom bee all honour, glory and praise, for ever and ever, Amen. Your sorrowfull Captaine, whose heart is heavy for you: Francis Drake.[4]

There remained two tasks to be done, to make the voyage pay, and to solve the problem of the northern strait. Drake was now alone. Supreme individualist that he was, no condition suited him better. Before him stretched that unknown ocean on which he had prayed to be allowed to sail. Soon news reached him through a native that there was a great Spanish ship at Valparaiso. As the 'Golden Hind' approached, the few Spaniards and negroes in the Spanish ship, taking her to be a friend, beat a welcome on a drum and prepared wine. The English ship came alongside and Tom Moone leapt aboard, shouting to a Spaniard 'Abajo, pèro'—Down, dog. Taken entirely by surprise, the Spaniards crossed themselves and allowed themselves to be stowed under hatches, except for one who swam ashore to give the alarm. The hamlet was abandoned. The Englishmen went ashore and carried off cedarwood to burn luxuriously in their fires, wine, and a Greek pilot, then sailed out to sea with their prize. They found in her 25,000 pesos of very fine, pure gold. Further north, at Tarapaca, they found on the quay thirteen bars of silver, with a man on guard lying asleep beside them. They left the man and took the silver, 4000 ducats Spanish. Not far off they landed for water, and found a Spaniard with an Indian boy driving llamas laden with leather bags—containing in all eight hundredweight of silver, which went to swell the proceeds. At Avila three small craft were rifled and in one fifty-seven wedges of silver, each the size of a brick, were found. The ships were riding unguarded, not a man with them, so unsuspected was Drake's approach.

The harbour at Lima had never been attacked. There were twelve sail moored there, which were rifled, and one yielded a chest of plate and some good silks and linen. In one of these ships they heard of a vessel laden with treasure, the 'Cacafuego', which was bound northwards for Panama, by way of Paita. They cut the cables of the ships in Lima harbour and set them adrift to prevent pursuit. Then they made off after her. They were too late at Paita, and the 'Cacafuego' was away before them. The 'Golden Hind' darted on. They picked up on the way another prize worth taking, for besides the ropes and tackle that formed her cargo, she had eighty pounds' weight of gold inside, and a crucifix of gold set with great emeralds. A chain of gold had been promised the man who should first sight the treasure ship, and about three o'clock one afternoon she was sighted by John Drake the younger. Drake dropped barrels on ropes behind his ship to reduce speed while keeping his canvas spread.[5] No hint of alarm must be given. Then, towards sunset, these were hauled in, and the 'Golden Hind' sped on again. As she came alongside, three rounds were fired, one of which struck down the Spaniards' mizzen mast. Then she was boarded. All that night and for the next day and night also they sailed with her westwards into the open sea, away from the coast and the route to Panama. Then they hove to, and the work began. The treasure she contained was never fully reported, but Pretty's account mentions thirteen chests full of reals of plate, thirty-six tons of silver, eighty pounds of gold with jewels and precious stones also. Drake had her captain to dine with him, and told him of three ways he had in mind by which to go home. One was the way he had come, one was the supposed route through the northern strait, the Strait of Baccalaos, as he called it, and one was the way that Magellan had followed.

About a fortnight later they captured yet another ship in which there was something of value, letters from the King of Spain to the Governor of the Philippine Islands and charts of the voyage thither. These were taken. They might prove useful. But meanwhile there was still the question of that northern route to be settled, and it was time now to consider such problems seriously. For we are told, the general thought himself 'both in respect of his private iniuries received from the Spaniards, and also of their contempts and indignities offered to our countrey and Prince in generall, sufficiently satisfied and revenged'.

Pretty, the writer of Hakluyt's main account of the voyage, describes Drake as having sailed 'northerly to get a wind'. Actually he was of course sailing in a north-westerly direction, and the course he took shows that he was after something more than a wind. Matters had been nicely timed. If a northern strait were navigable, it would be navigable now, when the year was drawing towards midsummer. So they sailed northwards from mid-April to early summer, till they were in the latitude of Vancouver or thereabouts. Drake's reckoning may then have told him that he was more than sixty degrees to the west of the eastern coast of North America in a similar latitude. The temperature had dropped suddenly, and it was now bitterly cold, so that six men could hardly do the work of three. The trend of the coast was still north and north-west, and if the mouth of a strait were to be reached now, the passage would be immensely long. He turned back, therefore, into an anchorage near San Francisco harbour, a 'fair and good bay'. Their welcome was enthusiastic. An elaborate ceremony was performed by the natives, at which, so it was supposed, Drake was asked to become their king, a crown being set on his head and chains about his neck. He 'tooke the sceptre, crowne and dignitie of the said countrey into his hands', in the name of her Majesty Queen Elizabeth; and Nova Albion it became. Centuries later pioneers were to make their way by land over those vast intervening tracts from East to West. But by that time Virginia itself was inhabited no longer by the subjects of an English sovereign.

There was also work to be done ashore. If he went south again by the way he had come, Drake anticipated that a watch would be set for him, and the bad weather he had encountered also deterred him. He had therefore determined to sail across the Pacific to the Moluccas, and home by way of India and South Africa. But it was an immense undertaking, for which everything must be shipshape, the 'Golden Hind' scraped and newly rigged from the Spanish prize he had taken, and fresh supplies of food and water secured. As a result of the preparations made, the voyage across the Pacific was uneventful. They were entertained magnificently by the Sultan of Ternate, scraped their ship once more at a small island south of Celebes where they paused for nearly a month, and then tried to make their way back north of Celebes into the Celebes Sea. But they failed to find a

VII. SIR FRANCIS DRAKE, aged 43

(National Portrait Gallery)

route, and after beating about off the coast for several days they turned again southwards. The monsoon was now blowing and they forged ahead merrily in the direction of home.

The voyage seemed as good as over. But the worst was yet to come. No sea is more treacherous, and as they sped forward, the ship suddenly ran aground late one evening on a shoal, a shelf so precipitous that though the bows were aground, the water by the stern was too deep for it to be possible to warp the ship off. No line they had would reach the bottom. They were many miles from the nearest land, and the ship's boat might have held twenty of the fifty men or more who were on board. Next day, after a night of watchfulness and prayer, Mr Fletcher administered communion to the company and preached to them. He had been sympathetically disposed towards Doughty, and had seen, in the disaster to the 'Marigold', a visitation of the Almighty on one of the witnesses against him. Now he was doubtless even more convinced of transgression and impending retribution. One man alone kept his courage. 'Our generall, as hee had alwayes hitherto shewed himselfe couragious, and of a good confidence in the mercie and protection of God, so now he continued in the same.' After service, the order was given to lighten the ship. Three tons of cloves—a duke's ransom—eight pieces of ordnance and some meal and beans were thrown overboard. The Almighty might not unreasonably have required a few of those tons of silver to go overboard too. But suddenly the wind changed, and the ship slipped off the reef, undamaged. The only person who was almost certainly not altogether pleased was Mr Fletcher. Drake solemnly excommunicated him and denounced him to the devil and all his angels. Then, somehow, they found the way through that barrier which closes the China seas from the Indian Ocean, it seems by Ombaya Island, and the way home lay open before him. He still had to sail half round the world; but there was little difficulty about that.

In England there had been some news of him, including a report that he had been hanged at Panama. Wynter had reached home full of forebodings, but not much later these had been dispelled, at least for those who had taken shares in the voyage, by news which reached the Spanish ambassador, which evidently made him very angry, and which made him full of anxiety to have immediate information of Drake's arrival. Drake had left behind him friends and admirers as well as enemies. St Juan de Anton and Zarate, Spanish commanders who had been entertained by him, could not disguise their admiration for the 'greatest captain of the world', and about his voyage as a feat of seamanship no two views were possible. But the financial losses he had caused were enormous. They threatened a financial crisis, so that after his return the merchants who traded with Spain and whose fleet was about to sail hesitated to risk their goods in view of the strained situation. Drake's friends on the Council, Walsingham and Leicester, were out of favour for the time being, and on his arrival he was unwilling to go to London without some sign of the Queen's disposition, for there was always a possibility that the Doughty affair might be resurrected by his enemies. But on receiving a personal message from Elizabeth he made his way to London at once. She supported him magnificently. Immediately on his arrival he was with her for six hours, and day after day she summoned him, in the face of Burghley's opposition, to discuss his voyage with her. Burghley regarded the whole venture as dishonourable, not without a shadow of justification, though there were things to be said on the other side as well. But whatever he might say to her, whatever policy the merchants of London might press on her, it made no difference. She went down to Deptford and was entertained by Drake at a magnificent banquet, such as had not been seen since her father's day, on board the 'Golden Hind'. There she knighted him; and when it was time to face the problem of the rich cargo of that ship, she gave instructions that when it was inventoried only those items should be included in the inventory which the admiral chose to declare. His sailors were treated handsomely. He himself was by modern standards probably a millionaire. The Queen did well too. And after the fashion of the time, Burghley and the new ambassador Mendoza were invited to share the proceeds, if they would keep their mouths shut. To their credit, they refused. But against success so triumphant protests were no use, and for the time being Drake's star alone was in the ascendant.

Chapter VI

THE WEST INDIAN EXPEDITION OF 1585 & THE EXPEDITION TO CADIZ

To men of the age which produced the first English prayer books, battle, murder, and sudden death were a part of the texture of their lives. England has enjoyed so many years of peace from the violence of foreign enemies, from persecution and from civil war, that it has been difficult to imagine an age when that peace was by no means a matter of course. When armoured cars rumbled through London on their way to the docks during the General Strike of 1926, the sight of them gave to many the sense of waking from an idyllic dream. A world of stability and peace was passing. It would surely leave not a rack behind. After it anything might happen; but at least it must be an utterly different world. By some miracle there followed not violence, but agreement, not recrimination, but co-operation. For a time the illusion returned. But it has been shattered finally and ruthlessly, not by that worst of all evils, civil violence, but by the war in the air. We can now more easily conceive what the insecurity and danger of sixteenth-century Europe was like.

For those whose business took them across the seas, hostile attack was an ever-present threat even in time of peace. In 1585 England and Spain were still nominally friendly countries. During that summer a ship, the 'Primrose' of London, was discharging her cargo at Bilbao. She had been there two days, and the work was quietly going on, when there came out to her a pinnace, on board which was the Governor, or Corregidor, of the province, with six others who were evidently merchants. They brought presents for the master of the ship, by whom they were hospitably entertained. After a time four returned to Bilbao. But three remained, and though they made themselves pleasant, something in their manner evidently struck the master as suspicious, and as the afternoon wore on he passed on his suspicions to members of his crew. Before long there came boats out to the ship with a further large number of merchants, seventy or thereabouts, together with the pinnace which had first come out and which now returned with twenty-four others in her. In the English ship there were twenty-nine men all told, and two of them had gone ashore with a boatload of her cargo. The master was now thoroughly disturbed, and he demanded that no other Spaniards should come aboard, beyond those who had already done so. This had only just been agreed, when there was a sudden rush. The Spaniards, armed with rapiers, leaped on to the ship and swarmed all over her, even entering the cabins, and the Corregidor called on the master to surrender, threatening him with death.

For the 'Primrose's' crew, however, there could be no question of surrender. They had little doubt what their fate would be, that they were like to 'taste of those sharp torments', as Hakluyt says, 'which are there accustomed in their Holy House'. Since the time of the engagement at St Juan, soon after which the activities of the Inquisition had spread to Mexico and brought punishment to many of those Englishmen who had been left behind from Hawkins' ships, the Holy Office had acquired a bad name among the Puritan English crews. Because of the master's suspicions, they had now set weapons ready. There were five calievers ready charged with small shot, and men under the hatches began to fire them at the Spaniards on the decks above. The boarding party had not expected resistance, and were not equipped to meet it. They were checked for the moment; they called on the master again to surrender, but things were already beginning to go hard for them. The decks were soon streaming with blood. The Spaniards were shot at from below and set on from every side; and as quickly as men clambered on deck they were swept overboard, so that scores of them struggled wounded in the water and were drowned. Four of them managed to lay hold on the ship's ropes, and they were taken up into the 'Primrose', one being the Corregidor himself. It was impossible, after what had happened, to complete the unloading of the cargo. The 'Primrose' weighed anchor at once and made her way back to London, taking the four prisoners with her. Her own casualties were one killed and six wounded, with the two men ashore left in Spanish hands. The numbers of Spaniards killed were never definitely ascertained but, relatively speaking, the Spanish losses must have been very heavy.

When the Corregidor was examined, it was found that he had on him his commission from King Philip:

Licentiat de Escober [it read] my Corrigidor of my Signorie of Biskay, I have caused a great fleete to be put in readinesse in the haven of Lisbone and the river of Sivill. There is required for the Souldiers of it, for the armour, victuals and munition that are to bee imployed in the same, great store of shipping of all sortes against the time of service; and to the end there may be choise made of the best...I doe require you that, presently upon the arrivall of this carrier and with as much dissimulation as may be (that the matter may not be knowen untill it be put in execution) you take order for the staying and arresting of all the shipping that may be found upon the coast and in the portes of the sayd Signorie, excepting none of Holand, Zeland, Easterland, Germanie, England, and other Provinces that are in rebellion against me....And the stay being thus made you shall have a speciall care...that none of the shippes or men may escape away. And send me a plaine and distinct declaration of the number of ships that you shall have so stayed in that coast and portes...to the end that...we may further direct you what ye shall do. In the meane time you shall presently see this my commandement put into execution...urging therein such care and diligence as may answere the trust that I repose in you, wherein you shall doe me great service.

Dated at Barcelona, the 29 of May, 1585.

This document,[1] throwing a flood of light on King Philip's plans, reached London at a critical moment. Since Drake's return from the raid in the Pacific, Elizabeth had been hesitating. Some of her advisers, like Secretary Walsingham, who was closely associated with Drake's designs and is addressed by him in his letters in terms of close personal devotion, were urging Drake's own plan of an immediate attack on Spain. But there were others who were more cautious. It had become known however that certain Spaniards were pressing King Philip in the direction of war against England. Some of them, and in particular the admiral, Santa Cruz, had realised the weakness of Spain as an oceanic power. Her magnificent success at Lepanto, the news of which had rung victoriously through Europe not so many years before, had been won by oared galleys. It was becoming apparent that the policy initiated by Henry VIII of giving England an ocean-going fleet had set her far ahead of Spain in the race for sea power. Santa Cruz, who knew what he was talking about, advocated the building of an ocean navy powerful enough to crush once for all that 'daughter of the devil', and to bring to a successful conclusion the enterprise of England. And here was evidence of a 'great fleete' being mustered in the Tagus and at Seville.

Still, it was impossible to be certain that Philip, who moved slowly, had finally accepted Santa Cruz' view. To take adequate precautions in England would mean spending money, and Elizabeth notoriously found that difficult. Spending money meant asking her subjects for more. In the old days she had managed well enough, partly on the proceeds of those royal 'progresses', like that into Essex and Suffolk in 1579, when she had been welcomed into Colchester by the bailiffs and aldermen in their fine clothes, and 'had been gratified from the town with a cup of silver double gilt, of the value of 20 marks, or 10 l. at the least, with 40 angels in the same'. But forty angels did not take long to spend, even if every town gave forty others as she passed through, and since 1579 there had been no royal progresses. To call Parliament and ask for money meant to be given not only money but advice. If there was one thing Elizabeth could not stand, it was being given advice unasked. Her parsimony was largely due to her dislike of listening to her Parliaments' good counsels and it was for that reason more than any other that she avoided summoning them. But she had nevertheless an unerring sense of popular feeling. She knew that a move against the Spanish power would be popular, and on Christmas Eve 1584 Drake's commission to command a fleet against Spain was signed by her. Throughout the first three months of the following year preparations went ahead: and then, in one of those moods that no one could understand and which became more and more frequent as she aged, she suddenly cancelled the commission and the whole plan fell into abeyance. The advocates of action were in despair. It was at this moment that the 'Primrose' returned to England with the Corregidor of Biscay and his commission safely stowed away under her hatches. There were many times during Elizabeth's reign when her seamen found her hesitations very trying. In judging her policy we are apt to look at it through their eyes. But she had a difficult task before her. She was like a circus rider with a foot on two horses; for there were not only Puritans, but there were also Catholics in her realm of England. In the Catholic estimates of the situation made at the time, it is more than once held that the Catholics were in an actual majority in England,[2] and in days when statistics were not available such an impression seems to have been easily formed by those who came into contact with the Catholic families. The estimates were wrong, but that they were made at all is an indication of the importance of the Catholic minority. The seamen, whose protests against Elizabeth's hesitation we have—'withal we were not the most assured of her Majesty's perseverance to let us go forward' wrote Carleill to Walsingham, to explain why they had left in a hurry in 1585—were mainly drawn from Puritan communities. They were anxious to see Elizabeth break once and for all with those of Catholic sympathies. But she was a trimmer. Both Catholics and Protestants were her subjects. At a moment when the greatest pressure was being brought to bear on her to declare directly for Protestantism, she insisted ostentatiously on the retention of the crucifix in her private chapel. And she was determined not to break with either till she was certain that she had not only the active Protestants, but the more or less indifferent also, on her side. She had a genius for procrastinating till her admirals thought it was too late, but till she knew the time was ready. She was proved right, and it was the instinct for this which gave her the overwhelming support of the country in the moments of real crisis that she had to face.

So far she had been hesitating. Her mind had not been made up. But the story that the 'Primrose' brought back from Bilbao cleared her doubts, perhaps because of the effect it had on that mass of indifferent opinion. In the following month Drake was authorised to impress ships for an expedition to rescue the vessels that had been arrested, and in July his commission was signed. If we find traces of hesitation in the Queen's actions after this it is partly because as the months went by the policy of 'appeasement' was gaining ground among her subjects as well as in her own mind, partly because of personal complications involved when Sir Philip Sidney, one of her favourites and just appointed Master of the Ordnance, became associated with the expedition. It was that odd lack of judgment which was going to appear later in so distorted a form in her relations with Essex. In such personal matters as these her mistakes were indeed disastrous, though her devotion to Burghley leaves the impression that there too she was right about the things that were supremely important.[3]

Before Drake left, he had discussed his plans with one of his friends, who summarised them the following April for the benefit of the authorities, perhaps because they were alarmed at the lack of news from him. This summary makes possible a fair estimate of the success that the expedition attained. It fell far short of what Drake had hoped to do. His intention was not only to extort reprisals by holding the finest of the West Indian cities to ransom. It was to paralyse the life of the Spanish empire by striking at the most vital spot. When he had finished with Rio de la Hacha and Santa Marta at the end of the year, and passed on to Carthagena in January, that was to have been only the beginning. From thence he was to go to Nombre de Dios once more. This time there should be no mistake. With the aid of the Cimaroons he would sack and ransom the city, and make his way up the Chagres river towards Panama. That, too, would fall into his hands, and perhaps the Isle of Pearls as well, and while his land forces were dealing with Panama he would return to the Caribbean and sweep from the seas the Spanish coastal shipping, it might be two hundred frigates. Most interesting of all, when this had been done, he would attack Havana, known as at that time the most important of the harbours through which the West Indian trade passed, and if the place were found tenable, he would leave there a garrison as a permanent threat to any revival of prosperity. It was a grandiose scheme. But the expedition was being planned on a great scale; Drake in the 'Elizabeth Bonaventure' of 600 tons, Francis Knollys in the galleon 'Leicester' of 400, Frobisher in the 'Primrose', Wynter in the 'Aid', and nearly twenty other good ships, great and small. Two were the Queen's own ships. Others came from London and others from Plymouth. There was a land force of over a thousand men commanded by Christopher Carleill. Some of the gentlemen adventurers were men who were later going to distinguish themselves in other fields, like Edward Wright, who published the first set of tables that provided the so-called Mercator's projection with its theoretical basis. And there were others who had grown experienced already in Drake's service, like Tom Moone, the ship's carpenter who had scuttled the 'Swan' and now sailed as captain of the 'Francis'.

Before the expedition left, the precise conditions under which leave was given for these reprisals to be taken against the King of Spain were laid down. Merchants whose ships or goods had been arrested in Spain were first to prove the losses they had incurred, before the Lord Admiral or before the Judge of the Admiralty. When such losses had been proved, it was to be lawful for those who had proved them 'to take and apprehend on the open seas ships or goods of the subjects of the King of Spain' equally as if the two countries had been actually at war. Ships or goods taken in this way were to be brought back to English ports intact (bulk not being broken on the return voyage) and then a full inventory was to be made. The proceeds of the operations were to be divided into three shares, the first for the owners, the second for the victuallers, and the third for captains and crews. It is noteworthy that in these letters of marque nothing was said about the right of reprisal against goods on land. Actually the chief damage done was done ashore, and a considerable amount of property was seized as well as destroyed. Such action is not covered by the letters of marque. It may be that the anomalous position of the King of Spain's West Indian possessions made this unnecessary. If they were regarded as part of Spain's dominions they were theoretically covered by trade treaties of nearly a hundred years' standing; yet since King Philip regarded them as excluded from the scope of these treaties, they might be considered from the English point of view to have no status in law whatever. But overmuch consideration was no longer being given to niceties of this kind. Not long before the expedition started, Sir George Carey, Governor of the Isle of Wight, wrote to Walsingham to say that a former pirate, one Flud, had just come to him offering his services for operations against the coast of Spain; the only condition was to be that if he did good service he was to be pardoned. Carey recommended that Flud should be given his chance, and the use of a man of this type does not suggest that the authorities at the time were straining at gnats. Indeed this expedition marks the opening of the war, which was in fact never preceded by any formal declaration.

The expedition, which sailed from Plymouth on 14 September 1585, did not wait even to take on board adequate supplies of water, such was the eagerness of Drake and of his associates to start before permission was countermanded. It was not many days before they began to fall in with French and Spanish ships. Sometimes it was not easy to decide their nationality, if as in one instance at this time the crew claimed their ship to be French, but had in their possession 'bulls of pardon from the Pope', printed in Spanish, with blanks left where the names were to be filled in. It does not seem that the English fleet were inclined to err on the side of caution, at any rate when the cargo looked like being useful for their own purposes; though in some instances receipts were given so that repayment could be made later if the ownership proved to be French. In the honouring of promises of this kind, Drake's record is good.

The first port of call was Bayona. It was necessary to make good at once the deficiencies which were due to the hurried departure from Plymouth, and in particular to water, before beginning the Atlantic crossing. But the opportunity was used to make a demonstration in force against the Spaniards. When port officials came out to examine the papers of the English ships, they were sent back to say that Drake's object was to demand the cause why so many Englishmen had been imprisoned, and their goods arrested. If war was intended, then the Spaniards might have it; but if not, and provided Drake's reasonable demands were satisfied, then he too would not break the peace. The ultimatum was forcibly put by an English officer, Captain Sampson, sent with them. He was chosen as a man whose judgment would tell him whether it was safe to deliver a message in such terms or whether they ought to be toned down. His opinion of Bayona's preparedness was apparently not high, for it is clear that he did not mince matters. The Governor answered that the embargo had been ordered by the King of Spain, but had already been countermanded, that his commission did not extend to questions of peace and war, and that if Drake liked to obtain provisions and water, he might certainly do so. Next day it was noticed that under cover of a storm that had sprung up during the night an attempt was being made to evacuate some of the treasures of the city up the river. An English force was sent to check the movement, and valuable plate from the churches was detained. Drake then met the Governor, and an arrangement was reached, with an exchange of hostages, by which Drake should get the supplies he wanted unmolested, on condition that he did no further damage and restored the property that had been taken. It was clear that the pleasure of the Spaniards was not unmitigated throughout the proceedings, and they were heard to say that if they could detain the English force for sixteen days they would wash their hands in English blood. But that was not provided for on Drake's programme, and when the necessary stores had been taken on board they left for the Azores. Don Alvarez de Baçan at once hastened to draw up for King Philip a forecast of Drake's intentions. The Spanish story was that he had a force of 5000 soldiers on board. De Baçan thought that he was planning a raid in force in the Pacific, and believed he might permanently occupy some point of vantage on the eastern coast of South America. He recommended the immediate despatch of a large force to the Indies to deal with him.

The English summary of Drake's plans to which reference has been made above was written after news reached England of Drake's doings in the Azores and we do not know, therefore, precisely what his plans for the earlier stages of the voyage included. But he was prepared to take opportunities for sacking not only Santiago, but also Palma, and for completing the military organisation of his forces; though not prepared to lose opportunities of a fair wind for the West Indies. At Palma he was met with a powerful defence, and his own ship had a couple of shot through her, though there were none hurt. He withdrew to plan a big attack by land and sea, but the wind was favourable for continuing the voyage and he therefore decided not to wait. He had landed six hundred men for a reconnaissance at Palma, and the same land force[4] was used at Santiago. There were fortresses commanding the harbour and defensive works commanding the land approaches. The city had been sacked by French privateers three years before, and its strengthened defences might make capture difficult. The landing force was set ashore late in the afternoon at a point some way to the east of the city, which lies in the gorge cut by a small river, flowing out into a bay facing south. Carleill, who commanded them, led them over a mountainous path to the plain north-east of the city, whence the plan was to attack next day. But the alarm had been given, and when they moved forward at dawn they encountered no sign of resistance, even when they reached the fortifications defending the city, and saw from the eastern edge of the gorge the six or seven hundred houses, the three churches, the hospital, and the market-place and trim gardens of Santiago spread out before them. Carleill sent his great ensign to be displayed in the city as a sign to the fleet that the occupation had been effected, and the guns that were found loaded in the fortifications were fired as a salute, for it was the anniversary of the Queen's accession.[5]

So far, so good. But the plan was to secure a good financial return for the investors in the expedition, and that meant plunder. There were stores with which to replenish the ships' larders in plenty, but apart from that not very much save what an eyewitness calls 'a great deal of trash'. They remained in the town nine days in the hopes of ransom being offered, and one or two prisoners who were captured were tortured, as was the regular practice of the times, in the hope of obtaining information as to the whereabouts of the treasure that was supposed to have been hidden. But nothing was discovered. A force was sent inland twelve miles to a village where it was reported to be, but that also was found deserted, and if there was treasure hidden, it was not discovered. During this expedition a lad attached to the force had strayed and been taken by the Spaniards. His body was found later, horribly mutilated. It was that perhaps which determined Drake to wait no longer, but to raze Santiago to the ground. One building alone was left standing, the hospital. But to make the destruction wrought more complete, a small force was sent round the headland at the eastern end of Santiago bay to the township of Prayo where there had been further reports of treasure being hidden, and this was also burned. Meanwhile time was being wasted, and there was some trouble, as it appears, between the soldiers and the sailors. At any rate, Drake thought it worth while to muster the whole force and administer to it the oath of allegiance to the Queen and to himself as commander-in-chief. It is all we hear on this expedition of trouble of this kind. Drake was easily suspicious of others, and this sometimes led him into serious mistakes. But it looks as if there were generally some reasons for his suspicions, however much his nature might magnify them, and apart from this one incident his leadership of the expedition, in matters both of tactics and of personality, was a triumphant success. He never condoned the questioning of his authority, but from those who accepted it without question he won a splendid loyalty, and he was their servant as well as their master. He had, so one of his soldiers wrote of him in this expedition, so vigilant a care and foresight in the good ordering of his fleet, with such wonderful travail of body, 'as doubtless had he bene the meanest person, as he was the chiefest, he had yet deserved the first place of honour'.

Santiago, where William Hawkins was said to have met with treacherous dealing, would not in a hurry forget the name of Drake. But the high promise of the expedition began to be diminished not long after. Two days out from Santiago sickness descended on the fleet and swept through ship after ship. At one time in Drake's own ship alone there were, so it was said, a hundred men sick, and in each ship the deaths sometimes numbered two or three a day. In three weeks they reached the island of Dominica, where they stopped for a few hours to refresh the crews, and would have waited longer if it had not been for the danger of native attack. Four days later they made St Christopher, and landed there; and as the island appeared to be uninhabited, it was decided to water and disinfect the ships, and attempt thus to shake off the plague that dogged them. In St Christopher twenty men were buried. Yet there was some good fortune when the expedition fell in with two Spanish ships, which were taken. In them were found provisions and a Greek pilot who knew the approach to San Domingo.

Thither it was decided they should at once move. It was the ancient capital of the West Indies and though it was by this time surpassed in importance by Carthagena, its prestige was still unrivalled. The body of Columbus lay buried in the cathedral, and the city was the administrative centre of the West Indies. The harbour was heavily fortified, and the coast, apart from the harbour itself, was difficult, so that a landing within easy distance of the town was thought to be impossible. Drake is said to have sent ahead to establish contact with the Maroons, and according to one report brought to Europe by a Spaniard a few weeks after the event, the Maroons overwhelmed those outposts that had been established by the sea side to watch for the English fleet, so that the attack took the city by surprise. The plan was for a landing to be made at a place shown by the Greek pilot, some miles to the west of the city. The landing force was taken there by night in the smaller vessels of the fleet, and a chart of San Domingo, published soon after the expedition returned home to explain the method of attack, marks the beacons lit by the watchers to signal the fleet's arrival—so that if the attack was actually a surprise, the Spaniards must have been aware at least of the presence of the English ships in the offing. The full force of one thousand or twelve hundred men that was available was set ashore. As they disembarked, Drake left them under the command as usual of Carleill, and went back himself to rejoin the fleet. Dawn broke as they landed, and in the early morning light the soldiers marched along an excellent road over low wooded hills towards the city that lay to the north-east. Reaching the plain in front of it, they deployed in elaborate battle order, the 'main battle' consisting of about six hundred pikemen, with musketeers and pikemen disposed round in smaller units in order to keep off the attacks of cavalry that were screened by droves of wild cattle.

Meanwhile a feint attack was being carried out from the sea by the fleet, which had come to anchor immediately off the town and within range of the guns of the fortress. The ships replied heavily to the fire from the shore which did some damage though it effected no casualties. It was impossible to enter the harbour for the mouth had been blocked by ships sunk in it. So the duel continued several hours, until suddenly the Cross of St George was seen floating over the city. The attacks of the cavalry had been ineffective, and the

Spaniards had retired on a position defended by artillery covering the town gates. At the first volley a few men had been killed, including one standing near Carleill. But before the guns could be reloaded, they were rushed, and in the vigour of the attack English and Spaniards together ran pell-mell into the gates. The English attack had been divided against those two gates that faced westwards. Both were taken, and the columns under Carleill and Powell, the 'Sergeant Major' or second-in-command, converged in the market-place. The defenders withdrew to the castle, which was in the south-east corner of the city, and commanded not only the narrow entrance to the harbour, but the whole anchorage. The English force barricaded itself in the market square, planning to attack next day. But when day came it was seen that the castle had been abandoned and the defenders withdrawn across the harbour. The attack had taken place on New Year's Day 1586—a New Year's gift, as the men said it should be called. As in other places, a quantity of cannon was captured here also, being booty of some value. Considerable stores were taken of food, wine, and sweetmeats, but here as elsewhere there was very little gold or silver to be had. Other captures included much shipping, with one specially fine French-built galleon 'the like whereof', according to a report sent back that summer, 'was not in all Spain'.

No attempt was made by the Spaniards to recapture the city. During the negotiations which followed for a ransom, an incident took place which is significant. One feature of English propaganda throughout the war was the reports of Spanish cruelty to the natives. Apart from the frequent mentions of such incidents that contemporary accounts of the campaigns contain, a book written many years before by Las Casas, a Spanish missionary who had been deeply concerned with the welfare of the native Carib population and wrote to expose the colonists' treatment of their native servants, was now republished in several languages, with lurid illustrations. Drake always adopted a different attitude towards the natives, and found their help of great value to him. He was warm-hearted and impulsive by nature, and several incidents in his career show him as a protector of the negro slave as well as of the Caribs or of the half-breed Maroons. Thus we find him in Santiago saying to a negro slave that if his master should be captured he would be handed over to the slave as his servant. It happened on this occasion that Drake sent a negro boy with a flag of truce to bear a message in the course of the negotiations—or, according to another account, that the boy was sent out to meet a party of Spaniards, themselves approaching under a flag of truce. The Spaniards took the matter as an insult. *Non sufficit orbis* was the motto blazoned at the head of the great stairway in the Governor's house. For Spain the world itself was not enough. Spanish pride is a traditional quality, and a man struck the lad through the body with his horseman's stave. The wounded negro struggled back to where Drake was, and died when he had gasped out what had happened. There were as prisoners in English hands some Friars, and Drake had two of them taken to the place where the boy had been wounded, and hanged them there. At the same time another was sent to the Spaniards, to say that until the offender was punished, two prisoners should be hanged there every day. The offender was brought forthwith, but the Spaniards were compelled to do justice on him themselves.

Meanwhile the negotiations moved slowly, and to hasten them the systematic destruction of the town by fire was undertaken. But it was a tedious business, and in the end agreement was reached on a ransom of 25,000 ducats. As with all the other incidents in this campaign, financially the results were disappointing. The fortunes of the expedition were yet to be made. Yet there hung over it like a pall the fearful mortality of the plague, by which its man power was being steadily diminished.

Still the job they had set out to do was as yet only half done. The last attack that was made, the attack on Carthagena, is also the most brilliant. It illustrates Drake's flair for a combined operation, by sea and land, when the force was small enough to be handled easily by his individual and personal methods. In some respects it is the climax of his career. The attacks which were soon to follow on Spanish ports in Europe were to achieve their fine successes, and that campaign as a whole is rightly regarded as a masterpiece. But the force he was then to have at his command was in fact too large for him. In the attack on Cadiz this shows itself in the objections raised by Borough, his second-in-command, who complained that no adequate plan of attack had been drawn up, and that the ships were led in to attack haphazard. There is a basis of justification in his criticism, though events proved him to have been wrong. When the time came for the Armada campaign, it was as a freelance that Drake did his most brilliant work. He did not remain throughout with the fleet as the Lord Admiral and his advisers, including Drake himself, organised it, but did his effective work on its fringes. He played the part of what would be called in the House of Commons a 'ginger group', and played it magnificently. But his co-operation with others, who were his equals, or technically his superiors, was always uneasy, and in the last campaign of all was to prove disastrous.

At Carthagena, however, conditions suited him absolutely. Carleill and he had no disagreement. The nature of operations was such that the brilliant apprehension of the one weak spot in the Spanish defence and of the right way of attacking it proved decisive. Like others of these West Indian harbours, that at Carthagena is formed by a long spit of sand, some three miles long or thereabouts, stretching out due southwards from the city, comparatively broad at the end furthest from the city, where it was covered with brushwood, but narrowing near the walls of Carthagena to some hundred yards or so of bare sand dune, eminently defensible by the wall that the Spaniards had built across it and had heavily fortified. The harbour was divided into two parts, an outer and an inner harbour, by another spit, running out almost at right angles from the first, due east from a point not much further from the city than that where the wall had been built. Thus the defence of the single neck of land, if accomplished, would keep off an enemy even if he had succeeded in landing on this second promontory within the harbour. Where the inner harbour was bounded by the sandy isthmus the Spanish commander had placed a pair of galleys, with the guns in their bows commanding the neck of land, so that it seemed any enemy who attempted to cross it must fare disastrously. The galleys themselves were safe enough, for the inner harbour was entered by a channel so narrow that, as a Spaniard describing the place for King Philip a year or two later said, 'sometimes one may cast a stone into the ships when they are coming in'. Moreover the channel was closed by a chain, and there was a strong fortification commanding it. On the other sides the city was defended by marshy ground and creeks, crossed by a long causeway, so that in these directions it was impregnable. The Spaniards had had a week's warning of Drake's approach, and the defence force, in view of the strength of the position, was a considerable one. There were fifty or so cavalry armed with lances, four hundred and fifty harquebusiers, one hundred pikemen, and an additional hundred and fifty harquebusiers in the galleys with a number of native troops besides. They had 'fortified and made such

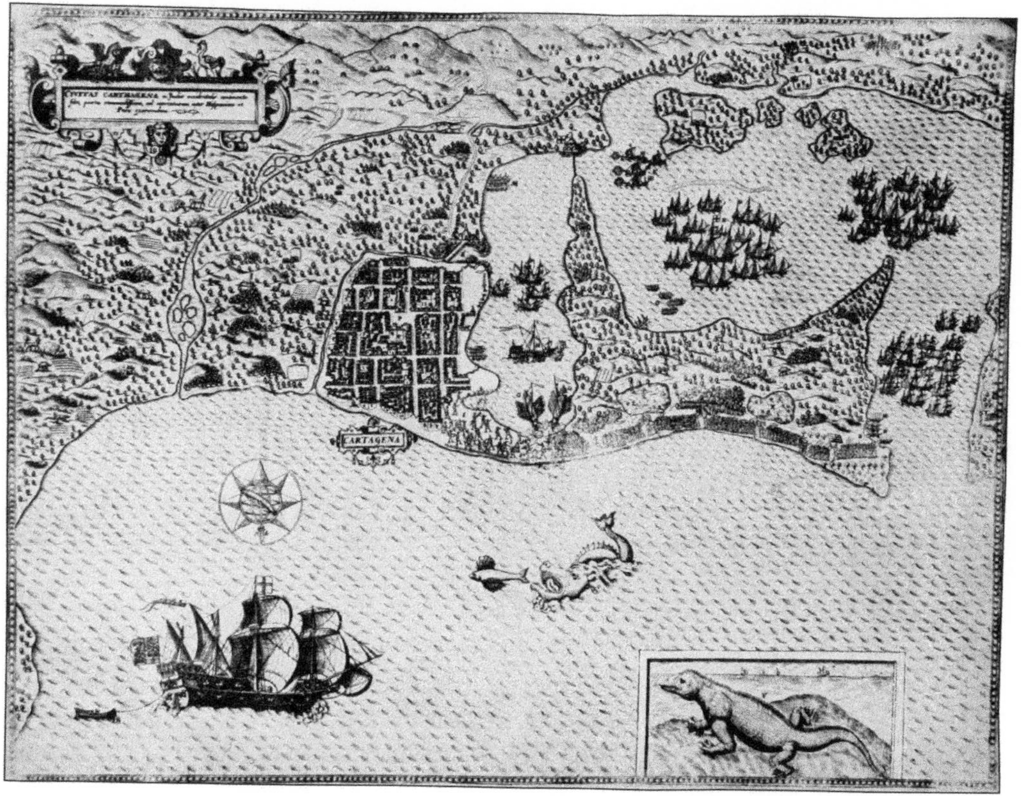

VIII. PLAN OF CARTHAGENA, TO ILLUSTRATE THE ATTACK MADE BY DRAKE

(Reproduced from a copy in the British Museum)

rampires', wrote one of the soldiers in the 'Primrose', 'that it was impossible by man's reason for us to win'.

Drake sailed southwards past the town batteries on the day before that fixed for the attack, near enough to draw their fire, and this time there was no real possibility of surprise. He must have had a general idea of the approaches before he reached that part of the coast, but it was that evening that the detailed plans were laid. The land force was to be disembarked on the southernmost part of the promontory running southward from Carthagena, at the inlet of the harbour. Not long afterwards this inlet, known as the Boca Grande, was filled in with stones as the result of an earthquake. When the English fleet attacked Carthagena in 1741 there was no inlet here, and they had to enter by the Boca Chica, or small mouth, six miles further south still, and a much more difficult entry. Sir Julian Corbett says that Drake himself entered by this Boca Chica. It is not mentioned by any of the English authorities. Its passage, as described in contemporary Spanish accounts, was hazardous even with a local pilot, and as one of the English accounts expressly states that the harbour mouth was some 'three miles' from the city (the distance of the Boca Grande, while the Boca Chica is eight miles or thereabouts) it seems unlikely that the Boca Chica can have been used at this time. The plan was to land the troops under cover of night, and make the attack early next morning. There was to be delivered at the same time an attack by the fleet on the fort at the mouth of the inner harbour. As this entrance was closed by a chain, this attack was most probably a feint, like that at San Domingo.

The troops were landed late in the evening, with instructions to move forward about midnight. Before they delivered the actual assault, they were to rest, and instructions were given that they should keep near the shore so that the way should not be missed. But the guide who was leading them was uncertain of the route and lost it, so that the night was far spent when contact with the enemy was first made. Some cavalry had been sent forward by the Spaniards among the scrub, and it was with these horsemen that the encounter first took place. The ground was, however, unsuitable for the action of cavalry, and they withdrew on the Spanish line of defence, giving the alarm. The Spaniards had anticipated a landing on the seaward promontory of the harbour mouth, and had dotted it with 'small sticks in great numbers half a yard long', 'all dressed with a most villainous and mortal poison'. These had apparently been avoided by landing within the mouth, but there was a further batch in the ground before the main defensive wall and trench. This wall was heavily built of stonework, and stretched all over the neck save that on the seaward side a gap had been left for the cavalry to pass through. Nor was this without defence, as wine butts filled with earth were then moved into place, and in this form the defensive line was carried right into the water. There were five cannon guarding the wall, besides those in the bows of the two galleys enfilading the advancing line.

As the English approached the narrow isthmus, they heard the noise of cannon from some two miles away and knew that, as arranged, the sea attack on the fort at the mouth of the inner harbour had begun. Though it was a feint, it was pressed hard, and some damage was done to one of the ships by fire from the shore batteries. But Drake had seen that the real weakness of the enemy's defences lay not here, but at the point where the line of the land defences came down to the sea, and had ordered that the land attack should be made here, by way of the shore. Thus the fire from the eleven cannon on the galleys and from the soldiers on them would be baffled by the camber of the neck of land. The tide was out, which made the plan the more effective, and in the early morning twilight the assault was made. Not a shot was fired by the attackers till they were almost on the wall. Then after a volley they threw themselves with pikes and swords against the butts of earth that formed the defences and hurled them to the ground. The English pikes were rather longer than the Spanish and the body armour better, and before long the Spaniards, heavily outnumbered, were retreating towards Carthagena half a mile away.

Once this line had been taken, there was only slight further resistance, before the English reached the market-place and the Spaniards withdrew entirely from the city. Some of the shipping taken in the harbour was burned, and the town was partly sacked as San Domingo had been. But here too the results were disappointing. After prolonged negotiations, the ransom offered was 110,000 ducats, and the plunder taken in the city amounted, in hard cash, to very little, though the loss of property to the Spaniards was great.

The negotiations had the same accompaniment of elaborate courtesy that accompanied all Drake's dealings with the Spaniards, and the Governor and the bishop were banqueted in their own city. But there must have been an undercurrent of misgiving. The force available for further operations amounted to seven hundred men only, little more than half of the original total, such had been the ravages of sickness. In honour much had been won, but in profit little, and Drake took what was for him the very rare step of summoning a council of war, attended by the officers of the land force only, and formally putting three questions to it. Was it possible with their present force to hold Carthagena permanently against all comers? Had the time come to cut losses and go home with honour satisfied, or should an attempt be made to carry out the original plan of an attack on the isthmus? Should the ransom offered for Carthagena be accepted? In answering that Carthagena could be held in spite of the depletion of their force, Carleill and his associates said that the opinion of the sea captains ought to be obtained on the degree of security from attack by sea which they could guarantee—a reply which incidentally confirms the fact which the few signatures to the document that have been recorded suggest, that the sea captains were not represented at this council. Their reply, or Drake's own opinion, may not have been altogether hopeful, for the decision was certainly taken to abandon the city. To the second question the reply was that it would be a mistake to follow the chimera of treasure still further. If the object was to damage the prestige of the King of Spain, then damage enough had been done. If it was rather to win plunder, then the sack of city after city, each apparently richer than the last, had shown that wealth could very easily be evacuated to safety. They might find, it is implied, that at the isthmus it was the same. Drake had told his friends, as we know from the draft plan, that Carthagena might be worth a million ducats to the expedition. In fact there was being offered a tenth of that sum. But the council recommended that the offer be accepted, and at the same time passed a resolution that showed how magnificently, in spite of the financial failure, Drake had succeeded in winning the confidence of his soldiers. The captains agreed to sacrifice their own share in the ransom for Carthagena in the interests of the 'poor men', the sailors as well as the soldiers, who had sailed with the expedition. That such a self-denying ordinance was issued by the army captains is an eloquent tribute to Drake's skill in eliminating the traditional hostility between sea and land forces. In everything but its financial results the expedition had been a superb achievement.

So they made for home. Four days later the Spaniards were horrified to see them coming back again, and packed up their belongings to return once more to the hills. But they were somewhat reassured when it was discovered that one of the prizes had sprung a leak and was to be unloaded and burnt, while Drake's only other need was to borrow ovens in which to bake biscuit. It was suspected that this biscuit might be a ruse and that the real intention was not to bake biscuit but to pull more chestnuts out of the fire by picking quarrels. The local justice came daily and nightly to see that no possible excuse for trouble was given. And what with the courtesy of the Governor's proclamation and the discovery of alligators in an uninhabited island a few days later, the return visit was a triumphant success. The final leavetaking was on 18 April 1586. The fleet made a last call on the homeward journey at a Spanish settlement in Florida, placed there recently for defence, which was wrecked. Thence it made its way up the coast to Virginia, where that historic attempt at colonisation, organised by Sir Walter Ralegh, of which we shall have more to say, had been begun the year before. Lane and his fellow-colonists believed at first that this must be another supply fleet for themselves. Drake offered to leave there a ship fully manned with pinnaces and boats and a month's provisions, for discovery along the shore and return to England later, and this was arranged. But at that time a storm arose and raged for three days, threatening to drive the whole fleet ashore. To wait yet longer when there was a chance of return seemed rash, so that the previous decision was withdrawn and the colonists were embarked forthwith. Two only were left behind. The storm was so fierce that it was not thought safe to wait for their return from an inland journey; and when they reached the coast they must have had to face that appalling certainty of isolation and death which has been the reward of so many pioneers. If endurance be part of the price of empire, then our fathers paid it in full.

As the fleet reached home, Drake sat down to write almost apologetically to Burghley. 'Let me assure your good lordship', he says, 'that I will make it most apparent unto your Honour that it escaped us but twelve hours the whole treasure which the King of Spain had out of the Indies this last year, the cause best known to God; and we had at that instant very foul weather.' Doubtless he had been reckoning up in his own mind the balance sheet of the expedition. He knew that Queen Elizabeth's Government had little patience with financial failure, reaping where they did not sow. And part of the unpalatable purpose of this letter was to ask for money to pay off the soldiers and sailors at once. When this had been done, the balance sheet would show a substantial loss. But Burghley had already had letters from Biscay which put the matter in perspective, and his secretary had made an abstract of them. 'The Bank of Seville is broke', ran these notes; 'the Bank of Valencia also very likely.... Sir Francis hath taken many and rich spoils, 250 brass pieces (i.e. cannon) and burned all the ships and galleys save such as were necessary for the carriage of victuals, and hath left them clean without weapons.... God send him well and a happy success in all his enterprises. It will be such a cooling to King Philip as never happened to him since he was King of Spain.' After all, there were other things than money. And Burghley, as he read through Drake's letter, may have reflected that the four thousand odd pounds which it cost her Majesty had not been too ill spent.

Yet clearly it was only a beginning. The correspondence arriving from Spain was full of the preparations which were being made. Every gentleman about the court, so it was reported, was 'building a ship or two to send after Sir Francis Drake'. It was being said abroad that 'England should smoke ere long'. It is true that the reports were not consistent. Some spoke of large numbers of ships being got ready, others said that there was 'but small preparation' and that it was 'only a Spanish brag' to speak of the great army of eight hundred sail which was to conquer England. But the reports were sufficiently widespread to prove that something on a great scale was afoot, even if as yet it had not advanced very far. What was to be done to prevent it? Was Drake to be given a free hand to attack the King of Spain in the ports of Spain itself, as he wished to do? There was a strong party in the Queen's Council that supported him. Or were the negotiations with Spain, through the Duke of Parma's agent in London, to be continued with the hope of a peaceful settlement? Elizabeth herself was still riding the two horses. She remembered still those Catholic subjects of hers up and down the country; and she may have thought that if she could maintain her position for a few more months, there was yet a chance that the two groups might be joined in harness together. For it was too early yet to say what might be the result of that climax in her cousin's tragedy which had just been reached the day that Drake came home.

The intrigues that had brought the Duke of Norfolk to the scaffold had not been the last episode of Mary's career. As she grew older, though she never ceased to hope for a turn of fortune that would make her Queen of Scotland once again, she knew well enough that she could expect nothing of her 'dearest sister' but close imprisonment and an ever more vigilant watch. That did not daunt her. Rather it made her more reckless, and the assurance of her letters became greater as the prospect of death itself became less unwelcome. After all, that magic season of youth was gone. She had tasted its triumphs, though they had been snatched away from her long before the appetite for them was satisfied. Now those tempestuous passions were abating. Her looks had long ago lost their bloom, wasted on her gaoler, her ladies-in-waiting, and her lap-dogs. She was now 'waxen far grosser', as one of the court secretaries brutally put it. Her retinue, once a Queen's court, had been reduced to a few retainers, and was still being whittled away. What remained was devotion to her faith, faith partly in her Church, partly also perhaps, even yet, in herself. Life itself was now not worth so much that it could not become part of the stakes. She regarded with serenity the prospect of a death which was a martyrdom. And she was not aware that, far away in Scotland, her own son, whom she had never known, was showing himself ready to bargain away his mother's life. She was 'ever a fighter' and, if she had known it, she might have been less prodigal with her life.

The story of the events that led up to her trial and death has often been told, though from the nature of things there can never be complete agreement as to the details. Walsingham had attracted into his service a young man named Gifford, of good family, who came from the neighbourhood of Chartley, where Mary was imprisoned. He was a priest who had apparently originally been sincere in his professions of loyalty to Mary, but for some undiscovered reason had transferred his allegiance. He continued to represent himself to her adherents, however, as a devoted admirer of the Scottish Queen, and he at length won their confidence and that of Mary herself, though she never actually saw him. His proposal to them was that he should organise a secret post, by which letters could be passed to and fro, without the knowledge of the authorities, between Mary and her friends. Once a week there was taken into Chartley a barrel of beer. With the connivance of Sir Amyas Paulet, whose task it was to guard Mary, a box was made to fit snugly into the bottom of this barrel,[6] and when the barrel had been delivered, one of Mary's retainers brought the box to her unopened. In it she found her letters from outside—those from overseas having reached England in the diplomatic correspondence of the French ambassador; and back into it she put the replies, to be taken out when the 'empties' were collected. What Mary did not know was that when the barrel had left the house, the box would be removed and taken up to London, and the letters copied before they were returned to their place and forwarded by Gifford in the 'secret' post to their several destinations. The letters were all in cipher. But Walsingham had in his employ one Thomas Philips, a man of 'singular skill' as Camden calls him, though—if we are to believe the description of him given by Mary, who once saw him by chance, knowing nothing of who he was, near Chartley—of unattractive appearance, with dark yellow hair and a lighter coloured beard, and a face marked with the smallpox. With Philips there worked Arthur Gregory, who could seal letters up with such skill that no one could judge they had been opened. These men had made a fine art of forgery. It is admitted that they added a postscript, pretended to be in Mary's hand, to one of the most important of the letters quoted at her trial. What can never now probably be known is how much else they forged.

The variation of the old plot that was now being concocted had most of the same elements as before. There was to be the support of a foreign army. There was to be a sudden attack on Elizabeth in London which would leave Mary, still heir presumptive to the English throne, in a position to step into that great inheritance. And while the assassins were at their work at court, a group of horsemen was to rescue Mary at Chartley. It might be done, she said, while she was out riding. Her guards, of whom there were usually some twenty, were armed only with pistols, and a determined attack on them by sixty men should be enough. Or if the stables at Chartley were fired, the confusion might give her an opportunity. Or a dray might be driven in at the main entrance and jammed in it, to make ingress possible for her rescuers, without that great gate which shut behind her as she entered irrevocably barring the way. All these suggestions were scanned eagerly by Antony Babington, the young man to whom the new initiative was due. He himself was in a sort of ecstasy of romance. And as he commissioned, for posterity's sake, the portrait of himself and the others who were to achieve this great deed, the man with the face marked by smallpox and the sandy beard deciphered letter after letter, and Walsingham silently waited for the moment to strike. Elizabeth herself was not so silent. She could never resist the temptation to let the cat peep out of the bag for a moment and then thrust it rapidly back into its seclusion. 'Monsieur Ambassador', she said to the French ambassador, Monsieur de Chateauneuf, 'you have much secret communication with the Queen of Scotland, but, believe me, I know all that goes on in my kingdom. I myself was a prisoner in the days of the Queen, my sister, and am aware of the artifices that prisoners use to win over servants and obtain secret intelligence.' No wonder Walsingham despaired of her. But she knew how far she could go. The French ambassador had a momentary qualm, perhaps, about that secret post. But it was unthinkable that those letters should have been read and no action taken. Anyhow, there was no trace, ever, that any hand had tampered with them. Here then was another of those brilliant guesses that caused one such acute momentary discomfort. But it must not be taken too seriously.

Even Walsingham's correspondence cannot tell us all that we should wish to know. It, too, might be read by eyes for which it was not intended; and so Mary was referred to by a cipher in it, and given, very often, the wrong gender. But there were other facts too secret even to be written down in cipher. What part was Gifford really playing on the fringes of this conspiracy? Was he, as Mary afterwards believed, its originator? Was the Government (certainly Elizabeth herself was not implicated) acting through an *agent provocateur* in its determination to secure evidence against Mary which, under the new law, would seal her fate? We do know that some of the means suggested were such that even Sir Amyas Paulet, who winked at the device of the beer barrel, could not bring himself to sanction them, though the character of the proposals which he rejected is no longer discoverable. As the weeks went by the secret post produced interesting material enough. There were all Mary's own plans for the rescue, for example, and all her letters requesting foreign assistance. One thing they did not give, and that was evidence, in her own hand, of knowledge of the plot to murder Elizabeth, and approval of it. Walsingham knew Elizabeth. Unless that was forthcoming, Mary's death would never be authorised. Gifford knew it too, and Ballard, one of the conspirators who was in touch with him believing in his honesty, played into his hands, urging the necessity to obtain Mary's 'hand and seale to allowe of all that should be practised for her behalfe'. But even with this help, the evidence never came. Mary was a shrewd woman, and she knew that to write such a note would be to sign her own death warrant.

Every one of her letters, though she trusted the secret post, shows the care with which she avoided definitely incriminating herself. Something had to be done. At last there came a long letter from Mary to Babington. It was deciphered by Philips, and then he scribbled on the back of his copy, which still survives, a note:

> The postscript of the Scottish Queen's letter to Babington.
> I would be glad to know the names and qualities of the six gentlemen which are to accomplish the designment; for that it may be I shall be able, upon knowledge of the parties, to give you some further advice, necessary to be followed therein; as also from time to time, particularly how you proceed, and as soon as you may, for the same purpose who be already and how far everyone privy thereto.

So far, so good. Philips' decipherment, so it appears, of Mary's postscript. But is it? Why then, after the word 'therein', can we now still read (though it has been scratched through) another sentence 'and even so do I wish to be acquainted with the names of all such principal persons, as also who be already...' etc. Here then is no decipherment of Mary's postscript, but the draft of a postscript to be added to the letter before it reaches Babington's hands. When he replies to it, he will return a true bill against himself and all his associates. It must be carefully worded for otherwise suspicions may be aroused. So Philips takes trouble on the draft, corrects it to make it more plausible, and then doubtless in that inimitable forger's hand to which there is contemporary testimony, adds it to Mary's letter. It was the copies, not the originals, that were produced against her in court. When she saw them, she was baffled to know who could have written those letters, and thought someone had been tampering with her secretaries.

For by now the drama was moving swiftly to its close. Something, the new postscript of this very letter, it may be, showed Babington that he was being watched. In desperation, he tried to change sides, and to give Walsingham the impression that he had stumbled on particulars of a far-reaching conspiracy and ought to be sent abroad to unravel its distant threads. The suggestion evoked no reply. In a panic he slipped away, and after a few anxious days, during which he was harboured in a Catholic household in Essex, he was apprehended. So were his fellow-conspirators, save one who escaped to France. There waited for some of them the torture that was the lot of all from whom the Government wanted to secure information, and after that, the death of traitors. Babington tried to lay all the blame on Ballard's shoulders, and it is Ballard whose superb courage shines most brightly at this time. He had been so severely racked that he could not walk and had to be carried in a chair. Yet to Babington's charge he replied: 'Yea, Mr Babington, lay all the blame on me. But I wish the shedding of my blood might be the saving of your life. Howbeit, say what you will, I will say no more.' He was right. Nothing could save him or Babington now from the frightful cruelties that were decreed to accompany a traitor's end.

Meanwhile, Mary had gone out riding one day with Sir Amyas Paulet, to see a buck hunt. As they rode, a knot of horsemen approached them. They had the Queen's warrant for Mary's arrest, and her papers at Chartley were immediately ransacked. Though there was probably no evidence that would to-day be admitted in a court of law on the specific point of her knowledge and approval of the assassination plot, a point which Mary saw to be crucial, she admitted fully her part in plans to escape, if necessary with foreign aid. And the Government were determined to be rid of her, once for all. A commission was formed to try her. 'So many counsellors,' she said of them, 'and not one for me.' For according to the custom of the time, she had to conduct her own defence. She did so with magnificent dignity. But the result was a foregone conclusion. She was condemned. Parliament met and demanded her death.

But Elizabeth would not consent. Few things are more puzzling than her treatment of Mary. There is none of the jealousy that might perhaps be expected. There may have been a lingering awareness that when Mary had expected help, through force of circumstances she had had to be kept a prisoner. And Mary too was a Queen, and

> Not all the water in the rough, rude sea,
> Can wash the balm from an anointed king.

To strike her down was an act almost of sacrilege that Elizabeth could not bring herself to commit. There was a delay of months. At last, after an agony of indecision, the death warrant was signed, though no authority for its execution was given. So her councillors took the law into their own hands; and Mary met her death with an untroubled resolution which speaks eloquently not only of her courage, but of the death of hope and of ambition in those years of waiting and of growing old. 'Lament not', she said, 'but rather rejoice; thou shalt by and by see Mary Stuart freed from all cares.'

Such were the events which coincided with Drake's return from the West Indies. Like others who shared his puritanical opinions, opinions which, if we can judge by the tone of his letters, grew stronger as time went on, he must have felt a sense of relief that the rallying point for the Roman Catholics of England had been destroyed. There would be less and less need now for Elizabeth to ride her two horses. She had such a chance, as never before, of unifying her kingdom. She took it, and by the time the Armada was fought there was a united England at her back. But she did not do it even now as the Puritans hoped she would, by establishing a Puritan ascendancy. She still kept to a middle course, on which she rightly hoped that many Catholics would be ready to follow her. Some of the Puritans themselves she liked well enough. But one may suspect that when she read a sermon by a Puritan divine preached in 1578—

> Will not a filthy play with the blast of a trumpet sooner call thither a thousand than an hour's tolling of a bell bring to the sermon a hundred—

her sympathies were on the side of the big battalions. At least she refused to let the days of Edward VI return, or to anticipate the Protectorate. Men might have their candles or do without them, as they pleased, in Elizabethan England.

When those who were associated with Drake saw, in Mary's death, the chance of pressing their advantage home, there were other good reasons for doing so. During Mary's lifetime, Philip's support of her cause had been in some ways equivocal. Her death removed doubts from him, for it meant that, after victory, he and not she could determine the future of England. The preparations that had been begun therefore of a great navy, either as was at first supposed to attack England direct, or as the plan in its final form provided, to convoy a Spanish army across the straits, were urged forward. If Elizabeth had wished it, she could already have had the Dutch as her subjects. But she had rejected the offer when it was made, and was on that account suspected by those who might otherwise have co-operated closely in the war against Spain. In the autumn of 1586 she was persuaded by Sir Walter Ralegh, whose star was now in the ascendant and who had lately been enriched by the estates of one of the executed traitors, to allow Drake to go to the Netherlands to negotiate with the Dutch. But the mission was a failure, and if anything was to be done, it must be done by England alone.

During that summer it had been deemed necessary to keep available in English waters such ships as there were, in case Philip should strike. Yet there was another possible plan, and it looks as if Drake had pressed it on the Council from the start, as he certainly did later. It was the plan of defence by attack. He believed that a resolute attack on Spanish harbours with the aid of a land force might do great damage to the King of Spain's preparations, and that if some point of vantage on the Spanish coast could be seized and garrisoned, there was a chance of paralysing the mobilisation of the Spanish Armada. For it was being built or mustered in all the great harbours of the Peninsula, from those on the Basque coast to Carthagena beyond the Straits of Gibraltar. Once united, it was a force to be reckoned with. In detail, it might almost be destroyed piecemeal, and should this not prove possible, if its concentration were prevented, it would be a negligible threat to England. The strategy of defence by attack was to become an integral part of the navy's tradition. Strike at the invasion ports, besides making preparations for the defence of the coasts, and for stopping the enemy while he crosses and for cutting his communications once he has arrived. But it was a revolutionary idea, far more so in an age when the intelligence that a fleet had set out might be received only with its own appearance.

What is remarkable about this campaign, indeed, is the revolutionary conceptions which mark its execution throughout. In his attacks on West Indian ports, Drake had encountered powerful land defences. He had never been faced with a naval force that could do him much damage. In Spanish harbours, and at Cadiz especially, there were powerful units which had in many ways ideal conditions for their work. But they were oared galleys, the old weapons which had been used with such success at Lepanto and before. The seamen brought up in the old tradition, like William Borough (who was attached to his expedition as second-in-command) had a healthy respect for them. Drake had not. He believed that the guns and gunnery of an English sailing ship of war could do so much damage to the galley, whose armament was much lighter, that she could never approach. Her powers of rapid movement would be of little use if this was so, even in the ideal circumstances of a calm. At Cadiz and elsewhere the galleys had such an opportunity, but the punishment inflicted on them as they moved up to the attack was so severe that it was never forced home.

Whether the campaign was planned as a whole before the start, or whether Drake only proved himself once again a great opportunist, it is hard to say. But in the event it was a faultless piece of work. There was, once again, that brilliant co-operation between the sea and land forces, and the same appreciation, in the assault on the forts at Cape St Vincent, of the details wherein the enemy's weakness lay. And above all there was the mastery shown in the general disposition of Drake's forces; the following up of that bold success in Cadiz harbour by the occupation of a semi-permanent base on land which prevented the concentration of the Spanish fleets and directly threatened the routes from the West and from the East Indies. If reinforcements had been available to make this occupation permanent, the Spanish position would have been perilous. Air attack has made nowadays the holding of such a base virtually impossible in a strong hostile country, but it could then have been held, and in Drake's occupation Cape St Vincent might have done incalculable harm.

If what he had in mind was to be carried out successfully, he must have permission to operate not only on the high seas, but also in Spanish harbours and on Spanish territory. The trouble was, however, that some of the Council considered the death of Mary to have removed the obstacles in the negotiations with Spain, and believed that war was by no means inevitable. Elizabeth disliked war, and she also sometimes veered, partly perhaps against her own better judgment, to the view that it could still be avoided. Changing reports from Spain account for her changes of mind, and when she heard rumours that preparations were slackening, she was liable to modify her own attitude at once in sympathy. What were the precise terms of the commission for Drake to which she at last agreed, we do not know. Two things, however, are clear. One is that Drake was fully satisfied with them, and that as the expedition included a powerful land force they must have envisaged operations on land. Walsingham, in a despatch written to Elizabeth's ambassador in Paris, mentions that in this commission he was 'directed to distress the ships within the havens themselves', to take, that is, such action as he took later at Cadiz; and that the general plan was to 'impeach' (i.e. to prevent) 'the joining together of the King of Spain's fleet out of their several ports, to keep victuals from them, and to follow them in case they should be come forward towards England or Ireland'. What Drake was sent to do in 1587, and succeeded in doing, was not merely to disorganise Philip's preparations, but actually to check them when put into effect, as it was expected they would be that summer. Drake himself wrote from aboard ship, after the attack on Cadiz, in a way which shows that he believed Philip's blow at England was imminent. 'I dare not a'most write unto your honour of the great forces we hear the King of Spain hath out in the Straits. Prepare in England strongly, and most by sea. Stop him now and stop him ever. Look well to the coast of Sussex....' It is clear then that, in the belief that the Spanish Armada was almost ready to set sail, Elizabeth had agreed to give Drake virtually a free hand in dealing with it. But it is clear also that he mistrusted her consistency. At any moment she might change her mind, and he hurried down to Plymouth determined to get away before such a disaster should occur.

As the last preparations were made, Drake was in high fettle. He found the ships that had joined him from London greatly to his liking. The captains who were to work with him he praises enthusiastically, including Borough, with whom there was to be friction before long. There was only one discordant note in his enthusiasm. His nature had been especially prone to suspicion since the treachery he believed himself to have experienced on the voyage of circumnavigation, and he now began to imagine that some of the men were having disaffection spread among them, presumably by that party in the Queen's Council whom he knew to be opposed to war. In place of the men who had deserted he enlisted soldiers and had letters sent to the country justices urging severe punishment for the delinquents. At a time when the biggest attack ever planned so far against England was imminent, it would be dangerous indeed to allow such conduct to escape unpunished. It is uncertain whether there were any real grounds for Drake's suspicions of secret opposition at this time. If it was there, it did not prevent him clearing Plymouth rapidly with a splendid naval and military force, very nearly but not quite ready. There were four of her Majesty's ships, two pinnaces and some thirty armed merchantmen. The fleet included five ships of 400 tons or over, among them his flagship, the 'Elizabeth Bonaventure' (a Queen's ship) and the 'Golden Lion', Borough's flagship. Half a dozen or more of the London-owned ships were the property of the Levant company.

Drake was not a moment too soon. Fresh news had recently reached London which suggested that Philip's preparations had slackened. The Queen's mind changed and revised instructions were sent down to Plymouth. He was to forbear to enter forcibly any of the King of Spain's ports, or 'to offer violence to any of his towns or shipping within harbouring'. His attack was thus to be confined to war on Spanish shipping on the high seas, and all the elaborate preparations of a land force to act with the ships were nullified at a stroke. Or rather they would have been if Drake had delayed many hours longer. As it was, he escaped the countermanding of his original commission. The new orders were sent after him in a pinnace. But she was commanded by a 'base son' of Hawkins, who evidently had orders to take his time and to encounter any storms or contrary winds that there might be. There proved to be enough to prevent his making contact with Drake and he returned with the letter undelivered. There was bad weather, it is true, which scattered the fleet for a time, though they reassembled unharmed off Lisbon. But he had managed to take a handsome prize on his way, and the circumstances do not suggest that the pinnace regarded the delivery as urgent.

Meanwhile Philip's preparations for the great campaign were becoming ever more complete. The Spanish King, an indefatigable administrator, was doing two things, both planning the fleet's equipment and also himself laying down the lines on which it must be used. Drake was lucky in having had his old captain, Hawkins, to do in England that job of organisation at which he himself did not shine. Philip, with a much more unmanageable problem, was trying to manage it all himself, and in some degree succeeding, thanks mainly to the affection which he won from those who worked with him. But the red tape was lengthening. Philip's endless minutes were becoming ever more complicated, and he was discovering, as do the military and naval commanders of to-day, who with their vastly more elaborate means of communication have vastly more elaborate tasks to do, that the successful organisation of such details is three-quarters of the battle. The commander-in-chief of the Armada, Santa Cruz, was at Lisbon, where the fleet as a whole was to muster. There were ships at Passages in the north. There were important units, including galleys and many supply ships, at Cadiz. At sea was a fleet under Recalde, cruising somewhere off Cape St Vincent; and in a Mediterranean port, Carthagena, there were not only ships and galleys, but also land forces assembling. On all these King Philip had to keep his hand, and his twofold problem was to equip them and to concentrate them in one harbour.

Drake had left Plymouth on 2 April. On the 19th he was off Cadiz. The port consists of two harbours, the approach to which was heavily defended by the batteries of Cadiz forts and by a flotilla of ten or eleven galleys under their shelter. There are shoals off the approach to the outer harbour, which faces north, and the passage through them takes a ship within about half a mile of the shore batteries and of the galleys moored there. Like a great breakwater guarding this harbour stretches out the rock on which the town of Cadiz itself was built, on a promontory (or rather an island connected with the mainland by a single bridge) which stretches northward some three miles. At a later date, at the time when the plan here reproduced was made, the narrow entrance into the inner harbour between the mainland and the neck of the Cadiz promontory, an entrance some half a mile broad, was defended by three powerful forts. In 1587 this entrance had no permanent defences, though a piece of ordnance was placed in position on the promontory and opened fire, at a critical moment, on Borough's ship, the 'Lion'. From this narrow entrance, the inner harbour broadens out into a fine haven with Puerto Real on its north-east shore, some five miles or thereabouts by water from Cadiz. In the outer harbour there were perhaps some sixty ships, large and small, and more in the inner harbour, including one great ship that belonged to Santa Cruz. Some of these ships were already laden with supplies for the Armada. Some were half laden, and others empty, waiting for their cargoes. Some were victuallers, laden with biscuit, wine, raisins, figs, oil and wheat. There was one large ship bound for the Indies, with ironwork of many kinds, but the great majority played some part in Philip's preparations for the English expedition.

Drake was off Cadiz in the afternoon, ahead of some of his ships. He summoned a meeting of his captains and told them what he proposed to do. He intended to attack immediately without waiting for the stragglers. Borough apparently demurred. The situation was ideal for the work of the galleys, and now, as certainly later, he was no doubt desperately afraid of them. But Drake had made up his mind and about five o'clock they moved in to carry out his plan. They were met by two galleys out from St Mary Port, the haven opposite Cadiz on the mainland. The fire from the English ships was

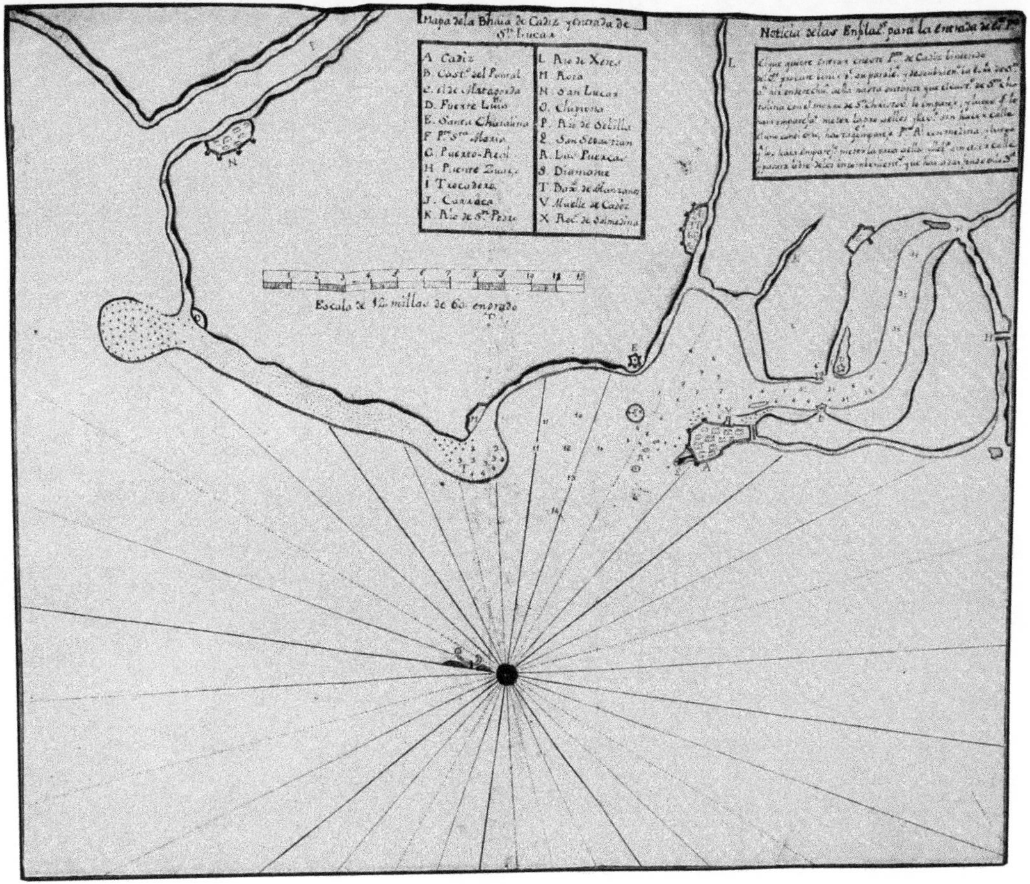

IX. THE HARBOUR OF CADIZ

(From a manuscript chart of about 1780)

enough to force them back without having inflicted any damage. As he entered the outer harbour, with the shoal known as the Puercas on his starboard bow, Drake could see galleys, eight or ten of them, near the first of the Cadiz forts. A few hundred yards beyond it was the second fort, and riding under its guns was a crowd of small ships, caravels and barks. A little further out in the channel lay the larger ships, and within the narrow opening to the inner harbour might be descried more shipping, and moored apart from the rest, the great ship of some 1200 tons owned by the Marquis of Santa Cruz. Many of the ships in the harbour were without sails and could not move. But some, when they saw what was happening, managed to slip away and through into the inner harbour, where they were comparatively safe among the shallows which defended Puerto Real. A few escaped into St Mary Port.

Borough afterwards complained that Drake issued no detailed orders for the attack. What in fact happened, however, was no doubt carried out according to his plan. The less well-armed ships in his own force attacked the hulks, Biscayans and merchantmen that still lay off the shore, while Drake and the other Queen's ships masked their attack from the galleys, raking these as they moved out with broadside fire. Drake says that two were sunk in this encounter, but it is possible that only one was actually sunk. The remainder withdrew under shelter of the shoal that lay eight or nine hundred yards due north from the promontory. It was getting dark. But fires were already blazing on the water which lit up the work. One big Spanish ship had been sunk by gunfire before her cargo could be got out of her. Before they were burned out the cargoes of most of them had been removed to the English ships. The work went on under the fire of the shore batteries, for by reason of the shoals it was not possible to get out of range. But the fire was comparatively ineffective. Late that night another council was held. Most of the fleet was moored further in towards the inner harbour to be out of the range of the town batteries, and Drake still screened them from a possible renewal of the galleys' attack.

Next morning he himself moved in towards the inner harbour. His eye was on the great ship belonging to the Marquis of Santa Cruz. He took in with him a flotilla of the smaller craft. It was dangerous work, for there were galleys in the inner harbour too, at Puerto Real. But this ship, like her consorts, was plundered and set on fire. Meanwhile Borough had been looking for Drake, as he said afterwards, to discuss with him the reprovisioning of the ships from the Spanish prizes, or, as Drake said, to urge him in panic not to proceed with his plan. There was probably something of both in their conversation. However that may be, as Drake went in, Borough's flagship, the 'Lion', anchored some distance outside the entrance to the inner harbour, and there she was fired on by a gun which the Spaniards had placed on the shore opposite. A lucky shot holed her above the water line, and broke the leg of the master gunner, who gave orders for her to be warped out. She was moving as Borough got back to her. He approved the order, and she continued out, till she was well outside the range of the Cadiz guns. Galleys from St Mary Port came to attack her, but Drake sent help and she beat them off. Borough indeed claimed that the purpose of his manœuvre was to cover the retreat of the rest of the forces. But a comparison of his own plan of the operations[7] with later plans suggests that he was actually further out to sea, by perhaps a mile, than he there indicates. For it is probable that the shoal on which the 'Edward Bonaventure', which was sent to his help, went aground, was the Diamante,[8] shown on the later plan, and that the 'Lion' was still further out to sea. When the charge of cowardice began to be made against him, Borough (as it appears) not unnaturally did not exaggerate the distance he had stood out to sea when the movement was made. The reasons for moving out, however, may have been sound. Drake does not seem to have blamed him at the time, and it was later that the controversy between them arose on the point.

The attack was a magnificent success in spite of Borough's fears. Though many of the Spanish ships were still intact and in safe shelter, an enormous amount of damage had been done, and the English ships had been revictualled at the Spaniards' expense. It was time now to leave, for this was only a beginning of what had to be done in Spanish harbours. Then the wind dropped; the English ships were becalmed, and the situation was ideal for the galleys to attack again. They moved forward gallantly to do so. But they were met once again by a broadside, which, in the completely calm weather, was more accurate than before. It was impossible for them to stand up to such a weight of metal, and they withdrew. Fire-ships were tried but they were equally unsuccessful. Then, at two o'clock in the morning, a land breeze sprang up, and Drake sailed out before it, round the headland and the shoals, to anchor eastwards of the city, in full sight of it but out of range 'upon a bravado'. There followed those demonstrations of mutual regard between one professional and another which always delighted him so much. He suggested an exchange of prisoners, which was refused. But he was sent presents of sweetmeats and paid other compliments, receiving a courteous letter from the Governor.

His plan on leaving Cadiz was unknown to the Spanish authorities, who suspected him of designs on the treasure fleet, and tried unsuccessfully to muster at Lisbon the military force that would be necessary to embark for the Azores to frustrate such a plan. But he was, in fact, after an even more important quarry. The attack on Cadiz had done serious damage to mobilisation plans, but it had not appreciably affected the Spanish fighting force. If Drake had been able to catch Recalde, who was at sea with a detachment of the Armada, and had been able to destroy it, that would have been a much more effective blow. But the weather which had kept him becalmed at Cadiz prevented him, and Recalde slipped away to Lisbon to join Santa Cruz there. Philip's urgent efforts to concentrate a military force there had left some of the Mediterranean galleys insufficiently protected. He wrote instantly to them, on hearing of Drake's whereabouts, to stop them from making northwards into the trap, and they were delayed therefore on the round voyage to Cadiz.

Realising that this plan had failed, Drake was faced with the problem which was the most serious difficulty for all those in charge of large maritime forces at this time. He had plenty of provisions. But disease was already beginning to show itself. By 26 May he had to send home two flagboats with the sick men, and there was a real danger that the success of the expedition would be prejudiced by sickness, as it had affected the venture in the West Indies. On 30 April Borough was summoned to the flagship. As he came aboard he overheard discussion among the men who were standing in groups on the deck, and the news which he heard from them struck him with alarm. He went in to see Drake himself, who confirmed his apprehensions. He intended to seize Cape St Vincent and occupy the anchorage below it. The pessimists said that water supplies there were inadequate. Borough saw every sort of objection to it. The Lord Admiral, so he alleged, had explicitly declared against any landing, though if this was so, it is difficult to know why Drake should have taken troops with him at all. Borough thought that it was all a piece of bravado, which would expose the fleet to the danger of the dreaded galley attacks. Some of his men had been seeing the ghosts of galleys in the storm that night. And he foresaw too the frightful difficulties of a force that had been landed, should the wind change and a storm blow up. It is possible that he had not listened to Drake's reasons for his proposal. It is equally possible that the admiral, seeing disapproval written all over Borough's face, and hearing his suggestion greeted with expostulation, never gave him any reasons. He was a man who kept his own counsels. If he trusted anyone with them it was as likely to be his master carpenter as his vice-admiral. But the reasons which had led him to the plan were unanswerable. A base on land would enable him to take in clean water, the only remedy against the spread of disease. And secondly, Cape St Vincent was magnificently situated to command the Spanish coasts and prevent the planned concentration at Lisbon. As Fenner wrote a few days later to Walsingham: 'We hold this cape so greatly to our benefit and so much to their disadvantage as a great blessing is the attaining thereof. For the rendezvous is at Lisbon, where we understand of some 25 ships and 7 galleys. The rest, we lie between home and them....'

There was only one objection to the plan. It was hopelessly impracticable. Cape St Vincent was heavily fortified with the castle at Sagres and other powerful defences which commanded the anchorage. The land approach to the promontory was from one side only, where a neck of land two hundred yards long was guarded by a battlemented wall with four towers commanding the gate. On the other sides, precipitous cliffs overhang the sea. Borough must have spent an anxious night. For next morning, Sunday, 30 April, he sat down and wrote his famous protest to Drake, criticising his conduct towards him from the start, and in particular urging him to reconsider this plan. He received back a reply which was evidently strong. For on the Tuesday he wrote again, offering to withdraw all he had said. But from that moment Drake was his implacable enemy, and Borough went in fear, as he said, of suffering the same fate as Doughty.

Whether it was as a result of Borough's protest[9] or of the weather or some other cause, the attack was not immediately made. Instead the fleet moved down to Lagos, a port which lies to the east of Cape St Vincent, after it has been rounded on the voyage towards the Mediterranean. A strong force was landed to attempt an attack, but it became apparent that heavy new fortifications would be encountered and so the troops that had been set ashore were immediately withdrawn, without loss. Then they sailed back to the Cape, and landed near one of the castles, while some of the ships attacked a village to the east, where houses and boats were fired. The first of the forts offered little resistance, though it had six cannon which might have done some damage. Its garrison withdrew to the main defences about a mile away. The position has already been described. Fenner says that the land wall was forty feet high. But Drake himself had landed with the attackers, and the Governor was summoned to surrender. He answered that he was in honour bound to defend it.

There was no siege weapon of any kind with the fleet. But by this time the attackers were thoroughly convinced of the necessity of securing possession of the castle, and any doubts among them had been resolved. There was only one possible means of entry, to burn down the gate. Bundles of faggots were collected for the purpose. About one o'clock they moved up towards it, subjecting the loopholes in the wall and towers to intense musket fire in order to make counter fire as difficult as possible. At last, in spite of casualties, the faggots were kindled and blazed up, and the fire was continually fed with fresh fuel for two hours. A lucky shot had wounded the Spanish commander, and suddenly it was decided to surrender, on condition that lives and equipment were spared. The place was naturally so strong that it seemed a miracle it had been taken. Other fortifications in the neighbourhood surrendered without fighting. Sagres castle was dismantled, the guns were tumbled down the cliffs and dragged aboard the English ships.

This sudden attack was to be followed by another, on Lisbon, and when the fleet had watered they sailed northwards. But Lisbon was too heavily defended for a direct assault to be possible, and it is a sure indication of Drake's judgment that he did not carry through the attempt, which he had certainly planned to do. Hoping that Santa Cruz might be enticed out, he worked all the havoc he could with coastal shipping under his very eyes. But his galleys did not stir. The Spanish watched the enemy depredations helpless to stop them unless they opened themselves to further attack, and the English fleet moved back, foiled in this last attempt, to Cape St Vincent.

On 17 May Drake wrote to Walsingham urgently for reinforcements. Like Fenner he believed that for the position to be held permanently would be a paralysing blow to the Armada's concentration. Then something made him change his mind. It may be that he realised already that the destruction he had effected in the Armada's supplies (for he had been capturing ship after ship since the attack on Cadiz, and burning their cargoes) made any attempt that year impossible. On the evening of the 21st, or early the following day, intelligence arrived through his spies which made him immediately change his plans again, and he made off south-westwards towards the Azores. Philip, hearing that Drake had left the coast, sent word to the Cadiz galleys to make their way round to Lisbon to reinforce the fleet there. But his plan was not to attack England, but if possible to defend the treasure ships which might arrive at any moment. And his heart was heavy, for he suspected why Drake had gone.

Those in the English fleet, however, did not know his objective, and with disease breaking out again, there was apparently discontent. Then a storm arose, the ships parted company, and opportunity offered to desert. Borough had been placed under arrest. But he succeeded, as it would appear, in persuading a ship's company to desert with him, save for the captain who was put off in a pinnace to make his way to Drake's ship. The admiral's worst suspicions of Borough seemed to be confirmed. In absence he was court-martialled and sentenced to death. But that was after all only an interlude. Some fortnight after they had left Cape St Vincent, Drake sighted what he was after, and at daybreak next day they made towards a great carrack which came to meet them dipping her flag. When they were within range they showed their own colours and instantly opened fire. The English pinnaces came right up under her, so close that the Spanish guns high above them could do them no harm. Her position was hopeless, and after a brief fight she surrendered. She was the 'San Felipe', a merchantman said to be the richest in all the East India trade, with rich oriental spices, silks, porcelain and jewels, King Philip's own ship, an incomparable prize. The voyage was made. Drake returned home, leaving Philip still wondering where he was about to strike next, and Santa Cruz setting out at last from Lisbon to convoy home the treasure fleet.

Drake's reception, when he returned, was comparatively cool. His actions had far exceeded the final instructions sent him, which he had expected indeed, but never actually received. Borough had friends on the Council, and Drake's condemnation of him was not upheld. We get at this time rather the impression of a popular hero, whom his equal associates find anything but easy; a man of quick temper, impatient of advice or criticism, infuriated with any sign that his authority is being questioned. But that lightning judgment is unimpaired, that immense energy unquenched. He is still the idol of those who follow him. 'We all remain in great love with our general and in unity throughout the whole fleet', writes Fenner, after Cadiz. After Sagres the ring of his despatches is one of still greater admiration. And indeed he had been privileged to view, at close quarters, the execution of one of the masterpieces of naval strategy.

Chapter VII

VIRGINIA: THE PLANNERS AND PIONEERS

The climax towards which King Philip's preparations, so disastrously disorganised by the Cadiz raid, slowly moved, was to involve the fate of Queen Elizabeth's far flung dependency, the second of the English colonies in Virginia. Late in August 1587, John White, Governor of the planters in Virginia, reluctantly left the eighty or so men, seventeen women, two children and two savages, who formed the colony, and returned to England to seek for supplies for them. His own writings show that he was loth to undertake this commission. He was leading an enterprise which had an uncertain future before it. The one thing which was clear was that new plans would have to be made within the next few months which needed his presence to make them. He had brought out with him all his most treasured possessions, including his books and maps. Even during a previous absence of a day or two from the colony these possessions had been disturbed by other settlers, and he anticipated that if he left them now to go back to England there would be little remaining when he returned. Years later he was to find them, the books tattered and out of their covers, the maps spoiled, the pictures—he was himself an artist—ruined, among the few relics of the vanished colony. But the settlers' request to him was urgent. They believed that he alone could secure a proper hearing at home. Because he felt that to leave them might savour of the desertion of his post, he asked them to set it down in writing.

May it please you [they said], her Majesty's subjects of England, we your friends and countrey-men, the planters in Virginia, doe by these presents let you and every of you to understand that for the present and speedy supply of certaine our knowen and apparant lackes and needes, most requisite and necessary for the good and happy planting of us, or any other in this land of Virginia, wee all of one mind and consent have most earnestly entreated and most incessantly requested John White, Governour of the planters in Virginia, to passe into England, for the better and more assured help and setting forward of the foresayd supplies: and knowing assuredly that he both can best and wil labour and take paines on that behalfe for us all, and he not once, but often refusing it, for our sakes and for the honour and maintenance of the action, hath at last, though much against his will through our importunacie yeelded to leave his governement, and all his goods among us, and himself in all our behalfes to passe into England, of whose knowledge and fidelitie handling this matter, as all others, we do assure our selves by these presents, and will you, to give all credite thereunto, the 25th of August, 1587.

So John White returned, and there is no doubt that he did his best to fulfil the trust imposed on him. But circumstances were overwhelmingly against him. English maritime enterprise was preoccupied by other tasks, and no one had leisure to spare for a few English settlers who might already have met death on an almost unknown coast of America. It was not till 1590 that he succeeded in making his way back to Virginia. There was that year a general stay of shipping that might have delayed him still more, but Ralegh himself intervened to obtain a licence from the Queen for the voyage. There were three ships, the 'Hopewell', the 'John Evangelist' and the 'Little John'. White was prevented by the owners and captains from taking with him any of the people or supplies that he thought necessary. It was regarded by the owners as a trading and privateering voyage. They captured a few ships and sacked a few villages in the West Indies. When they reached Virginia at last, the season was late and the weather foul. They landed near the site of the old settlement. When White left in 1587, he had arranged that if the settlers had to move elsewhere, a notice should be left giving the name of the place where they had gone, and if it was by reason of distress, a cross should be carved over the name. The place had, since his departure, been heavily fortified with a palisade of trees, and on one of the gate-posts the name CROATAN was carved, with no cross above it. But it seemed nevertheless that the site had been plundered by savages. It was agreed to follow the settlers to Croatan, the whereabouts of which was known to White. But before they could do this, the weather worsened, and what with the failure of supplies and loss of water casks in a storm, the seamen, who had never had much heart for the real objects of the endeavour, determined to return home to England. Beyond that carved name, no certain intelligence was ever heard again of the settlement. 'Wanting my wishes,' wrote White in 1593, 'I leave off from prosecuting that whereunto I would to God my wealth were answerable to my will.' Not till 1602 was the deserted village visited again by Englishmen, once again under Ralegh's auspices, and then every trace of this second settlement was gone.

Thus, in the year of Cadiz, Ralegh's second Virginian settlement met disaster. But it is time for us to examine the antecedents of these events, the voyages of the first pioneers, and the history of the first settlement which they made possible. Ralegh, whose name is rightly connected by tradition with the founding of Virginia, though he himself never visited the colony and though the attempts sponsored by him ended in failure, was half-brother to Sir Humphrey Gilbert who had been concerned, long before the planting of the first colony in Virginia, with American exploration. Gilbert's immediate interest was in the discovery of a north-west passage to China and he wrote a famous memorandum or 'discourse to prove a passage to Cathaia and the East Indies'. He used the familiar arguments: of the three brothers who had passed through it and had given the name Fretum Trium Fratrum—the Strait of the Three Brothers—to it; of the Indians mentioned by Latin writers as having been stranded on the German coast in 57 B.C., who must have come by it; and the like. But he had some not unimportant things to say about the advantages which the discovery of a passage would bring. Not only would it provide direct access to the supplies of gold, precious stuffs and spices in the Far East, but also employment in England; for the children of the poor could be set to make the 'trifles' which savages valued highly, and settlements could be made of needy people 'which now trouble the common wealth, and through want here at home are enforced to commit outragious offences, whereby they are dayly consumed with the gallowes'—a shrewd observation of the cause of social unrest, at a time when most people ascribed it, more simply, to original sin.

Gilbert did more than write a memorandum on the matter. He set himself to discover the north-west passage, and to found some settlement which should guard the way to it. In its final form, as reached in the summer of 1582, the plan was for a group of Catholics to explore the coast of what was later to be New England and settle there, while Gilbert was to follow with another colony, modelled on the lines of English society, with parishes three miles square, churches, gentry and yeomanry. Ralegh's contribution to this expedition was the bark 'Ralegh', on which he spent £2000—for the great estates which the Queen had granted him and even more the privateering ventures which he promoted, were already making him rich. The Queen, who was beginning to maintain that constraint over her favourites' movements which Philip Sidney and Ralegh and Essex all found so galling, forbade Ralegh to sail, and just before Gilbert left, he received a letter from his half-brother:

Richmond, 17th March 1583.

Brother,

I have sent you a token from her Majesty, an anchor guided by a Lady, as you see; and further; her Highness willed me to send you word that she wished you a great goodhap, and safety to your ship, as if herself were there in person: desiring you to have care of yourself, as of that which she tendereth; and therefore for her sake you must provide for it accordingly.

Further she commandeth that you leave your picture with me. For the rest, I leave till our meeting, or to the report of this bearer, who will needs be messenger for this good news. So I commit you to the will and protection of God, Who send us such life or death as He shall please or hath appointed.

Your true brother,

W. RALEGH.

At the instance of Hakluyt the Hungarian scholar Parmenius sailed with the expedition as its chronicler. When it was about to set out, he addressed to his captain in Latin hexameters what he called a song for embarkation. In all his travels, so he says in the preface to it, no place has pleased him so much as England, which has almost banished from his mind the desire for home. 'For these reasons it has been my intention, time and time again, to give some proof of these my opinions and feelings.' He is not the only stranger from abroad who has paid for his devotion to this country with his life.

Gilbert was later than he should have been in starting, and it was mid-June before his ships were at sea, five of them, the largest the bark 'Ralegh', mentioned above, and the smallest the 'Squirrel' of only 10 tons. It appears that in spite of delays provisions were still regarded as inadequate, and instead of taking a southerly route, therefore, their course was northerly. They would thus fall in with the fishing fleets and hoped that when the season was over and the fishing fleets turned for home, they would be able to spare supplies for revictualling Gilbert's ships. The figures given of ships found in the harbour of St John's by Gilbert when he arrived are impressive, and a clear witness of the results of the earliest voyages made by Bristol seamen to America. There were between thirty and forty sail, English, Spanish, Portuguese and others, and in the presence of their captains and masters Gilbert read his commission from Queen

Elizabeth giving him licence to found and govern a colony on the North American coast. Henceforward those who visited St John's regularly were to hold their drying grounds on lease from Gilbert and his heirs and assignees for ever; and a tax in kind was levied on both foreign and English ships, the proceeds of which furnished full provisions for Gilbert's crews, so that they had excellent entertainment there. Parties were sent along the coast and inland, to obtain information of the lie of the land and of its economic possibilities. In the account issued after the return to England the wealth of the fisheries was rightly emphasised, but the view was also maintained that many things such as pitch, timber, hides, and flax for linen, might be obtained there, while as usual the soil was described as metalliferous. The furs which were afterwards to play a large part in the commercial development of the northern regions of America are also mentioned, and it was observed that the climate was colder than might have been expected in that latitude.

Towards the end of August, the fleet, which was now weakened by desertions, put to sea and made south-westwards from Cape Race, towards Cape Breton and Sable Island. The weather was for some days fair, though there was uneasiness among the crews, who imagined that during the night they heard 'strange sounds i' the air', as Shakespeare called them; they thought they heard the noise of trumpets and fifes, and the roll of drums, and took these as ominous. Then the wind rose and a sea mist descended, so that visibility was barely a cable's length. Sounding, they found that they were in shoal water, and people thought they saw white cliffs ahead, though it was probably only the whiteness of the wave crests. As they turned out seaward, one of the ships struck a shoal, and broke up almost at once. Not a man was found from her, though all that day and the next her consorts beat up and down searching for survivors. Aboard her had been Parmenius, and she was the supply vessel for the fleet, so that her loss was a disaster that could not easily be repaired. Another who was on board was an assayer, a German. It is interesting to notice a German technician, as early as this, sailing with an English expedition. Her captain up to the last moment was cheering on the crew, urging them on to fresh efforts, exhorting them not to despair. He was last seen 'on the highest decke, where hee attended imminent death and unavoidable'. 'How long', says the narrator, 'I leave it to God, who withdraweth not his comfort from his servants at such times.' Although they were not then found, fourteen men had escaped in a tiny pinnace. They were adrift six days and nights without food or water; and the boat was so heavily overloaded that a suggestion was made (but rejected) to cast lots for some to be thrown overboard. Two died, but the rest reached the shore, and were taken home by Frenchmen who at that time were fishing off the coast.

Those who remained in the other ships grew daily more depressed, with the thought of approaching winter and supplies running very short. A conference was held at which Gilbert agreed to return to England, saying that he was satisfied with the results of the voyage, even if they could not do all that had been hoped. One thing, however, that had been lost besides all his notes he particularly regretted, and it was believed afterwards that this must have been proofs obtained by the assayer of gold deposits. At any rate, it is clear that whereas Gilbert had had little use for a northern settlement originally, except as a station on the way to Asia, he now regarded it as having possibilities. But he was never to see them realised. He was himself sailing in the tiny frigate, the 'Squirrel', which had been overloaded with cannon from the other ships, when they first set out from St John's. On 9 September, the weather being very stormy, the frigate was almost overwhelmed by the heavy seas. As she approached the larger ship, they could see Gilbert sitting in her stern with a book in his hand, reading; and being within earshot he cried out to them through the storm: 'We are as neere to heaven by sea as by land.' That night, about midnight, the watch saw the lights of the 'Squirrel' disappear, and she was never seen again.

Thus one ship only returned. She had on board a brief description of the country, in a letter written in Latin to Hakluyt addressed from St John's in August by Parmenius, and more detailed information was set out in a report made by Edward Hayes, the only one to return of the 'gentlemen' who had sailed with the expedition.

This information was soon set out in a pamphlet written by a distinguished Catholic, Sir George Peckham, who had been largely responsible for the financing of Gilbert's expedition. His purpose was to show the possibilities which 'planting' offered in North America, prove Queen Elizabeth's title to any lands that should be discovered, and to enumerate the advantages that would accrue to England. Dr John Dee had been elaborating the arguments for the Queen's title for some time, and contended that America had been visited by a Welsh chieftain Madoc, who was said to have sailed thither about A.D. 1170. These arguments Peckham used also. Some of Madoc's followers were said to have stayed in America, and it was pointed out that Montezuma, Emperor of Mexico, claimed to be descended from a foreign stock. Two and two were put together, and the English claim was manifest. Peckham emphasised that the conversion of native populations justified their conquest, quoting Saint Paul: 'If we have sowen unto you heavenly things, do you think it much that we should reap your carnal things?' This same argument was put forward by many of those who favoured colonial expansion in Tudor and Stuart times, and though it often has, as in Sir George Peckham's pamphlet, a too specious look about it, it was often set out in sincerity and earnestness and was undoubtedly an important motive in these enterprises. Besides mentioning the possible mineral resources of the country, the writer follows a line of argument that had been developed by the elder Hakluyt, who had done more thinking and had learnt more about the economic possibilities of planting than any other man in the country. The area in which colonisation was proposed lay in the same latitude as Portugal, Spain and North Africa. Therefore it might be supposed that the climate and products would be the same, and that by exploiting its resources England might obtain within the limits of her own possessions many things for which she now depended on foreign trade. It was assumed that climate was governed almost entirely by latitude, and one of the interesting features of Edward Hayes' report on Newfoundland is his information about the coldness of the winters, so difficult to understand, on a comparison of latitudes, in contrast to those of Western Europe. For St John's is in the latitude of Cornwall.

Gilbert's death, followed by the Queen's transfer of his rights to Ralegh, meant that the movement passed more definitely under the influence of that group of theorists which was led by the two Hakluyts and Dr Dee. Their contribution is characteristic of that of theorists to such a movement: a mixture of good sense and of nonsense. In the planning of details of expeditions they often gave sound advice, and their collection of data, economic, geographical and linguistic, was of real value. But their cosmography was still worked up from phrases picked out of the Bible, the Latin classics, and to some extent the early fathers. The practical seamen who had none of it were in some respects lucky. Dr Dee, with his brilliant maps and his conviction that the philosopher's stone would be found in China, was in some ways the most typical of the group. By his immediate acquaintances, and by himself, he was regarded as a second Aristotle, and his work had a deep influence on the mathematicians of his day. By many of his fellow-countrymen he was thought to be in league with the devil. His house was once fired by an angry mob. Ralegh, who was his friend and was evidently interested in his theories—for Ralegh loved a scholar, and endangered his own skin more than once by pleading for tolerance for persecuted scholars—introduced him to the Queen, and she treated him graciously. That unattractive monarch who succeeded her, who, as is well known, was an expert on witchcraft, refused when Dee appealed to him to clear him of the suspicion of magic practice, and the philosopher, who had undoubtedly made a contribution to his age, died in poverty.

The original plans for Gilbert's expedition had been drawn up before Drake's voyage of circumnavigation was over. When Wynter returned from the Straits of Magellan, the younger Hakluyt interviewed at least one of his crew, and wrote a pamphlet advocating the seizure of the straits by an English force which might be based on some settlement on the Atlantic coast of South America. It was believed that one settlement, St Vincent, in Spanish hands, was already sufficiently disaffected to be won over, and someone was actually sent to look into this possibility. But the Spaniards, warned by Drake's success, took the initiative in sending an expedition to guard the straits, and Hakluyt's plan, therefore, came to nothing. At the time, his first great book on American exploration, *Divers Voyages to America*, was in preparation, and was published in 1582. This book, and the scores of works that followed it, such as a translation of de la Laudonnière's *History of Florida* published in 1587, did more than anything else to keep the possibility of American settlement before the public mind. More confidential plans were drawn up for the eyes of authority, for we have already had occasion to notice that in published work suppressions were sometimes thought desirable. In 1584 the younger Hakluyt drew up, for the Queen, Walsingham, and a few others, the tract generally known as the *Discourse of Western Planting*, not actually printed until a generation ago, but an influential document among the group for whom it was prepared; and the following year the elder Hakluyt drew up his *Inducements to the liking of the voyage intended towards Virginia.* His views of the economic possibilities of that region may have determined Ralegh more than any other single influence.

During the next twenty years Ralegh spent a fortune on this great enterprise, and though he did not succeed, yet he lived to see Virginia an English nation as he had believed he would. He is one of those men whose money may have been, at least by later standards, ill-gotten, but who spent it on ends that were almost wholly good. Both as a seaman and as a coloniser, his best work was rather as a promoter and planner than in action. He sailed to Guiana, but never actually touched Virginia himself, though he hoped to do so. Yet his instructions to those who took part in the first two settlements prove not only his interest, but his shrewdness; and it was certainly not his fault, for instance, if, in the clumsy but vigorous hands of Sir Richard Grenville, the plans he had made for a careful treatment of natives and the avoidance of any action designed to terrorise them were frustrated. In this particular he was on his own expeditions to Guiana signally successful. He may have learnt from Drake's experience.

The report made to Ralegh on the first voyage to Virginia under his authority might well give him hope for the future. He had taken great care about the drafting of instructions. The two ships sailed from London, but further details were sent later when they touched at a west-country port. Their cargoes consisted of those trinkets and trifles which the elder Hakluyt recommended. The narrative shows that they had received strict orders to treat savages well, and the accounts of the contacts made with them are, in fact, almost idyllic in character. The explorers, led by Captain Philip Amadas and Captain Arthur Barlowe, were formally welcomed by a local chieftain and his entourage and given generous entertainment in a native village. 'We were entertained', stated the report, 'with all love and kindnesse, and with as much bountie (after their manner) as they could possibly devise. We found the people most gentle, loving and faithfull, voide of all guile and treason and such as live after the maner of the golden age.' Two were brought back to England, and played a not unimportant part in the later history of Ralegh's endeavour.

The expedition had evidently been instructed to report on the fertility of the soil, the topography and the possibilities of trade, and in all these matters a rosy picture was painted. Even those who had seen vines on the continent of Europe had never seen such grapes growing. More than five hundred years before, Leif Ericsson, the first European to visit America, had called his discovery Vinland by reason of the grapes which he saw in that same region. Fish was abundant, and there were valuable supplies of timber, such as sassafras (which fetched high prices) and a kind of cinnamon-bearing tree, specimens of the bark of which had recently been brought back from South America by Wynter. The natives wore strings of pearls and some gold and copper ornaments. Grain, especially maize, grew luxuriantly, and the skins which had been brought back were of considerable value. The place where they had landed was not actually on the mainland of America, nor was it in the modern state of Virginia. Roanoak Island, off North Carolina, was one place they had touched, and it was to this group of islands lying off the coast of North Carolina that the report referred.

With such prospects of development, it was important that the next expedition should have men of ability staffing it. While he was as yet by no means rich, Ralegh had become patron to a brilliant young mathematician named Hariot, who was later to make an important contribution to algebraic methods and to win distinction as an astronomer. He taught Ralegh mathematics and remained his life-long friend, visiting him constantly even during the years of his imprisonment in the Tower. Hariot agreed to accompany the expedition, and the report which he made on it, which was splendidly published in 1587, illustrated with finely executed maps and engravings with versions of the text in several languages, is one of the most important 'Americana' of the modern collector, and was an admirable piece of advertisement. The new colony was to be in charge of Mr (later Sir Ralph) Lane. Of the hundred and seven who stayed in Virginia for a year, thirteen in the recorded list are given the title of master, and are presumably therefore to be reckoned as 'gentlemen'. There is no indication of friction between the gentlemen and the rest of the company, and conditions in Virginia must indeed have made it impossible for the gentlemen to stand aside from the jobs that had to be done. Sir Richard Grenville sailed with the expedition, but did not remain in Virginia. There were seven sail in the fleet, including the small pinnaces, and apart from the setting ashore of the planters, the expedition was a typical privateering venture. In the Spanish West Indies a port was established in Porto Rico while another pinnace was being set up. Soon afterwards two Spanish frigates were taken, one with important personages aboard, who were ransomed for 'good round sums'. At Isabella, a meeting was arranged with the Spanish Governor and an al fresco banquet given him in great style by Sir Richard Grenville, followed by a bull-fight and some profitable exchanges of goods. Then Grenville sailed up the coast to Virginia, set the planters ashore with the promise to return with further supplies by the following Easter, and went back home, picking up another good Spanish prize on the way. One of his ships carried a letter from Ralph Lane to Hakluyt, reporting as enthusiastically of the prospects in Virginia as Ralegh's first explorers had done.

Lane was to discover that the life of a planter was no bed of roses. There were two great difficulties, lack of food and the hostility of the natives. The colony had arrived in August, too late in the year to plant its own crops, while the supplies of corn that had been brought were anyhow too musty to germinate; and though there was for the moment food in plenty, fish and fruit, autumn and winter made the position very difficult. Men had to be sent off in groups to different parts of the coast to live off shell-fish, and though Hariot's report makes it clear that the potential food supplies were abundant, one after another of the plantations made in America was reduced to desperate straits in its first season from famine. What was chiefly responsible for native hostility it is difficult to say. Probably it was, as Lane remarks, the growing realisation that the English were not gods, nor, so it seemed, under the direct protection of gods. Hariot has indeed a story of the plague that struck all those villages which were opposed to the English, and his account of this shows that Ralegh's instructions were still being followed; 'We sought by all meanes possible to win them by gentlenesse.' Still, one tribe took the initiative in attacking the settlement, and in the ensuing fighting a number of Indians were killed.

Hostilities had just come to a head in the late spring of 1586, and the shortage of food was still acute, though the new harvest was within a fortnight of reaping, when a large fleet was sighted. It was uncertain at first whether the ships were Spanish or English, but (as we have seen already) they were in fact Drake's fleet returning from the West Indies' expedition. According to Lane's account, Drake agreed to leave a 70-ton bark, the 'Francis', with the settlers, with food for one hundred men for four months, and new equipment such as weapons, tools, clothing and the like; with two pinnaces also and four small boats. Two master craftsmen were to be left and other skilled men too. But suddenly a storm blew up. It raged for three days. The 'Francis', with all the new supplies on board and the men who were to have stayed, was carried far out to sea. There was as yet no sign of Grenville and his fresh supplies. It was mid-June, and they had been promised for Easter. So Drake left a ship of 170 tons, the 'Bark Bonner', to carry the colonists home. 'The very hand of God', as it seemed to them, 'was stretched out to take them from thence', and they reached Portsmouth towards the end of July. To another, writing at the same time as Lane, a different interpretation suggested itself. 'The hand of God came upon them', he said, 'for the cruelty and outrages commited by some of them against the native inhabitants of that country.' Immediately after their departure, so we are told, the provision ship arrived, but finding the settlement deserted returned to England. She had been followed by Grenville himself, with three ships. He left fifteen men on Roanoak Island with provision for two years, in order to maintain the English claims to the coast. Some time later, as their countrymen learnt a year afterwards, this small group was attacked by Indians. One of them was killed outright in a trap set for him. Then the house in which the rest had taken refuge, and where all their stores had been stacked, was fired. A few escaped in a small boat. But where they went was never known.

Such were the earliest settlements in Virginia. In the winter following the return of the first colony, preparations were pushed forward actively for a second, to be led by John White. This time it was fully intended that the settlement should be permanent, and besides the men concerned there were seventeen women also, one of them White's daughter, who was accompanied by her husband thither on the enterprise. That summer a daughter was born to them, and she was named Virginia, the first European to be born in that fair country. Towards the end of the summer, John White, as has been mentioned, returned to England to obtain help for the settlement. But the following year was the year of the Armada, and nothing was done for the planters of Virginia, with such urgent matters on hand at home. So it was also the next year and the next; and when at last an attempt was made to help, it was too late. Yet those sacrifices were not in vain. Pioneers were to learn at last by the mistakes of their forbears. Part of the coast had been mapped, and an idea had been obtained of its products and its possibilities. There was a legacy, the legacy of native hostility, that proved well-nigh fatal. Ralegh had done his best to avoid it, but it must remain doubtful, even if those first planters had been saints, whether it could have been avoided. Ralph Lane wrote that the discovery of a gold mine or a passage to the South Sea, and nothing else, could make Virginia desirable in the eyes of English settlers. The great lesson that had to be learnt was that he was wrong; and that even more precious than a mine of gold or trade in spices was to prove the opportunity of founding a new nation in the tradition of freedom.

Chapter VIII

THE ARMADA AND AFTER

(i) THE GREAT CRISIS

DURING the years which followed the planting of the second colony in Virginia, the national endeavours of England were focused, to an unprecedented degree, on the war with Spain. Drake had been returning from one of the most brilliant phases of the campaigns, the West Indian expedition, when he took back to England Ralph Lane and the settlers from the first colony. This same Ralph Lane was a member of Drake's expedition to Lisbon in the year following the Armada's defeat, and wrote an important despatch about it. Several of the ships which fought the Spaniards, including the Lord Admiral's flagship the 'Ark Ralegh' (later called the 'Ark Royal'), had been built for Sir Walter Ralegh, who played a large part also in the organisation of the second line of the country's defences, the land defences along the south coast and the Thames estuary. In Spain also there had been an enormous concentration of effort on the preparation of the great Armada which was to convoy Parma's army across from Flanders for the invasion. King Philip and his officers, certainly no less than those who served in the English fleet, thought of it as a mighty crusade demanding the country's whole resources, and the Spanish flagship displayed a sacred banner to inflame the Catholics with ardour, and the Protestant seamen opposed to them with fury. It was as near a total war as anything had yet been.

The course of the fighting illustrates many problems that tax the brains of strategists on sea and land at present: the division of authority between the civil power and the soldiers and sailors; the changes brought by new weapons and new techniques, with the difficulties of convincing the powers that be of those changes; the co-ordination of sea and land forces, made easier to-day by the development of mechanical methods of communication, but infinitely more difficult by the addition of a third arm and by the vast increase in the scale of operations; above all, the administrative difficulties of the supply both of materials and of men when considerable forces are employed. These difficulties more than anything else were the undoing of the Armada, and these too destroyed Drake's chances of success in the Lisbon expedition of 1589. The Queen had little appreciation of such things, but she was ready to listen to her admirals, when they were actually present to urge their point of view; and Burghley's letters and notes show that he sometimes put the blame for what was in fact his own policy on his mistress, protesting the difficulties she was making about maintaining supplies, for instance, when he himself was the author of her policy. The admirals, on their part, did not appreciate the political problems. It is easy now to condemn Elizabeth for not realising earlier that her plans for appeasement, with demonstrations of strength, were doomed to failure. Much of her seeming hesitation was due to these plans, and to her belief that they could still be put into effect.

For Drake, after the attack on Cadiz, the issue was simple. He knew the scale of King Philip's plans. He disapproved wholeheartedly of the landsmen's policy of waiting till these plans matured, dividing meanwhile the English fleet into three sections, one to operate in the narrow seas, one in the western opening of the Channel, and one off the Azores. This could ensure the defence of England, so the Council thought, whether Philip should decide to attack direct, or should arrange for a junction between his fleet and the Duke of Parma's forces in Flanders. To adopt this plan, so Drake maintained, would be to offer the opportunity for the fleet to be attacked piecemeal, and destroyed squadron by squadron. He believed in taking the offensive, and in attacking the fleet in Spanish harbours or off the coast of Spain. If the English ships were operating off the coast of Spain and the Armada got to sea between them and the Channel, so much the better, for any wind that took the Spaniards northwards would mean that the English had the advantage of the wind for a fight. 'If there may be such a stay or stop made by any means of this fleet in Spain' (wrote Drake), 'so that they may not come through the seas as conquerors—which I assure myself they think to do—then shall the Prince of Parma have such a check thereby as were meet.' Drake saw rightly that if Philip's command of the seas was thus challenged, an invasion by Parma had no hope of success. Barges carrying troops could not cross the narrow seas undefended. A few ships operating off the Kent coast could destroy them. These conclusions were clearly right. What was not so well justified by events was Drake's confidence in the power of the English ships to wipe the Armada from the seas. After a week's hard fighting in the Channel, though the Spanish ships had been severely handled, their losses were not considerable.

Drake's faith was naturally unbounded. But the factor that gave him reasoned confidence was the new technique of fighting which the English ships of war were adopting. The Spaniards still regarded a ship of war primarily as a barracks for soldiers. Their hopes of success in a naval action depended on the chance to board. If they could grapple, the sea fight could be converted into a land battle; and the Spanish infantry was famous. We have already seen the beginnings of a change in the English fleets. The sailor was beginning to acquire an equal status with the soldier. In the Spanish fleets this had not begun, because the soldier was still the more important element in the fighting, even at sea.

The new answer found to grappling was gunnery. Ralegh was going to insist later, drawing his conclusions from the Armada's fate, that armament and gunnery were all-important. This view came from Drake. Drake was indeed reprimanded for wasting ammunition in gunnery practice. But Hawkins was now at the Admiralty, and he, like Drake, knew the importance of heavy guns. The Queen's ships thus fired a far heavier broadside far more accurately than the Spanish ships, and both such figures as are available, and also the English and Spanish stories, make clear the terrible effect of these broadsides on ships that were crowded with soldiers. The lessons that the English gunners learnt in the course of the fighting were two: one that they had over-reached themselves with long-range guns, which were never really effective in comparison with firing at close range, and the other that the number of gunners to every ship could be yet further increased, if each unit was to exert its full power.

Another difference between the fleets, which impressed opinion at the time, was the towering structure of the Spanish, as contrasted with the lower build of the English, ships. The Spanish practice was a relic of medieval construction. Some men taking part in the action were impressed by the moral effect of these lofty works—which would undoubtedly have been a great advantage if the Spaniards had ever succeeded in grappling—and urged that English ships should also be built lofty. But Hawkins had had experience, in the 'Jesus of Lubeck', of such a high built ship, and if the more rakish lines of the English ships were due to him, he was undoubtedly right. Here again, all accounts show that the English ships were handled far more easily than the Spanish. One Spaniard after another pays tribute to their qualities of movement and speed, and as naval architecture they represented the new, and the Spanish ships the old, tradition. 'The worst of them', said one Spanish captain, 'without their maincourse or topsails can beat the best sailers we have.'

When the action was over, Howard ordered a series of tapestries to be woven to commemorate it, and though they were destroyed a century ago by fire, they had been reproduced by engraving in 1739 and we know, therefore, how the fights were pictured on them. In one after another in the foreground was prominently shown one of the great oared galleasses of which there were four in the Spanish fleet, generally disposed two on each wing. Evidently, therefore, these also impressed the English. They combined the qualities of a sailing ship with the possibility of free movement in a calm or into the wind, for they could be rowed as well as sailed. There had been in addition ten oared galleys when the Armada set out, but the first storm was too much for them and they went back home. Yet though the galleasses impressed the English, it is surprising how little harm they did, and before the battle of Gravelines was fought one of them was a casualty. To some slight extent the English ships had it both ways. For when the fleets were becalmed, English ships were towed into action by their long boats, which were only stopped when the oarsmen got within musket shot of the Spaniards. And the advantage gained by the galleasses, if not counterbalanced by this bold move, was not great enough for the authorities to demand oared ships in future for ocean fighting. Drake thought little of the galleys at Cadiz, and events vindicated his confidence. Here again it was a contrast between old and new methods of fighting. It has often been pointed out that the legend of the enormous superiority in numbers and size of the Spanish fleet is not justified by the figures available. But while this is so, if we reckon all the units that took part in the fighting on the English side, it is doubtful whether many of the merchant ships of which the force was largely composed were very effective. Thus Wynter, writing to Walsingham on 1 August, before the final issue was known and with the Channel fighting fresh in his mind, said:

> I do assure your honour, if you had seen that which I have seen, of the simple service that hath been done by the merchant and coast ships, you would have said that we had been little holpen by them, otherwise than that they did make a show.[1]

X. FLEMISH MAN OF WAR AND GALLEY

(*About* 1565)

The Spanish accounts make it clear that 'making a show' was important in the destruction of morale. The Spaniards saw constant reinforcements coming to the enemy, and none to themselves. But the battle was primarily between a small force of warships built according to the new ideas, heavily armed and better supplied than their opponents with ammunition, and a bigger, but more unwieldy force, the units of which were the last word in a tradition now out of date. Because the English naval force was smaller, its equipment was more complete, and the 'coast ships' which slipped out from the harbours of Hampshire and Sussex had not taxed the organisation of the Navy Office, but had been fitted out individually by their owners and masters. At a time when the difficulties of supply on a large scale were so great, with the slowness and inadequacy of transport and smallness of reserves, this was a real advantage. No government machine has been more elaborately tied up with red tape than that of King Philip. Mobilisation was a business of months, almost of years, for a Spanish armada.

The task of the English officials was smaller. But it was well done. Hawkins knew well the importance of wages and of decent conditions. He suggested, and carried through, a reform that consisted in reducing the crews of the ships and paying them at correspondingly higher rates:

> By this mean her Majesty's ships will be furnished with able men, such as can make shift for themselves, keep themselves clear without vermin and noisesomeness which breedeth sickness and mortality, all which would be avoided. The ships would be able to continue longer in the service that they should be appointed unto....

Wages had been raised on his recommendation, and, compared with later practice, were punctually paid. The contractor for the fleet's food supplies similarly did a very competent job, and it was not his fault that typhus ravaged the crews. Beer went bad, and there was too little food here and there, but considering the machinery at his disposal he achieved much.

It was to the credit of Hawkins and the navy officials that an efficient force was ready when at last the blow fell. For they had had a difficult winter with the Queen and her Council. Her plans were constantly changing as the political situation changed. Philip had still believed, after the affair at Cadiz, that it would be possible for the Armada to sail that summer. But the months dragged on, and the concentration of the fleet was not effected. Summer became autumn, and though Philip pressed for an attempt even during winter, his admiral, Santa Cruz, thought this impossible. Englishmen, too, thought that a start late in the year was unlikely. The Queen refused to mobilise the fleet, and opinion at the time endorsed her decision. At last news arrived that the Armada was likely to sail early in 1588. Accordingly, just before Christmas 1587, Lord Howard's commission as Lord Admiral was signed and the fleet's mobilisation began. It had hardly been carried through when the order came to reduce crews by half—a wise order in view of the havoc caused by disease among large numbers. Though it was naturally a blow to the commanders, it did not mean the undoing of the work of mobilisation. A skeleton fleet was still ready if the unthinkable should happen and the Armada sail in January.

In addition to the Lord Admiral's commission, a separate commission was sent to Drake at Plymouth (Howard being at Queenborough in the Thames) giving him authority to take a fleet at once to the coast of Spain to repeat if possible the devastation of Cadiz elsewhere should he find concentrations of ships. Should the Armada be assembled ready for sailing, he was to harass it on its voyage northwards. Seven of his ships were to be supplied from the Royal Navy, and one was the 'Revenge', in which later Sir Richard Grenville fought his immortal action. Work was pressed forward urgently at Plymouth to make the ships ready for sea. Even at night, under the flare of torches, the yards were busy. But the same news that had decided the Council to reduce Howard's crews—that there was widespread disorganisation and even demoralisation among the soldiers and sailors concentrated for the Armada—determined them to cancel Drake's instructions also: with far less justification, since they had authorised action on his part, and there was no question of avoiding the dangers of inaction. The explanation must be that the appeasement party for the moment held the ear of the Queen. There was a new reason for their hopes to revive—Santa Cruz was dead. His gigantic task had mastered him. All Elizabeth was prepared to do now was to use Howard's squadron to make a demonstration off Flushing, where peace terms were being discussed with Philip's representatives. Yet peace, however much Elizabeth desired it, was not to be. News constantly reached London to show that the work though interrupted had not been abandoned. Santa Cruz' successor, the Duke of Medina Sidonia, was reorganising the Armada's supplies, which he had found in a state of wretched unpreparedness.

In February the Council laid down their plan of campaign, the triple division of the fleet. It was in the following month that Drake wrote the letter that has already been quoted, urging an attack on Spain itself. Backing his plan at the Council table was Walsingham. And Howard, whose appointment was magnificently successful, soon became infected with the ideas of the great seaman with whom his office brought him into contact. His actions in this memorable year triumphantly showed the rightness of having in command at that time a man who could compose the differences between these impetuous individualists and reconcile them to serving under one flag. He succeeded because his instinct told him, in technical matters, what was the best advice; because, though an amateur, he had unbounded enthusiasm for the sea, and admiration for the seamen; and because he could, as the times went, be trusted, better perhaps than any of that brilliant group of men who, led by Elizabeth, made the Elizabethan age. In April Howard was authorised, perhaps partly as the result of Drake's advice, to take the bulk of his squadron round to Plymouth and form there a great concentration. Early in May Drake was summoned to court, and the Council's plan was radically overhauled. Supplies were to be made available large enough for an attack on the Spanish coast to be possible, and Howard was authorised to make such dispositions of the fleet as he thought necessary. As soon as he was ready he made his way down the Channel, leaving behind a force under Seymour to guard against any sudden attempt by Parma to cross from Flanders. Drake on 23 May struck his flag as an independent commander and became Howard's vice-admiral and chief of staff. For the operations that followed both can claim a great share of the glory, but the planning of the general dispositions was no doubt Drake's.

Meanwhile the Armada's new commander was gradually working his force together. In those 130 ships were to be 19,000 soldiers in addition to the 8000 seamen, soldiers who were not intended as a reinforcement for Parma but whose primary job was, as has been seen, to board the English ships. By the time that Howard joined Drake, the Armada was almost ready to sail, and the English admirals were aware that it was now a matter of weeks, perhaps only of days. A council of war was at once held, and Drake's plan was accepted. The combined fleets were to sail at once for the Spanish coast. Then the weather prevented them. The winds were contrary. And though supplies of food had been authorised, they were not forthcoming. At the end of the month the wind changed, and with such provisions as were available the fleet put out to sea. But before they were out of the Channel a south-westerly gale blew up, and after a few days' fighting with it, they put back to Plymouth. There they found despatches from London, urging that the decision to sail for Spain should be reconsidered, and the safer policy, as it was thought to be, of lying somewhere off the entrance to the Channel 'to protect England, Ireland and Scotland' was pressed. Howard was in despair. 'Sir Francis Drake, Mr Hawkins, Mr Frobisher and others that be men of the greatest judgment,' he said, 'and also my own concurring with them in the same, is that the surest way to meet with the Spanish fleet is upon their own coast or in any harbour of their own, and there to defeat them.' His protest was admitted. But the weather frustrated a whole series of attempts to make southwards, and so it was decided to wait in the Channel. This time it was Drake's turn to protest to Howard, and Howard's answer was to give the order to move southwards once again. For three days the wind was fair, and some of the English ships were almost within sight of the Spanish coast. Then the sou'wester came on to blow again. The last chance of carrying out Drake's plan was lost. Unknown to the English, the wind that carried them back to Plymouth was bringing with it Philip's 'invincible' Armada.

Howard's immediate task seemed to him to be the revictualling of his ships as soon as might be, and then to put into operation some fresh plan. Burghley meanwhile was scanning anxiously the dossiers of the fleet's expenses, finding mistakes in the contractor's calculations, and wondering how long the country's finances would stand such a burden. But his prayer that if something was going to happen, it should happen quickly, met with a speedy answer. Almost as soon as it was made, news came into Plymouth that the Armada had been sighted off the Lizard. A ship of St Mawes in Cornwall, bound for France to load salt, encountered with nine sail of great ships between Scilly and Ushant, bearing north-east. Fearing that they might be Spaniards (for they had already been warned by a flyboat that there were Spaniards about) the ship's master kept her to windward. The Spaniards gave chase, and almost caught him. But he escaped, after seeing clearly the red cross, the ragged Burgundian saltire which looks in the engravings like a St Andrew's cross, that was the flag of the Spanish fleet. A ship named the 'Golden Hind', Captain Fleming, was before him with the news. The Spaniards were in English waters.

'The commanders were at bowls upon the Hoe at Plymouth', says a writer in 1626, so secretly did the Armada reach England. Drake finished his game. There was time for that and to beat the Spaniards too. The problem needed thinking. What was needed was to get the weather of the Spaniards. All along the coast beacons were lit, and so the message leaped from hill-top to hill-top that the Spaniards had come.

Then the admirals acted. With the wind in the Spaniards' favour, an attack with fire-ships on the English fleet in Plymouth Sound might have led to disaster. So all that night, in the light of a sliver of moon that shone dim through the mist, ships were warped out of harbour, and, as morning broke, beat out to sea southwards, across the bows of the Spanish fleet which lay away there to the west. One small group of ships, as they left the Sound, turned westwards, and worked along the coast tacking into the wind, in the attempt to get to windward of the enemy. But the bulk of the fleet was with Howard, who intended to turn north-west, when he had made far enough southwards for this to be possible. In the afternoon, through the mist, those on board these ships could see dimly the forms of Spanish ships, away to starboard. Howard was leaving Plymouth to its fate. It had its shore defences. His advisers rightly thought that the paramount necessity was to secure the advantage of the weather. The wind was still in the south-west, and with the exception of a few brief hours it was to remain in that quarter for the next week.

The Spanish admiral saw through the night the light of the ship leading those that moved along the coast. But he took no step to stop them, nor did he realise that the main body of the English fleet was passing east and south of him. He did not even know that Howard had joined Drake. When he saw the English fleet astern and to windward, at dawn on 21 July, the sight was so unexpected that it was thought at first this must be another fleet that had come out of Dartmouth. Thus the first great victory was won without a shot fired. English seamanship had recovered the weather-gauge at the start. In his instructions to his admiral, King Philip had told the Duke that he must at all costs keep it. It was lost.

The precise formation in which the Spanish fleet was drawn up on that day and on the following days also, for fighting, is a matter of doubt. Certainly it gave the English the impression of being a crescent.[2] An elaborate order of battle had been drawn up before the expedition started, but we have seen that the galleys, an important element in the force as planned, had turned back. Philip had written to his admiral to dispose the heavy 'urcas', or supply ships, at the centre where they would have greatest protection, and it looks as if his orders were obeyed. In the Howard tapestries several things can be observed. There was usually a screen of look-out vessels, feluccas probably, thrown forward in advance. The oared galleasses were posted on the wings, at the points of the crescent. And the fleet maintained regular formation. The English council of war evidently thought that this had played a large part in the comparative success of the Spaniards in keeping English attacks at bay, and the highest tribute they paid to it was to attempt themselves a much more definite organisation after a few days' fighting. We must imagine, therefore, an apparent crescent, formed by the fighting rear division of the Spanish fleet, the horns being squadrons thrown back, on the defence, in *échelon*, and the oared galleasses on the actual wings; and we must imagine the centre thickened by the van of fighting ships that led the way eastwards, and the supply ships behind them. It was a formation planned when the possibility of attack from both east and west was anticipated. Massed behind the van were the hulks and victuallers, and deployed in front of these the van division of the fleet which from the following English ships was not visible.

The serious defect in the Spanish fleet, indeed, was not its squadronal dispositions, which could hardly have been bettered, if we may judge by the course of the fighting. Rather it was the lack of a feasible plan of campaign. Medina Sidonia's orders were not to fight unless he met first with only a division of the English fleet,[3] but to bring the Armada through the straits to the shores of the Low Countries, whence it could convoy Parma's army across to the Thames. 'It was openly spoken of', said Vicente Alvarez, captain of the 'Nuestra Señora del Rosario', when the prisoners were later examined, 'that the place of their landing should be within the river of London.' But no machinery had been devised for co-ordinating the Armada's movements with those of Parma. What if he were not ready? More than one distinguished Spanish officer had asked this question, and suggested the securing of a base, such as the Isle of Wight, on the north side of the Channel, as a preliminary. Medina

Sidonia may have had it in mind to do this, in spite of Philip's instructions. But the event proved that his plans were not clear cut. He was prepared to make his way up the Channel and see what happened next.

On the morning of 21 July, at about nine o'clock, Howard sent forward his pinnace, the 'Disdain', to give the Duke of Medina defiance; to make, that is, a formal declaration of war with a gunshot. Almost immediately, perhaps even before this, the northern horn of the crescent formed by the Spanish fleet was engaged. The English accounts make little of this engagement, but the Spanish show that it was important. They blame a change of the wind for their ill success. This shift was a few points northwards, and with Drake and Howard coming up from the south-east, and other ships to the north of the Spaniards, it may well be that this shift gave this northern squadron an advantage which the Spaniards had expected to be theirs, unaware that there were ships waiting to sweep up from the south also. The Spanish admiral had hoped to make for Plymouth. But the attack on his landward wing, pressed home with a fire that from the start was intensely effective, checked that movement completely. Some of the ships began shifting towards the Spanish centre, away from the danger that threatened. Recalde drove up into the wind to help. But he was cut off and severely handled. Things might have gone very badly with him had not Medina Sidonia rallied his fleet and beaten back into the wind to his assistance. Many of Howard's biggest ships were not in company. The recent shift in the wind had at last made it possible for them to leave the Sound, but they were not yet available to help. So he signalled to discontinue the engagement. His captains, Drake, Hawkins and Frobisher, had been putting into practice tactics afterwards set down on paper by Ralegh—whose seamanship it is now the fashion to decry: attack the weathermost ships of the enemy only, where it is hardest for him to send help. They had been rewarded by doing severe damage in the first contact. Moreover, in a moment of confusion in the Spanish fleet, the galleon of Don Pedro de Valdes had fallen foul of another ship, so that her foremast and bowsprit were borne overboard; and almost at the same time a barrel of powder exploded in a great Biscayan ship. Her decks were blown up, her stern blown out, and she could not steer. She was rescued by the galleasses from immediate destruction.

That afternoon a council of war was held on board Howard's

ship. Drake was given the job of leading the fleet and keeping in touch throughout the night with the Armada. Late that evening, however, as the English line silently followed him, his light suddenly went out. He had sighted a number of sail far to the south, and putting out his lantern so that he should not lead the whole fleet off on some wild goose chase, had gone off to see what they were. Howard criticised him for this action, but it is difficult to see what else he could have done. The ships might, so he supposed, have been Spanish ships, trying to recover the weather-gauge. In fact, they were German merchantmen, and having spoken to them he let them pass. When morning broke, he found conveniently near him Pedro de Valdes' ship, which as a result of the damage she had received had dropped out of her place and was separated from the rest of the fleet. Medina Sidonia had left her to her fate. She was taken, with all her treasure, so that Drake was accused of having turned aside for that reason. Howard, indeed, had been left in some difficulty, for at dawn he was isolated, with only the 'Bear' and the 'Mary Rose' with him, almost within range of the Spanish fleet. His own ships were far to the west, so that the nearest might 'scarce be seen half mast high'. Still the day was not altogether unprofitable for him. The wind remained steady, so that he came to no harm. The Biscayan, on which the explosion had taken place on the previous day, was abandoned by the Spaniards. Lord Thomas Howard and Hawkins, in a skiff from Hawkins' ship, the 'Victory', went on board, and a grim sight greeted them. About fifty men had been killed, and their bodies were strewn over the wreck. Captain Fleming, in the 'Golden Hind', was given the job of towing her into Weymouth. Meanwhile Drake's exchange of compliments with Pedro de Valdes was at last complete, and the captive taken to Dartmouth. Drake rejoined the main body of the fleet that evening.

The Spanish admiral was a landsman, as indeed was Howard. He had been warned to beware of the English gunnery. He must have known the apprehensions which his great predecessor, Santa Cruz, had felt of the Armada's success. The difficulties of supply which he had himself found when he took over the command had been only partly solved, and the storms he had encountered in the Bay of Biscay cannot have increased his optimism. Yet after these two days he may have felt not dissatisfied. He had suffered two important casualties, but both were due primarily to misadventure. The English captains had done brilliant things, but though they had had for two days the advantage of the weather, it had led to nothing that could be called a decisive success. The Spanish formation had remained unbroken. Medina Sidonia may have reflected that discipline and organisation were again vindicating themselves triumphantly against brilliant individual valour and clever seamanship. Soon, perhaps, the 'Ark Royal' would be isolated completely by the accidents of the chase. And then his galleasses might show their worth. That very night it was dead calm. A few small ships lay apart from the main English fleet, and the watch from the fleet saw the four galleasses moving out as if to attack them. They were helpless to assist, motionless in the calm sea of the summer night. But it was a feint. The galleasses' commander was after bigger game. He was ready to bide his time.

The Spanish admiral was by now convinced that King Philip had been wrong and that his own flag officers were right in saying that a base must be occupied on the English coast. The Isle of Wight was the obvious choice, a choice as obvious to the English as it was to himself; and during the next phase, therefore, it was the Spaniards' objective. Howard on the other hand, was determined to hustle them on with constant pressure, driving them on to Portland race, or pressing them northwards towards the Owers sands, but always urging them on nearer the anchorage at Calais where they would be stranded, with no army awaiting them. On the Tuesday morning the wind, after the calm of the night before, sprang up north-east, giving the Spaniards for the moment the advantage that the English had so far enjoyed. Frobisher, in the 'Triumph', attempted to get round the Spanish northern wing by a movement towards the coast, northwards and eastwards. At once the Spaniards fell upon his ship with the galleys, cutting her off, with the five other ships in company with her—three of them large merchant ships, but built for the Levant service and so well armed. They fought gallantly. At first the rest of the English fleet was prevented from coming to Frobisher's help by an attack in force by the Spaniards, and to avoid boarding, Howard and the ships with him had to move away before the wind, with the Spaniards in pursuit. But all the luck was on Howard's side, for after an hour or two's fighting, the wind shifted right round again into its old quarter, and once more the English were free to bring Frobisher help without having to beat into the wind. And more reinforcements, probably led by Drake, attacked the seaward wing of the Spanish fleet so fiercely that Medina Sidonia withdrew, and by evening was moving once more, his fleet still in good order, towards the east. It had been a day of intense fighting. Such gunnery had never been seen, and if the cannon had been muskets, they could not have fired more ammunition. Howard's supplies were running low, and next day he sent the small ships in the fleet into harbour to get more powder and shot. Then a council was held, and it was determined to reorganise. The steadiness of the Spanish formation had saved the enemy so far. Now it was hoped that by a more systematic organisation of the attacking force that advantage too would pass to the English fleet. It was divided, therefore, into four squadrons, that inshore led by Frobisher, next Hawkins, next Howard himself, and then the vice-admiral Drake on the seaward wing. That very night, it was arranged, six merchant ships from each of the squadrons should attack the Spaniards, so that even by night they should be harried. But the night was windless, and the plan could not be carried out.

The need to press forward the Spanish fleet ever further and further eastwards was now critical. For they were, next morning, off the Isle of Wight, fifteen miles or so to the south of it. The English had edged in, so it seems, to lie between the Spaniards and the island, and though they had not entirely succeeded it is probable that the fleets lay deployed along a line running roughly north-east and south-west, with the English fleet inshore. The squadron on the left of the English line was led by Frobisher in the 'Triumph'. On the right was the 'Revenge', Drake's flagship, and Howard's and Hawkins' squadrons were in the centre. At dawn on the 25th there was still no breath of wind. But Howard was resolved not to allow the Spaniards a day's respite for that. Two of the Armada's ships, so it happened, had fallen away from the Spanish fleet and lay south-westwards of it. One was Recalde's flagship, the 'Santa Ana', which had been severely mauled on the 21st, and may perhaps have hoped to slip away that night to a French port. The other, a Portuguese galleon, had been told off to help her; but with no wind they could go no further. At once Howard decided to tow to attack them, and Hawkins followed, till the longboats of the two ships were within musket shot of their opponents. Here was the galleasses' chance, and three of them dashed out to help. But they suffered terribly from the fire of the 'Ark' and the 'Lion', and though they rescued Recalde for the moment from almost certain destruction—his ship eventually became a total wreck on the French coast—'they were

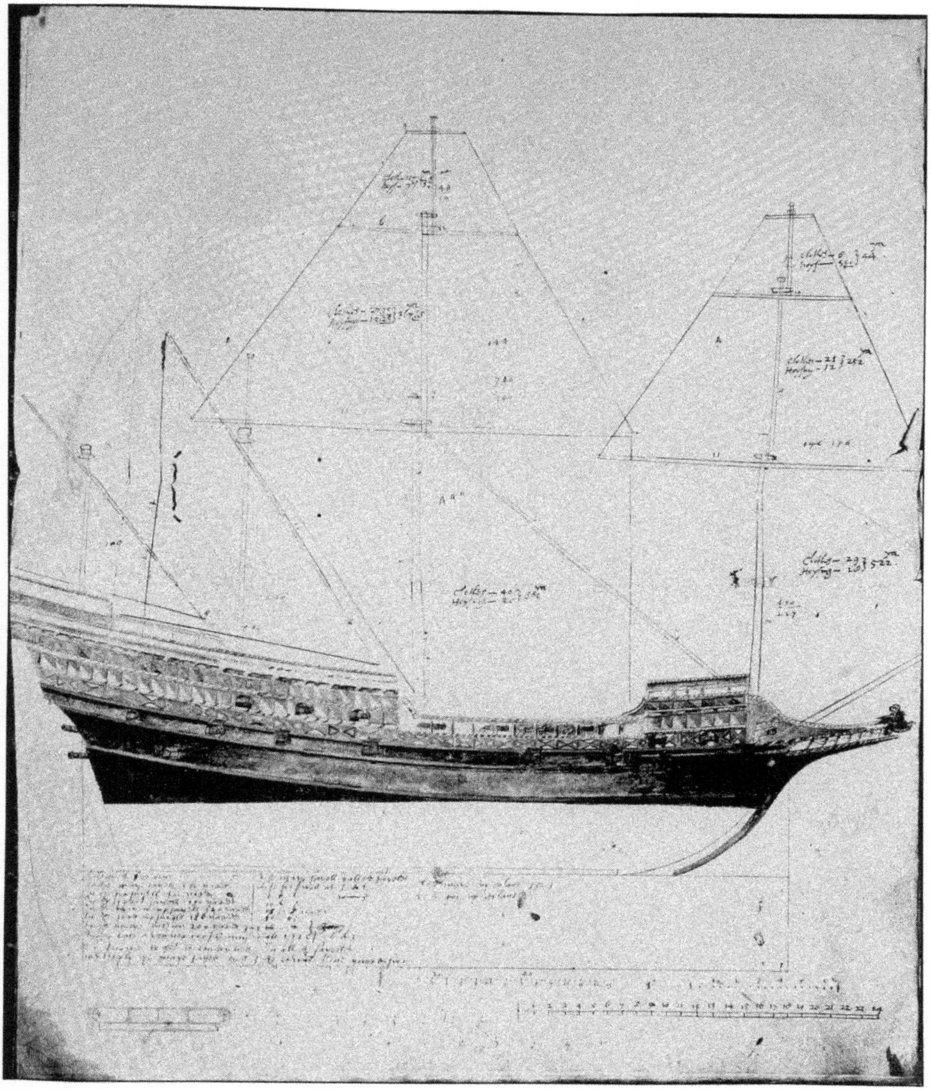

XI. AN ELIZABETHAN GALLEON, PROBABLY THE 'ARK ROYAL'

(From a manuscript in the Pepysian Library)

never seen in fight any more, so bad was their entertainment in this encounter'.

Meanwhile Frobisher was fighting at the other end of the line, and as usual he was in difficulties. He too had been towed out to attack the Spanish admiral's own flagship and had damaged her rigging, killing some soldiers. But other ships were supporting Medina Sidonia. Frobisher believed he might be cut off, and fired three guns to call for help. Then his ship was towed back towards the English ships with eleven launches. It looks as if the first day of the squadronal organisation had been a failure. The four flagships had each, apparently, acted almost without the help of their squadrons. The 'armies looked on and did not approach', says Howard of the fighting round his own ship, 'for the "Ark" and the "Lion" did tow to the galleasses with their long-boats'. Frobisher, like his three colleagues, seems to have fought unsupported. Nothing is specifically heard of Drake during this battle,[4] for, in Howard's account, his part in all the fighting—after the incident of the German ships—is glossed over. But two of the ships of his squadron, the 'Nonpareil' and the 'Mary Rose', are specially mentioned by Howard for a gallantly sustained attack. Drake must have been with them, and it was probably this attack (which must have been delivered from the starboard wing, possibly from a south-westerly direction so that this wing of the Spaniards had actually been turned) that forced the Spanish admiral to disengage and withdraw to the east. He may well have feared being driven north-eastwards on to the Owers banks. The wind had now risen in its old quarter, the south-west. So he sailed on, reforming no longer in the roundel formation which was normal when there was to be no fighting, but in the apparent crescent of his battle order. For at any moment he might expect a new attack.

Howard, too, reorganised into his old squadrons; and there may have been some plain things said of the need for maintaining formation. For the present, since the shortage of ammunition looked like being acute, it was determined not to force more fighting, but to save supplies for when they might be more urgently needed. For the fighting had been almost as severe as that of two days before, and ammunition was, as Howard says, 'well wasted'. So both fleets, reorganised, sailed eastwards through the next day, the Spaniards in their crescent, with the galleys at its horns, the English in their four squadrons. Over to the north tiny sails could be descried, coming out of almost every haven to join Howard, like small boys following a troop of soldiers; from Southampton, Portsmouth, Chichester, off Beachy Head, from Rye and Winchelsea. By these ships the captains of the castles and forts were sending powder, shot and food. The Spaniards watched with growing misgiving. Nor did they yet know that to the east Seymour waited with a squadron of great ships as well as small. And there were other preparations, besides the army at Tilbury. Walsingham at the court at Richmond had already pictured what would happen, and had sent down to Dover six dozen barrels of pitch. The Spaniards would anchor to wait for Parma. They would have to be dislodged. That would mean the need for fire-ships.

On Saturday morning, the 29th, the coast of France was sighted near Boulogne, and the Duke of Medina Sidonia had to make up his mind what to do next. On the Thursday he had sent an envoy to Dunkirk to tell Parma of his arrival, urging that there should be as little delay as possible before Parma joined him. On the Friday another pinnace had gone to Dunkirk to ask for powder and shot, and for forty flyboats, his own ships being so heavy to handle that they could not hope to match those of the enemy; also to press again for a quick meeting. Medina Sidonia hoped to find Parma waiting at Dunkirk. But he suspected and feared that there might be delay. With Howard pressing on his heels, delay would not be easy. Calais was reached about four o'clock on the Saturday afternoon. Many of his advisers urged him to go on. But he was told that the currents would sweep his fleet out to sea if he continued, and so the fleet anchored. Three hundred and fifty-two years later a host of tiny boats from the Thames and from the English south coast harbours thronged to Dunkirk to take off a British army. Those who manned them speak of these currents sweeping across, dragging at the moorings. The Spanish admiral had good reason to avoid them. He now sent his own secretary to Parma saying where he was, and that delay meant extreme danger. Then he got into touch with the Governor of Calais, and next day some of his officials went ashore to replenish stores. On the Saturday evening a squadron of thirty-six ships was seen joining the English fleet. Medina Sidonia imagined it to be Hawkins, Acles as he called him. It was of course Seymour, who had had instructions from Howard, and had rightly decided not to wait till the previous orders sent down from the court had been countermanded. He had had to beat across the Channel in the teeth of the wind.

The next day was one of increasing apprehensiveness for the Spaniards. Captain Rodrigo Tello, who had been sent off to Parma a fortnight before, arrived early that morning to say that Parma was at Bruges, and that nothing had yet been started there. Neither men nor munitions had begun to be embarked. In desperation the Duke sent once again saying that something must be done at once. He heard that night from his secretary that Parma had not even yet arrived in Dunkirk, and that it would probably be a fortnight before anything could be done. Looking back on them, Spaniards remembered those hours as a time of foreboding 'with a great presentiment of evil from that devilish people and their arts'. They were warned that 'the currents and counter currents of that channel were very strong', and that it would be dangerous to attempt to remain. But to leave would be to throw away without chance of recovery the hope of conjunction with Parma, to fail in the Armada's whole object. They must remain, but every precaution must be taken. As the admiral debated what to do, he saw a small pinnace detach itself from the English fleet. She bore down towards his own ship, fired four shots into her from almost point blank range, went about and escaped with nothing but a single shot, from one of the galleasses, through her sail. It was an astonishing piece of bravado, though she may have obtained in the process useful information of the position of the ships. About that same time, the Spaniards noticed movements among the enemy. One squadron seemed to be taking up new positions, dead to windward. Medina Sidonia and his officers remembered those terrible 'explosion machines' that had been used against the Spaniards in Flanders, fire-ships with huge quantities of powder aboard to bring fearful destruction to any who attempted to grapple them and tow them from harm's way.

During the morning a council of war had been held on board the 'Ark Royal'. To use fire-ships to dislodge the Armada was an obvious decision, and a messenger was sent across to Dover for materials. Then someone said that it would take too long. Ships must be sacrificed that same day, to be set ablaze and drifted down among the Spaniards with the tide that night. Drake offered one of his own ships, Hawkins one of his; and there were others, eight ships in all. There was no time fully to dismantle them. Their cannon were charged. About midnight the Spaniards heard a shot. It was the signal for the ships to be fired, and from the Spanish admiral's flagship the glow of two fires, blazing in the darkness, gradually increased to eight as the other ships kindled, was seen. When they were alight, the men aboard them slipped off into the boats. Medina Sidonia had suspected according to his own account that fire-ships would be used. He had ordered that an officer from his own ship should take out a pinnace to tow away to shore any that approached. But the sight of these eight, with their guns firing and their canvas set and lit up with the red light of the flames, and the knowledge that at any moment magazines might explode within them, was too much. Orders were given in a panic for the fleet to weigh. The flagship of the galleasses in the confusion became entangled with another ship and so badly damaged that she could not move. But considering the difficulties, this one mishap was a low price to pay, and the wind and tide that were bringing down the fire-ships swept the great Armada out of their path. The fire-ships could be seen away to the east, burning harmlessly. Not a Spaniard had been touched by them. But the Armada was caught now by the currents of which the admiral had been warned. He fired a shot as a signal to anchor once more. It was impossible. The fire-ships had scattered the whole fleet from the roads.

The Duke and one or two other galleons succeeded in anchoring again. But in the morning he saw that it was impossible for his fleet as a whole to come back into the wind and anchor. Most of the ships were now drifting towards the banks of Dunkirk. Their only chance of reassembling lay in a move northwards, and this he determined to make. The English admirals were under no illusions that their work was complete. The Armada had suffered loss, but had not yet suffered disaster. Howard wrote off to court to say briefly what he intended to do, and added a postscript that the stranded galleasse had fallen into English hands. Behind that statement there lay a curious change of plan on his part. It had been arranged after the flight of the Armada had been observed that Howard should pursue them and make the first attack, after which Drake's squadron should follow. But seeing the galleasse in difficulties, Howard turned on her and left the immediate pursuit of the Spaniards to others, and it was not till the battle was half through that he rejoined them. The galleasse lay stranded under the guns of the French forts of Calais. When the 'Ark Royal' tried to approach, the water was found to be too shallow, but boats were launched to attack. The huge ship towered high above them and casualties in the boats might have been heavy. But a lucky musket shot hit the captain of the galleasse between the eyes and killed him. The crew was struck with panic, and those who could struggled ashore. English sailors swarmed aboard to plunder, but there was an altercation with French officials and the commandant of the fort opened fire. So the Englishmen retired, not however without a rich reward of booty.[5]

While the 'Ark Royal' lay thus off Calais, Drake had led the fleet to the attack. By the time that this had been delivered, the incredible had been accomplished, and the Armada was once again in formation. It is indeed one of the marvels of the campaign that the Spaniards succeeded in maintaining this compact formation day after day in the fighting, and shows the remarkable quality of Spanish discipline and organisation. Englishmen who took part in the campaign witness constantly in their letters to the order of the Spanish ships, and in a solitary passage in which their order is described as bad, the writer is referring to the lack of equipment and provision actually in the ships, not to their conduct in battle. Flaws in discipline can be noticed, and it is on record that the admiral of the galleasse was reprimanded by Medina Sidonia at one stage in the campaign for not carrying out orders. But the reason was personal pique, not lack of courage. The fighting at Gravelines is indeed a striking testimony to the bravery of English and Spaniards alike. Its general character seems to have been a series of individual attacks, led by Drake, recklessly pressed home at short range with devastating effect. From time to time Spanish ships were cut off and suffered terribly; but again and again they struggled back into formation, or were somehow reabsorbed into it. Some of them, like the Portuguese galleon 'San Felipe', which evidently fought back magnificently, became total wrecks. She was eventually stranded on the Flanders coast with several others. Some were sunk outright, and the disasters that followed made it impossible for an accurate reckoning of the losses ever to be made. But on the whole the chief impression the accounts leave is of the desperate bravery shown on both sides, of the 'Revenge' 'riddled with shot', of Medina Sidonia's flagship, the 'San Martin', turning back again and again into the fighting, 'transfigured and shrouded in the smoke of her guns'. But because of the training of the English crews and the design and armament of the ships, the casualties that they suffered were a fraction of those suffered on the Spanish side. Later in the afternoon, when the fighting still continued unabated, a squall broke over the fleets with torrential rain. It lasted for a short time only, minutes rather than hours. But it ended the battle, for the English admirals had achieved their objective. There was no hope for the Spaniards of returning to Dunkirk. And throughout the fighting they had been drifting eastwards, towards the sandbanks off the coast. A high sea was running. It looked as if Providence were bent on completing the work that had been so effectively begun.

At two o'clock next morning, with the strong north-west wind blowing, it seemed that the 'San Martin' must be driven on to the shoals. When day broke, the English fleet was half a league to windward, and the force of the gale had somewhat abated. Eastwards, strung out with their formation at last broken, were the galleons of the Armada, driving into waters ever more treacherous. The pilots on board the 'San Martin', which brought up the rear of that struggling column, told Medina Sidonia that there was no hope of saving a single ship. It was the eve of the feast of San Lorenzo, the Duke's patron saint; and 'suddenly', said the Duke, 'God was pleased to change the wind to W.S.W., whereby the fleet stood towards the north without hurt to any ship'.

The English ammunition was spent, save for a reserve that must be kept in case Parma tried still to cross; for there was a theory that he was waiting until the English fleet had been enticed away into northern waters. Howard and Drake both believed that the peril was not yet over, though they knew that the Spaniards had suffered a heavy blow.

'We have the army of Spain before us, and a mind, with the grace of God, to wrestle a pull with him. There was never anything that pleased me better', wrote Drake, 'than seeing the enemy flying with a southerly wind to the northwards. God grant you have a good eye to the Duke of Parma, for with the grace of God, if we live, I doubt it not but ere it be long so to handle the matter with the Duke of Sidonia as he shall wish himself at St Mary Port among his orange trees.'

When he wrote this to Walsingham, Drake had been up all night watching. And the watching and waiting went on, even in port. The English crews were kept standing by for weeks, and there was an epidemic of typhoid among them. At last there came certain news that the Armada had not made for Denmark, nor yet for a Scottish port. The ships had been seen to the west of the Orkneys, and were struggling back by way of the Atlantic. Before they reached home the coasts were strewn with wreckage of some that would never return, and thousands of their crews were massacred in Ireland. *Flavit deus, et dissipati sunt.* On the medal struck to commemorate the Armada's destruction, it was to God that it was ascribed.

The defeat did not shatter the power of Spain, nor did it even end the war. But the English were right in believing that it was in some ways decisive. The conquest of England, followed as it must have been inevitably by the crushing of Holland by King Philip, would have checked, probably for ever, that great tide, which rising ever higher was making England, as it was making the Netherlands, a nation. Both nations had things in store for them which were going to be of some account, not to themselves only, but also to others. Elizabeth was capable of playing ducks and drakes with the fortunes of the Dutch, as of toying with the idea that a pretender should be restored in Portugal. But none was more sensitive than she to public opinion, and she knew that she could not consent, in the end, to leave the Dutch in the lurch. As at other times, what England accomplished, she did not only for herself—for self interest was paramount—but also, in her blundering and often self-righteous way, for the service of others. Her motives, seldom clearly seen, but rather instinctively realised, would be reckoned by her critics wholly selfish, and her methods wholly deceitful. If it is selfish to champion freedom and law, then she is selfish. They are her interest, as they are the interest of the citizen in a society. But had Parma crossed to the 'river of London' the English nation might perhaps never have happened, and those outposts of it, to the history of which we shall recur in a later chapter, might never have been planted.

(ii) THE CONTINUANCE OF THE WAR WITH SPAIN

The two most celebrated victories in English history, the defeat of the Armada and Trafalgar, were at the beginning, not at the end, of wars. Elizabeth had responded magnificently to the crisis. She was never greater. But when the immediate crisis was passed and when with its passing the national feeling, interpreted by her with consummate skill, became less intense, she slipped back further and further into petty jealousies, into hesitation, appalling indecision, and fear for her dignity and authority. These latter were never seriously questioned, except possibly by Essex; but as she aged she began to believe that they might be. It is probable that she was affected by age more than almost any other of the great figures of history; so much had she relied on the charm which was now vanishing. And though she was able enough to be revered for ability alone, for that she did not care. She had always liked having about her a court of brave and handsome young men, Knights of her Table, who should be devoted to her with a chivalrous love. And as the bonds by which she had held that court together were loosened, she insisted on maintaining it, nevertheless, as a sort of fiction. 'Paradise is grown wilderness, and for green grass are comen gray hairs.' It is her own phrase in a letter to Burghley in 1591, a phrase written in mockery—but it has a ring of anguish.

When the Armada was known to be in final retreat, a thanksgiving service in old St Paul's was held, a service which was in some ways strangely modern in sentiment:

> We cannot but confess, O Lord God, that the late terrible intended invasion of most cruel enemies was sent from Thee, to the punishment of our sins, our pride, our covetousness, our excess in meat and drink, our security, our ingratitude and our unthankfulness towards Thee for so long peace and other thine infinite blessings continually poured upon us....

And when the tumult and shouting died, Elizabeth began at once to plan Philip's final defeat. Success should be followed up immediately by an expedition to the Azores to strike at the treasure fleet. Drake, whose influence with the Queen was at its height, hurried to court to explain that it would take months for the ships to be got ready. In the ensuing period we find Howard and Hawkins urging the scheme in an extended form. Hawkins had indeed mapped it out before the Armada sailed. Let the English keep a dozen ships, great and small, cruising on the treasure routes. They must be regularly relieved by similar squadrons, and the results would not only finally cripple Spain, but would represent also a good profit. But Drake had a more ambitious project. He had lately had under his wing Don Antonio, pretender to the throne of Portugal. Drake planned an expedition to set up Don Antonio in Lisbon or possibly in the Azores, and to strike at Spanish power by repeating at Lisbon on a far more grandiose scale and with land support the operation that had been effected at Cadiz. Early in 1588, while the Council had hesitated, Drake had been scheming with Essex. Now Essex, the last object of the Queen's extravagant favours, secretly entered this new project. To a wiser head than Drake's this ought in itself to have spelt disaster.

And for a large-scale expedition of this kind, Drake was not the right leader. He was not an administrator. Things went wrong with the food supplies of his expeditions as regularly as they did with those of King Philip himself. Furthermore, there was no trained English army to carry out the military side of such an operation. Sir John Norreys had won a reputation in Ireland. Sir Roger Williams had done brilliantly in the Low Countries, and Elizabethan England did not lack men who could perform the most extraordinary feats of individual bravery. What she could not produce was an organised and disciplined military force with the necessary equipment, in particular a siege train. The need was partly met by recruits from the Low Countries. But their number was disappointing, and the bulk of the soldiers were men of no adequate experience. Drake was determined to control the expedition himself. Howard had nothing to do with it, to his intense and legitimate mortification. His great qualities might have made all the difference to it. But it was one of those strange privately subscribed ventures, with the Queen holding shares, which we have met already. One thing the promoters had learned by experience—to insist that if sailing orders were countermanded, the Queen should pay the costs of the delay. The expedition that left Plymouth was magnificent in scale, comparable with the Armada, a nominal 23,000 men and 130 ships. 'There was never army in better order than this,' wrote Drake to Burghley, 'nor greater hope of good, if God grant relief of victual, which I mistrust not.'

The wind changed immediately the fleet was clear of Plymouth Sound, and they had to put back again. Then came the first disaster, a message to say that Essex had left word that he was sailing with the expedition, and had disappeared from court. After him to Plymouth came post-haste the Queen's messenger, but Essex was not to be found, having slipped off with Sir Roger Williams in the 'Swiftsure', and taken the wise precaution of not returning to Plymouth, but putting in at Falmouth. And there was a further misfortune. When the wind changed and they got away again, it was with new instructions from the Queen. Her Council were afraid of what was left of the Armada in the Spanish harbours. Before anything was attempted at Lisbon, these ships should be destroyed.

It was, presumably, these instructions that led Drake to postpone the attack on Lisbon and forgo the advantage of surprise which might have been decisive. In his next campaign, he was, of his own act, to make the same mistake. He passed by the Biscayan forts, where many ships were known to be in harbour, and attacked Corunna. A landing was made without loss. The base town was captured and sacked, and the shipping in the harbour destroyed. An action, marked by fine acts of heroism, was fought and won outside the town. But the High Town itself was not taken. There was no adequate equipment for an attack on a heavily fortified position, and in the course of the attack that was made, when the walls were being mined, there were by ill luck heavy losses. And much worse than this, the recklessness of the men in the sack of the base town was the beginning of epidemic disease, which worked havoc when the men were back on shipboard.

Still, shipping had been destroyed and the affair might be reckoned not wholly unsuccessful. No plan of campaign for the Lisbon attack had been devised before the start. Drake was in favour of an attack with sea and land forces in close co-operation. But he was apparently outvoted at the Council table, and had perhaps lost the touch of which Borough complained before Cadiz; or perhaps set much more store by the judgment of Norreys and Williams. It was agreed that a landing should be made at Peniche, fifty miles or so from Lisbon, and the army was to march overland. Drake was to attack by sea when the critical moment arrived. But it was inevitable in this scheme that sea and land forces should get out of touch, and there was no way for him to discover when the critical moment came.

If the Portuguese people had rallied to the pretender's flag, as Drake no doubt hoped, all might yet have been well. But the ground had been carefully prepared by the Spaniards. It was rumoured that all the bishoprics were to be filled with English Catholics, if Don Antonio succeeded, and that he had agreed to a twelve days' sack of Lisbon and a huge indemnity. Such stories had done their work, and there was scarcely a finger lifted in support of him. After a difficult march, the army reached the suburbs of Lisbon. But Drake had not yet attempted to move in past the enormously strong harbour defences, for to do so would have jeopardised, if by chance he had been weatherbound there, land as well as sea forces. Moreover, when it was needed, the wind was contrary. All that could be done was to seize Cascaes Castle to cover the army's retreat. It was now that further supplies arrived from England. But they brought with them an extraordinary letter from Elizabeth for the generals. She told them that Essex' escapade and their connivance were 'no childish actions'. He must be sent home at once. 'We look to be obeyed.' Essex had to go.

Not long after this, which was in itself a blow to the crews' morale, the fleet was becalmed off the Tagus. No adequate precautions against surprise were taken. It was just the day in a thousand for action by galleys. Twenty-one of these dashed out in the calm weather, and three or four English ships were cut off and destroyed. The plan was now to make for the Azores. But the weather did not hold. Seventeen days after the embarkation at Cascaes, they were still at Vigo, and so fearful had been the losses from wounds and disease that it was said that there were not more than two thousand sound men in the expedition. Then a storm arose in which Drake's own ship was seriously damaged. It was with difficulty and some ignominy that he reached England. For though some things that had been done were remarkable achievements, public opinion was right in reckoning the whole enterprise a failure. It had shown, among other things, that the problem of operating far away from a home base with a fleet transporting an army was as far from solution by the English as it had been by the Spaniards themselves.

The essential feature of the Hawkins plan was that no extensive land forces should be used. This would make it possible to provision fleets for six months' service, and in 1590 Hawkins was sent to sea so equipped. But the Council could not make up their minds to allow him to cruise only off the Azores, when there might be hostile Spanish ships in the Channel ports. So he was given orders to watch Corunna also; and soon after reaching the Azores he was summoned back urgently to dispel imaginary dangers in the Channel. The plan was not completely abandoned, however, and in 1591 Lord Thomas Howard, with Grenville as his vice-admiral, was sent to the Azores. For months he waited for the treasure ships, but they did not come. At last it was necessary for him to clean out the filthy ballast from his ships and take in fresh, for after months at sea the sand and shingle used as ballast became foul with the ship's refuse. When the process was only half completed, and many of his sick men were ashore, a pinnace came to tell him that a Spanish fleet of fifty-three sail was approaching. Spain was beginning to recover from the disaster of three years back, and this fleet had been sent out to convoy the treasure ships on the last part of their journey.

The men, sick and whole alike, were tumbled back into the boats and taken aboard. There was no time to finish the job of getting in ballast. Howard's small force was lying at the northern end of the island of Flores. The Spanish admiral attacked with his whole force from the east, and so quickly did its approach follow the warning that some of the ships had to slip their moorings to escape. But all did escape except Grenville, the vice-admiral, in Drake's old ship, the 'Revenge'. He was cut off and surrounded, being by virtue of his office the last to leave. If he had chosen to do so, he might have escaped westwards. But he was touched with that audacity and recklessness of which the time has so many great examples, and preferred to stay and fight. Howard's ships, six ships of the navy, six victuallers, and two or three other smaller ships, were in no condition to help, and gave him very little support. Exactly how much it is difficult from the accounts to say. About three o'clock in the afternoon, Grenville found the wind taken out of his sails by a huge ship of 1500 tons that towered above him, the 'San Felipe', a three-decker with eleven pieces of ordnance on either side of each deck. Other ships also crowded round, and as fast as one was put out of action, another came up to take her place. The first broadside from the 'Revenge', of crossbar shot, damaged the 'San Felipe' severely, but there were others to press the attack, and after a fierce exchange of gunnery, attempts were made to board. Of the 'Revenge's' normal crew, many were sick, but she beat off every attempt, and throughout the night she fought on, giving much worse than she received. Two Spanish ships were sunk beside her, one sank when she reached the island of St Michael on her way home, another was stranded and became a wreck. Next morning, with all her upper works shot away, and not a barrel of ammunition left, the 'Revenge' was still unbeaten. Grenville himself had been twice wounded. The surgeon dressing his wounds had been killed; and so the vice-admiral called on his master gunner to sink the ship. But the ship's master had reached terms with the Spanish admiral, under which the 'Revenge' surrendered honourably. Grenville was carried aboard a Spanish ship to die. It was a superb action; but Howard had failed in his object, and that year the treasure convoys got through to Spain according to plan. And Spanish technicians had worked out other means of solving the menace of blockade.

XII. THE LAST FIGHT OF THE 'REVENGE'

(From the tapestry formerly lent to the National Maritime Museum, Greenwich)

The treasure began to be carried in specially designed ships, 'gallizabras' as they were called, fast sailers, armed heavily enough to give a good account of themselves. These proved more effective than the convoy system, and in the end the blockade was able to do comparatively little harm.

So Elizabeth and her Council turned again to those great men whose names had been magic ten, fifteen, or twenty years before, to Hawkins and Drake. They should lead an expedition for her once again to the West Indies, the heart of Philip's power. Hawkins had aged prematurely. Even before the defeat of the Armada he had cried out against his job in the Navy Office, and had begged to be relieved of it. But there was no one who could do it but he, and though he had been promised a year's holiday after the Armada's defeat, it never materialised. All the time he had probably been longing to get to sea again with an independent command. He said once that he had never had the chance of doing any 'royal thing'. It was in his mind that, before he said his last good-bye to the sea, the chance might still be his. After the fiasco at Lisbon, Drake had been in disgrace at court, throwing his overpowering energy into a landsman's job in Devon, superintending the fortifications at Plymouth, and completing the arrangements for its new water supply. But he was itching to go to sea again, for the sea was his calling, and his mind went back to those days when the West Indies were a 'delicious and pleasant arbour' in which he had played. Perhaps there was still one last great game to play among those sunny islands. Since the days when Drake in the 'Judith' 'had forsaken Hawkins in his great misery' outside St Juan de Ulua, close co-operation between them had come to an end; the royal things that Drake had done, the voyage round the world, Cadiz, the Indies' voyage, had thrown into yet deeper shade the dull work of administration that Hawkins had done so well. Yet neither could be made admiral over the other's head. The command must be shared; and in that there lay the first fatal error of the plan. On paper it looked well enough. There was Hawkins to see that stomachs were properly filled and tackle was trim; and Drake, still a comparatively young man of fifty or thereabouts, only a few years older than Beatty at Jutland, to provide the dash, to sweep everything before them. And so it seemed at first to be. The word that Drake was putting to sea again spread like fire through Devon. He had but to stamp his foot and soldiers and sailors came flocking to his standard.

Yet when the decision to send them had been taken, there was the paralysing difficulty that everyone now had to face of the Council's policy. Elizabeth could not or would not see what harm its advice had already done; how it hamstrung one enterprise and then another. There was news of another Armada building in Spain, and then at last, when Drake and Hawkins were due to start, came the horrifying intelligence of a Spanish landing in Cornwall. It was a tip-and-run raid, hardly more than the putting ashore of a few men on the Flemish coast not many days after Dunkirk in 1940, to show that it could be done. But it had showed that. So they were told to make their way round the southern coast of Ireland looking for an invader, then on to the Spanish coast to look for him there; then to watch out for the treasure ships; then to guarantee their return in time to defeat the Armada next year. A military and naval expedition had been planned. Now the suggestion was that ships full of soldiers were to cruise for a month about the Azores, after goodness knows how many weeks in the Atlantic. Drake was never patient with people—only, sometimes, with his own purposes. And here at any rate Hawkins agreed. The expedition might thus have ended in an unholy outburst of discontent and anger, if news had not come of a rich ship stranded for the season in Porto Rico harbour. In her hold was a vast amount of treasure, three million ducats it was afterwards said by prisoners, with thirty tons of silver. The Council's mind was made up. The risk was worth taking, and Drake and Hawkins sailed.

At the first important council of war trouble began. Drake's foot had been stamped a little too hard. Too many men had come and he could not gainsay them. There was not food to take them across the Atlantic; so Drake pressed for a landing in the Canary Islands to secure further supplies. Then and there, four days from Plymouth, there was an open quarrel, almost a final breach. But the matter was patched up and Drake's demand was accepted. Everyone sided with Drake. Hawkins was 'old and weary' (or possibly 'wary') 'entering into matters with so leaden a foot that the others meat would be eaten before his spit could come to the fire'. Yet it is hard not to sympathise with Hawkins here. When a landing was attempted at Las Palmas, there was a heavy sea running. It failed; Spanish colonial defences had been strengthened beyond anything that Drake dreamed of. The place might have been taken, but it was decided to water elsewhere in the island. In the process a party of men was cut off and made prisoners. So soon did failure put its mark on the enterprise.

They reached the Indies, Guadaloupe. By ill luck, a squadron of the new gallizabras reached the island that same day, cut off two of the smaller English ships and captured from one of them the plans for the expedition. 'Howbeit', says one account, 'they had intelligence from the King of all our voyage the eight of August, which was three weekes before we set foorth of England: as also by a Fleming that had seene all our provision at London.' However that may be, the Spaniards crowded on sail for Porto Rico harbour, to give the alarm. Unless action was taken at once, everything was lost. But Hawkins, old and weary, would not act quickly. Pinnaces must first be set up, tackle trimmed. Apple-pie order had been what they had in the Navy Office. They should have it in Guadaloupe. This time it was Drake who had to give way, so that the enemy knew what was coming and got things ready.

In preparing the descent on Porto Rico, there is nevertheless a touch of the master hand once more. The first surprise had been lost. But surprise of a sort there could yet be. Drake knew that the channel by Neckar Island passage would be watched. He set out to find a new way through, and without charts he found it, and slipped behind the Spanish scouts. But the defences of Porto Rico were ready. A boom had been stretched across the harbour, and the narrow channel into it was guarded by the batteries on the promontory, west of the harbour mouth, on which the town was built. East of the channel were two small islands, unfortified and uninhabited, in shoal water. The isthmus joining the town with the mainland ran westwards, a sandy spit, barely a quarter of a mile wide in places. At the western or mainland end of it there were more fortifications. It was said that there were seventy guns in the defences.

As the English fleet approached, Hawkins lay dying in his cabin. He was muttering to his friend, Captain Troughton, his wishes. Let him tell the Queen of the 'perverse and cross dealings of some in that journey'. He died foretelling that the voyage would end in disaster, and such was the omen under which the fleet felt its way along the western shore towards the harbour mouth. There were pinnaces leading, instructed, when the guns fired, to show flags. They did so, and made out to sea, and the fleet stood in towards the batteries, hoping perhaps to surprise them. They were met with a destructive volley from the guns. A shot went through Drake's own cabin and two of his officers were killed as they sat there. Drake put out to sea again, along past the city, then slipped in where no commander but he would have gone, among the shoals on the eastern side of the harbour mouth.

Still that was not within the harbour, where somehow he had to penetrate. His immediate objective, however, was five treasure frigates, ready to take the precious cargo from the stranded ship. They were beached under the batteries of the point, outside the boom. For a day he waited, scouting the coast eastward. Then, after nightfall, a flotilla of twenty-five boats slipped out silently from his anchored ships. He was going to burn the frigates. The shore batteries opened fire, but in the darkness they did no harm, and fireballs were rained down from the small boats on to the frigates. Fire after fire was extinguished by the Spaniards, but still they came until one ship, the rear admiral, burnt into a blaze that lit up the water, the frigates, the shore, above all the English sailors working their destruction. Then the defences had their chance. The guns began to find their mark, then again and again and again, smashing the light craft, killing the men in them and those struggling by the ships till it was a murderous inferno of fire, a hundred and eighty-five great shot, so it was afterwards said, besides musket fire. So with their work only half done, one ship gutted and others burning, the boats were driven off, forty or fifty men being killed. It was another failure.

Drake's confidence remained until those last moments when he saw death staring into his eyes. Even then he was not daunted, but angered. A council of war was held. 'I will bring you to twenty places', said the admiral, 'far more wealthy and easier to be gotten.' He had in mind the old eldorado of the treasure road across from Panama to Nombre de Dios. Nombre de Dios was taken without difficulty. There were a bare hundred men holding it with three or four small guns. Two days later, Sir Thomas Baskerville set off along the Panama road. Five days later he was back. He had marched more than half-way across the isthmus, 'the most sore march', it was said, that Englishmen had ever taken. The forest crowded by the road, and from the trees the Spanish snipers were active. Then on the crest of the ridge there was a fort built, so strongly placed that there was no hope of taking it, for behind it, as it became known, there were other forts besides. So he could do nothing but return.

Still Drake was not beaten. He would take them to Honduras, to Tuillo. But the weather brought them to the mouth of the San Juan river and stayed them there. Making a virtue of necessity, they landed to clean the ships. The place was fever stricken. Disease spread. One man after another succumbed to it. Then Drake himself sickened, kept to his cabin; then in delirium got up and dressed himself, 'using some wild speeches'; and at four o'clock in the morning of 28 January 1596 he died.

Long before that, the spring had gone out of the year. The age was growing old. The great fighters of that generation were gone, and it was for the new men to show what they could do. That same year, and in 1597, Ralegh and Essex showed it, at Cadiz and in the Azores. At Cadiz Drake's own feat was repeated, even more brilliantly. A landing was first attempted on the spit leading out to the town, on the seaward side. But the weather was rough. It failed, and disaster seemed imminent. Ralegh pulled the chestnuts out of the fire. He planned the attack on the harbour, and with the captain of each ship striving to outdo his fellows in bravery, almost as if it were a competition in some spectacular games, victory was achieved. But, apart from the burning of ships and the plunder of the town which was afterwards also taken, exactly nothing was gained by it. 'If any man presume so farre, as to inquire how it chanced', wrote Purchas, 'that the Lord Generall rested so long at Cadiz and went no further... I will not answere him with our common English proverbe, as I might, which is, that one foole may aske moe questions in one houre than ten discreete men can well answere in five dayes.' But it is a pertinent question. The answer that Purchas goes on to give shows indeed how pertinent it is. The towns that might have been stormed were not worth it. There was no plan of campaign. The taking of Cadiz was typical of these later heroes, a sensational exploit, done for the sake of itself. And in the islands' voyage that followed next year, almost the only result was the quarrel between Ralegh and Essex as to whom the credit for the one exploit belonged.

So the war died of inanition, and it was left for Elizabeth's successor to make peace. It might seem that nothing was gained by it, not the right of entry into the West Indian trade, for which Hawkins had hoped, not the smashing of Spain's might which Drake had believed possible. Spain emerged from the war a first-class sea power, strengthened rather than weakened. And here, as so often, what the war did was to show that there is no real division between 'haves' and 'have nots', that there are magnificent opportunities and to spare for all. If England secured no footing in the treasure lands, she found greater things elsewhere. But to realise what the war did, we have to look, not at its end, but at its beginning. By the armadas England was doomed to destruction. Resistance by force alone could save her, and it was the flow of that tide of resistance which had carried her ships to the gates of Lisbon and Cadiz.

Chapter IX

THE LAST ELIZABETHAN AND THE FIRST AMERICAN

Thule, the period of Cosmographie[1]
Doth vaunt of Hecla, whose sulphurious fire
Doth melt the frozen Clime and thaw the skie—
Trinacrian Ætna's flames ascend not higher;

These things seeme wondrous, yet more wondrous I
Whose hart with feare doth freeze, with love doth fry.

The Andelusian Merchant that returnes
Laden with Cutchinele and China dishes,
Reports in Spaine how strangely Fogo burnes
Amidst an Ocean full of flying fishes;

These things seem wondrous, yet more wondrous I
Whose hart with feare doth freeze, with love doth fry.

So sang the poet, or so he wrote for others to sing, and Mr Weelkes set to music his words, with their charming references to distant oceans and distant lands, in 1600. In the years when this poem and its music were written, peaceful maritime enterprise had been largely checked by the war against Spain. Yet some peaceful victories were being won that were going to affect the course of trade almost as much as the more heroic successes of war; notable journeys, like that of Ralph Fitch which we shall here mention briefly; the founding (partly as a result) of the British East India Company; but above all the placing of maritime enterprise on the map of English thought. For the man who wrote these lines we may be sure that the talk of the town had recently been the arrival of a cargo of spices or china from the east, or the return of Davis or Frobisher from the north-west. That this was so was the achievement of Hakluyt more than anyone. By his lectures at Oxford, his books and pamphlets, and his industry and enthusiasm in making contact with the navigators and collecting their records, he had made the mind of England turn to the sea. In his early life, few men except those who occupied their business in great waters were concerned with the sea, the lands beyond it, and the chances they offered. When this madrigal appeared (and its publication coincided in date with that of the great second edition of Hakluyt's *Principal Navigations, Voyages, Traffiques and Discoveries*) Englishmen were beginning to assume that they could also do what Spaniards and Italians could do, and perhaps do it better. A year or two later *Macbeth* was acted with its allusion to the sailor's wife, whose husband sailed to Aleppo as 'Master of the Tiger'. It need not worry us that Aleppo has no more sea coast than Bohemia. Ralph Fitch and his friends took ship in 1583 'in a ship of London called the "Tyger", wherein we went for Tripolis in Syria: and from thence we tooke the way for Aleppo, which we went in seven dayes with the Caravan'. No wonder this voyage was remembered. John Newbery, one of those who took part in it, had been commissioned by Hakluyt to find a copy of 'the book of cosmographie of Abilfada Ismael', an Arab geographer, and wrote from Aleppo to say that there was no copy in Aleppo to be had, but that he would look for it in Babylon and Basra. At Ormuz the travellers were imprisoned by the Portuguese, then sent on by the authorities to Goa in India, where one of the company went into a monastery, 'which life he liketh very well'; and the rest, thanks to the intervention of English and Flemish padres, were released. One was a jeweller and remained in India, with a house, five slaves, a horse and a very good income. John Newbery belongs to the number of those pioneers who never returned. But Fitch got back to London eight years after he had started out and lived to see the British East India Company founded, and to advise its promoters. And whoever wrote the *Macbeth* lines, Shakespeare, or Middleton or some other, wrote them when that journey was a topical theme. It is about this same time that the Indian boy creeps in, by the back door as it were, into *A Midsummer Night's Dream*:

> His mother was a votaress of my order
> And in the spiced Indian air by night
> Full often hath she gossiped by my side
> And sat with me on Neptune's yellow sands
> Marking the embarked traders on the flood.

We need not enquire too closely whether this young squire was from the West Indies, whence what some of the Elizabethans called 'salvages' had been brought back for their edification, or from the East, whence Ralph Fitch had come. For the point is simply that talk about these things was in the air. So was gossip about another voyage when *As You Like It* was written, and there was put into Jaques' mouth that vivid metaphor about a brain 'as dry as the remainder biscuit after a voyage'. From other allusions in the play, it seems to have been talk of a South Seas voyage that was then on Shakespeare's mind. So too when the news of the adventures that had been encountered by the 'Third Supply' to Virginia in 1609 arrived in London, with the story of Sir George Somers' shipwreck on the coast of the Bermudas in the 'Sea Adventure', several of the printed accounts came into Shakespeare's hands and suggested ideas that he used in *The Tempest*. The same play has reminiscences of Ralegh's writings about Guiana. In Shakespeare's early manhood England had been reading the chronicles of its own historic past. Now England's eyes were searching beyond the oceans.

In this search there are two phases which it remains for us to tell. Both are connected with the imperialist Ralegh's name. In the expeditions to Guiana—'the large rich and bewtiful empyre of Guiana' as he called it—he played a leading part. The expeditions which finally consolidated the English settlements in Virginia were not directly sponsored by him, but it was he who had planned and provided for the original settlement, the records of which had shown some of the country's possibilities and problems—especially those of supply and native hostility.

Last of the Elizabethans, as he has so often been called, his personality is as puzzling as any of that intensely living and intensely individual group of men. We know too much about him. We can still read the letters he wrote when he was intriguing to secure pardon for a traitor who was bribing him for his help; and there are not many men whose correspondence and thoughts could thus be laid naked without our shuddering at some of them. One critic has applied to him words originally written about his friend Marlowe's *Faustus*:

> Alternating moods continue with increasing violence up to the last scene; a macabre and sombre series of contradictory passions; triumph, mirth, terror, repentance, despair and recklessness, until Faustus is beyond repentance, beyond salvation, and looks back on his last delusion with clear eyes.

The secret of Ralegh, which Elizabeth knew, was that he was an artist, with the temperament of an artist. So she would never accept him as what he wanted to be, a statesman. Yet he was a statesman and a planner as well as a poet. He never ceased to feel the sting of ambition, ambition for power for himself and equally for his country. The moods which were briefest were the moods of disillusion with material power, or contentment with spiritual things, which he sometimes expressed in his splendidly moving prose:

> Neither have those beloved companions of honor and riches any power at all, to hold us any one day, by the glorious promise of entertainments; but what crooked paths so ever we walk, the same leadeth on directly to the house of death; whose doors lye open at all houres, and to all persons. For this tyde of man's life, after it once turneth and declineth, ever runneth with a perpetuall Ebbe and falling Streame, but never floweth againe; our Leafe once fallen, springeth no more, neither doth the Sunne or the Summer adorne us againe, with the garments of new Leaves and Flowers.

So he wrote during his imprisonment in the Tower. And what is probably the best known of his poems, where he asks for his 'scallop shell of quiet', suggests in its opening stanzas a mood of acceptance and resignation, which was, nevertheless, itself the most transitory of all the things in his life.

There are characteristics that remain unchanged with him besides his tireless energy and his clarity of thought. They are his constancy in championing unpopular causes, in championing men who were his friends but were attacked by the heresy hunters with which the age abounded; his courage in condemning publicly measures he believed to be wrong; his love for his wife, which had first brought on him Elizabeth's displeasure, and for which Elizabeth never wholly forgave him; and some quality about him which made the ordinary man who served him or served with him hold for him an extraordinary devotion. And there was one constant thing about his ambitions too, which remained till his death. It was his striving for, and his faith in, an English empire beyond the seas. His half-brother, Sir Humphrey Gilbert, had believed in an English colony in North America, as a fishing station, and port of call on the way to the Far East. Ralegh's ideas were different in conception as well as in scale. He believed not only in a settlement in Virginia or in South America for its own sake, but in a great English empire that would stifle the empire of Spain and ensure a splendid future for his countrymen. And however much he may from time to time have been entranced with the legend of El Dorado, the 'gilded man', and of that city with the wealth of the Incas somewhere in the unexplored wastes of the Amazon or the Orinoco basins, the real power behind his efforts was this imperial idea. He refused to accept failure in Virginia. The hopes of gold in South America may have tempted him, but he used them rather to tempt Elizabeth and James, so that he might have the chance of undertaking the far greater enterprise he had in mind. He spent much of his energy on amassing money. But he used his fortune without stint to help his friends and to further his imperial projects.

Ralegh's plans for empire were grounded in the belief that Spanish power was already undermined by native hostility. From the first sketches of the Virginia scheme till the plans for the last voyage to Guiana there was always that central assumption. Drake had shown that it was justified, and that a determined attack on the isthmus cities with the support of the Maroons was as dangerous a menace as the Spaniards ever had to face.

> The offers to be made to the Guianians [wrote Ralegh] and performed on our partes may be these: 1. First, that we will defend them, their wives children and countryes against the Spaniards and all other intruders. 2. That we will helpe them to recover their country of Peru. 3. That we will instruct them in liberall arts of civility behooffull for them that thei may be comparable to any christian people. 4. And lastly that we will teach them the use of weapons, how to pitch theyr battells, how to make armor, and ordnance, and how to manage horses for service in the warrs.

The third clause is a remarkable statement for its period. And it was not only theory. Ralegh associated with native chiefs in Guiana, liked them and was evidently worshipped by them. He had found the Achilles' heel of the Spanish empire. One thing only made his plan impossible, that James and his ministers were veering between a policy of opposition to Spain and of co-operation with Spain. Ralegh had to bait the plan with gold for them. And the bait failed him.

Still, he might well reckon it a powerful motive. It had driven imperiously both Spanish and German adventurers already on frightful journeys through the depths of that dark continent. This legend of Eldorado in its first form was of an escaped remnant of the Inca power that had fled from the Spaniards, carrying the knowledge and skill of Peru somewhere eastwards towards the lands from which, it was supposed, the Incas had obtained part of their riches. In quest of this lost remnant, expeditions had been led eastwards from Bogota and down the Orinoco river, eastwards from Peru across the high passes of the Andes to the Amazon. But the objects of their search always eluded them; tantalisingly near, for the Indians whom they captured came to know that unless they gave them stories of this mysterious kingdom, their fate was sealed, and they played up to this necessity. There were trinkets enough, some of them of fine workmanship—probably from Peru itself—scattered among the tribes, to give colour to these reports. And the story gained currency, which Ralegh records in his *Discoverie of Guiana*, of men with

> ...their bodies annoynted al over with a kinde of white Balsamum (by them called Curcai) of which there is great plenty and yet very deare amongst them, and it is of all other the most pretious, wherof we have had good experience; when they are annointed all over, certaine servants of the emperor having prepared gold into fine powder blow it thorow hollow canes upon their naked bodies, untill they be al shining from the foote to the head....

It seems that this story originated in an actual ritual practised in one of the Andean regions, in the period before the Spaniards reached Peru. The story had lately gained a new currency through the report of a Spaniard who had 'gone native', returned many years after to the cities of his countrymen, and invented for their edification tales of what he had seen and heard. It chanced that one of Ralegh's privateer ships in 1594 captured letters which spoke of 'a land newly discovered called Nuevo Dorado...they write of wonderfull riches to be found in the said Dorado and the Golde there is in great abundance'. There was also in his hands a document intended for the King of Spain which specified where the region of Nuevo Dorado was situated. As these stories had fired the imagination of the Spaniard Berrio, who had been appointed Governor in that region to follow up the discovery, so Ralegh, out of favour with the court, kicking his heels and bursting with ambition (as all Elizabethans always were) to do 'some royal thing', was fired by them. With him was associated a young Oxford scholar, a Fellow of Balliol named Keymis, who was to devote himself body and soul to the prosecution of Ralegh's designs in Guiana. As Ralegh pieced together the various details that he learnt, he imagined a great inland sea situated south of the mountains of Guiana, between the Orinoco and the Amazon.

The reports of this lake, which was shown on maps of Brazil into the nineteenth century, originated apparently in vast floods that at certain seasons may appear along some of the rivers in that region. Ralegh compares it in size with the Caspian. At the eastern end of this island sea, called the lake of Manoa, or Parima, was situated the city of Manoa. This was Ralegh's goal. His ideas can be pictured with precision because Hariot, who had drawn a map of Virginia for him, drew maps of Guiana, based on Ralegh's sketches, for Ralegh himself and his friends. One such manuscript map, showing some of Keymis' discoveries in 1596, is in the British Museum. Another was in the Percy Library and was no doubt given to Henry Percy by Ralegh.

These ideas had helped to crystallise the plan of a great empire in Guiana. We shall misapprehend Ralegh's achievement if we regard him as an explorer, or as a mere adventurer in search of gold. Keymis did some useful work charting the coast of Guiana, but the route that Ralegh traversed was well known to Spaniards. Ralegh's interest in it was that of an imperialist, not of a gold seeker. The ground for the first voyage had been carefully prepared. In 1594 he had sent Captain Whiddon to Trinidad (which had been occupied by Berrio as the most convenient base for his operations in Guiana) on a voyage of reconnaissance. Eight of Whiddon's men were killed by Berrio. But he had obtained some information, and Ralegh had also learned something from another of his captains, Captain Parker. Ralegh's expedition left England early in 1595, and besides his own ship it included the 'Lion's Whelp' (Captain Gifford, owned by Lord Charles Howard) and another ship commanded by Keymis. Making for the West Indies by the usual route, they reached Trinidad six weeks later. There Ralegh waited for a few days, scouting off the island in the small boat, mapping the coast and the outlets of the rivers, and sampling the mangrove oysters that fasten on the roots of the trees by the shore, and are left uncovered by the tide. Then contact with the Spaniards was made, and although Spain and England were enemies, Spanish actions showed that they did not wish to meet Ralegh with violence, but to trade peaceably with him. But one evening two natives, one a Cacique or chief, stole on board and told Ralegh what was the strength of the Spanish forces. Ralegh saw the folly of leaving an enemy at his back while travelling up the Orinoco. He heard too that Berrio had sent for reinforcements. So a few days later he set upon the Spanish guards and massacred them, and went on to capture almost without a blow the city of St Joseph and Berrio himself.

He treated him well. The two men had conversations about Guiana, during which Berrio fenced dexterously to avoid giving away too much, and if possible to dissuade Ralegh from the enterprise. Berrio told him that Guiana was six hundred miles up the Orinoco, and Ralegh claims to have travelled four hundred miles towards it. Actually the highest point he reached is not more than 250 miles allowing for the windings of the river from the coast. The narrative he has left is a full one, and many of its incidents give a clear impression of the character of the undertaking. At one stage they had to turn off the main river in a small boat to find a village where supplies could be replenished. Night fell, the river narrowed, with tropical trees overhanging on either side so that they had to cut a way through with swords. But after midnight they found the village and secured fresh stores; and when they began the journey up the main stream once more, the country opened out into fine grassland, with deer feeding by the water. Still, for all the attractiveness of the country their goal seemed to get no nearer. The river was beginning to flood; and at last Ralegh, who was impatient and was also intolerant of the discomforts of the journey, decided to turn back. The only tangible result was a few specimens of minerals. Ralegh remained convinced of the great wealth of Guiana, and of its magnificent possibilities for development. But his report of it, though widely read, did not impress the authorities. He was back in England seven months after he had left, and his critics (so he tells us) accused him of having got no further than Cornwall and having invented the rest. Actually his observations are vivid and the best of his descriptions magnificent. He has embodied in his book legends and travellers' tales, but the truth of South America was so strange that it is hardly surprising if one who lived in the age of the conquistadors failed to distinguish legend from reality. And his purpose was a lofty one, to be realised (though not in Ralegh's way) in the fullness of time.

The next few years were crowded with distractions for him, for they saw, first the climax of the rivalry between him and Essex, and then Ralegh left almost alone to hold the stage during the last phase of the ageing Queen's great reign, when, in his words, she was 'surprised by Time'. Almost any month might have brought a crisis. Men in high places were already intriguing with her successor, and it is not to be wondered at that Ralegh did not follow up his belief in Guiana with another expedition. And not long after James' accession all hope of doing so was suddenly snuffed out. Ralegh was arrested on a charge of treason. The evidence was as flimsy as it could have been, and he was condemned for treason by men who were already in the pay of Spain. His fault was that he had not hastened from his audiences with Elizabeth during those last declining years to worship the sun that had not yet risen. And so he went to the Tower, to eat out his heart there, year after year, and to add another to that illustrious number of Englishmen who while they were in prison wrote great books—Malory, Bunyan and the rest. 'None ever employed Enlargement worse', so it was said, 'that knew so well how to advantage himself and his country in Imprisonment.'

The *History of the World* which he then wrote is a superb work, and was one of the formative influences among the Parliamentarians of the next period. But his mind was still turning to the imperial theme, to Virginia and Guiana. For a time he had the ear of the young prince Henry, and at one time it looked as if the patronage of Henry and of the Queen was going to be enough to secure him the opportunity for another voyage to Guiana. Then Henry died; and his death, disastrous in so many ways, ended Ralegh's hopes of release. Yet at last, when he was too old to profit by it, the chance came. James was desperately in need of money. Ralegh claimed to have brought back from Guiana specimens which an assayer had said were auriferous. Perhaps, thought King James, he was right. Perhaps there was after all untold wealth waiting to be picked up in Guiana. James was carrying out delicate negotiations with Spain. He seems to have thought that if Ralegh succeeded this would in itself be a solution for the financial problem, but if he failed his fate might be used as a piece in the negotiations that were taking place. It meant playing a double game, which James played with a vengeance. He seems on the one hand to have suggested to Ralegh that, though he must not commit any overt act of violence against the Spaniards in the West Indies, it might be possible to arrange for a French force to do it for him; and on the other hand, it is certain that he supplied to the Spanish ambassador details of the force which Ralegh was taking and of its objective, a force that was almost bound to meet with Spanish resistance if surprise did not succeed. It was afterwards alleged that Ralegh's note relating the particulars of his force, in his own hand, was found by his men when San Thomé was taken. This may not be true, but it is beyond question that James had given the details to the Spanish ambassador—as he had given many other things, like that splendid medieval gold cup from the royal treasure of the kings of England, which was to find its way back at last into this country's keeping.[2]

The story of this last expedition gives the impression that Ralegh's leadership had lost its power, and lacked the dash to which even his enemies had paid tribute. Nor does it seem that there was ever any clear-cut plan in Ralegh's mind for the operations when Guiana was reached, though possibly it is because secrecy on some points had to be maintained to save the King's credit that no sufficient plan comes out in the documents as we have them now. Recent investigation has shown that Ralegh thought he knew of two mines in Guiana, some miles apart, one close to the settlement of San Thomé, a hundred and fifty miles up the Orinoco river, where the Caroni flows into it, the other further downstream, so that its approaches were not covered by that settlement. Drake when faced with an analogous problem had entered Nombre de Dios the year before his attack on it and had reconnoitred the coast time after time. Ralegh's knowledge of these mines was based on little more than hearsay. His plan seems to have been to make for the nearer of the two mines (a plan which there was a chance might not involve a clash with Spanish forces), and to secure from it enough ore at least to give proof of its quality. It was indeed possible that in doing this he might be attacked, and he proposed to land troops to form a screen for the operations. They were not to take the offensive. After his return his enemies and in particular Gondomar alleged that Ralegh had wantonly sacked cities in the Canary Islands and taken the offensive in Guiana, massacring innocent Spaniards. But this was diplomatic technique. 'Exaggerate as much as you can Ralegh's guilt' were the instructions given to Gondomar by his sovereign. Pressure must be brought to bear on King James of England, and when Gondomar interviewed King James a few days after the first news of San Thomé reached London, he simply repeated melodramatically a single word, 'Piratas, piratas, piratas'. James was not one to stand up to pressure, but he knew that such allegations were fantastic. Ralegh had in fact been scrupulously careful to avoid unnecessary conflict with the Spaniards. Twenty years before, the experience of the last West Indies' expedition had shown that Spain was not to be trifled with in the Indies. Ralegh's strict orders had been given that the offensive must not be taken; and when he learnt of the failure of Keymis to obey, he saw disaster staring him in the face.

The King must also have been aware of the existence of the Spanish settlement at San Thomé in Guiana, though it cannot now be said whether the matter had been tacitly ignored in his conversations with Ralegh before the start of the expedition, or whether some arrangement had been reached which could not afterwards be published. Ralegh contended after his return that this settlement did not constitute Spanish possession of the country. It was a single village in a vast wilderness of river and mountain and plain and forest, the sovereignty over which had been transferred years before by the natives to Elizabeth through Ralegh himself. To work a mine, therefore, if it could be done without disturbing the Spaniards, would be a crime against nobody; and if the Spaniards attacked, well then they must be fought off in self-defence. Such at any rate is the argument as it emerges at his trial. Ralegh is inconsistent, his quick mind darting now this way, now that way, in the effort to escape. But that is not surprising. For the one thing he could not say was the whole truth, the truth of the King's treachery. It is that which makes the trap so sure and so baffling for him. He was trying always to find what he could say without laying bare the truth—which would explain all, and yet inevitably prove his own irrevocable undoing.

On 19 March 1616 Ralegh was released from the Tower, after paying £750 each to the brother and half-brother of King James' favourite for the time being; released 'to make provision for your intended voyage'. He had been in the Tower twelve years, and was probably now sixty-two years old. He and Lady Ralegh somehow raised the thousands of pounds which the expedition cost, and a fine ship, the 'Destiny', was built specially for it. Her very name suggests how well her admiral knew that he was stretching the strands of his own fate. We cannot enter into the story of the intrigues which preceded the voyage. Those with the King have been sketched already. They were based on the fiction that an armed expedition could penetrate regions where Spaniards were settled without them taking action, and on the King's side it was a question simply whether Ralegh would make enough for it to be worth while to back him. He sailed with six ships, the 'Destiny' of 440 tons, five others ranging from 240 to 80 tons, and a 25-ton pinnace with eight men in her. As he started, an indiscretion put papers and a map into hands from which they were to pass ultimately to Madrid, and King James is not wholly responsible for Ralegh's disaster. *Quem Deus vult perdere prius dementat.* Ralegh had never ruled his tongue. Now once again in his new freedom he was talking too freely. And yet it was not true freedom. He had not been pardoned, only released as it were on parole, released to get gold for King James or to die for Gondomar. He left the Thames just a year after he had left the Tower. His captains have been described not unjustly as a 'scratch lot', and indeed the leader who had shouted that famous word of triumph at Cadiz never came out of the Tower. It was an unstable shadow. Ralegh's son, Wat, sailed with him, and Keymis, whose life was bound up with Guiana even more than Ralegh's own. They left England finally on 19 August. Ten days later Ralegh started a journal. There are twenty-three sheets of it written in a tiny hand, and it ends suddenly on 13 February 1618. On that day must have come the news which showed Ralegh that his fate was sealed.

At Gomera in the Canary Islands, which were Spanish territory, they stopped to water. There was, as so often, sickness raging aboard the English ships, but they were allowed to take in water unmolested, and the Governor's wife sent Ralegh a present of fresh fruit which may have saved his life, for he also was desperately ill. Between a fifth and a quarter of the men in the 'Destiny' died on this outward passage. Ralegh, writing to his wife, when Cayenne was reached, talks about the 'hell fire of heat'. It is not surprising that there was already defeatist talk, but that too is a sign that the touch of the leader was no longer sure. Ralegh himself could not, by reason of his sickness, go up the river to look for the mine. He was to wait off Trinidad while Keymis, George Ralegh (a nephew) and his son Wat made the journey. They were to bring back ore, even if only a basket or two, to satisfy the King that here was something more than mere imagination. When it had been obtained they might get a cargo of tobacco from San Thomé.

The party sailed on 10 December up that great river with a month's provisions, while Ralegh waited. The weeks went by. Then from Indians he heard a report that there had been a fight and that two English captains had fallen. Ralegh was in an agony of anxiety and suspense. But Keymis put off writing to him day after day, for he could not bring himself to tell his master what had happened. At last the news came. In the fight with the Spaniards, which the

Spaniards were said to have begun, San Thomé had been taken, but Wat Ralegh had been killed. No mine had been found, and Keymis was returning.

Keymis, it seems, had not carried out Ralegh's orders, in that he had never attempted to find the mine that lay away from San Thomé. As he approached its supposed site, he may have realised how fantastic was the attempt to find it without more precise information; and may have felt that the neighbourhood of San Thomé was the most likely place to hear something. But that meant the risk—almost amounting to a certainty—of a clash, unless, as there was some slight reason to hope, traitors in San Thomé handed it over. He took the risk and landed. In the darkness, soon after midnight, a Spanish patrol attacked. They were driven in to the gates of the city. There was another force waiting there and for a moment the English wavered. But Wat Ralegh dashed forward and the rest followed him. By morning the settlement was taken. Ten men, five English and five Spaniards, were killed. The two English captains who had been killed were buried in the cathedral church. Some of the Englishmen waited at San Thomé while George Ralegh went on up the river on a prospecting voyage. But nothing could come of it, and the only thing to do was to go back, for they were harried constantly by Spanish snipers from the woods and lost heavily.

When Keymis returned Ralegh at first seems to have received him kindly, then to have realised that Keymis had disobeyed his orders. In spite of his sanguine temperament, which even after this at times let him feel that all would somehow be well, at that moment the blackness of despair seems to have come down on him. He cursed Keymis for the death of his son and for his own undoing; and then Keymis, who was devoted to him, said he would wait on him presently and give him better satisfaction. A few moments later Ralegh heard a pistol fired. He went out to find what had happened. Keymis was lying on his bed, but said he had discharged the pistol because it had been so long loaded. A few moments later he was dead. A knife had completed the work that the bullet, breaking a rib and so deflected, had failed to do.

We need not follow the sordid story of the return, the efforts to escape—those strange alternations of twisting and of courage—their betrayal (the work of the Government's spies), and the trial at which Ralegh was accused of the offence for which, by James' proclamation, he had already been condemned; of the 'scandalous and enormous outrages' with which he had 'broken the peace'. The King, though it seems almost incredible, had actually given an undertaking in writing, before the trial began, that Ralegh and some of his associates on the voyage should be sent to Spain to be hanged there. But he was frustrated. For on the evidence conviction was impossible. There was only one thing that could be done. Ralegh could be put to death on the count of treason, fifteen years old, on which he had been once reprieved, and the imperial idea thus be scotched.

On 29 October 1618, sentence was carried out. The night before, as Ralegh sat and smoked, the lines of a love poem he had written many years before kept repeating themselves in his head:

Oh cruel Time, who takes in trust
Our youth, our joys, and all we have,
And pays us but with earth and dust:
 Who in the dark and silent grave
When we have wandered all our ways
Shuts up the story of our days....

He wrote them down again as he sat thinking; but a new serenity came over them. Time after all was not cruel. Now he could survey his life, he could see that the weariest river was winding at last, safely, to sea. And so he began afresh:

Even such is time, who takes in trust
Our youth....

And there was something more to it too, now that all the changes and chances were almost over. Two new lines should close it:

But from that earth, that grave, that dust
The Lord shall raise me up, I trust.

Nearly a hundred years before, a greater figure than Ralegh had waited in the Tower till he suffered death at the decree of a ruthless sovereign. In Thomas More's mind also there had run, in those last few days, verses about Fortune that he had written many years before. He too had added an epilogue to them 'with a coal, for ink then had he none':

Trust shall I God, to enter in a while
His haven of heaven....

Ralegh also was dying in a great cause. And however uncertain his steps had been before, in these last hours they did not falter.

Everyone next day noticed the serenity of his manner and the evident lightness of his heart. But after it was all over, after that unforgettable scene on the scaffold was done, there was one at least whose heart was not light. Lady Ralegh wrote that day a letter, often quoted, to Sir Nicholas Carew:

> I desiar, good brother, that you will be plessed to let me berri the worthi boddi of my nobell hosban, Sur Walter Ralegh, in your chorche at Beddington, wher I desiar to be berred. The Lordes have geven me his ded boddi, though they denied me his life. This nit hee shall be brought you with two or three of my men. Let me here presently. God hold me in my wites.

* * *

It would be difficult to find a personality that contrasted more strongly with Ralegh's than that of the man who was responsible for the realisation of his hopes in Virginia. 'Brass without, but gold within', says the writer of the lines on an almost contemporary engraved portrait of Captain John Smith, admiral of New England; and the description fits well that sturdy enterprise he showed. Some who have written about him are incredulous of much of the detail of his life. But his solid achievements are great enough, even if there were not, in almost every instance when other information besides his own writings is available, confirmation of his strangest adventures. To have produced his American maps would be in itself a sure title to fame.[3] Geography was indeed a passionate interest with him and in one of the critical moments of his life he found this interest of practical use. This was when he fell unarmed into the hands of an Indian chief, but gave him a 'round Ivory double-compassed diall' which he had with him:

> They much marvelled at the playing of the flye, which they could see, and not touch, by reason of the Glasse cover; but when he had read a Cosmographicall lecture to them of the Skies, Earth, Day and night, with the varietie of Nations, and such like, they were all amazed; notwithstanding which sudden wonder, they tide him to a tree within an houre after, and as many as could stand about him prepared their fatall Arrowes to his death, which were all laid downe when Opechankanough held up the said diall; and they led him in a kinde of triumph to Oropaxe.

It is typical of the adventures which Captain John Smith went on having. And the extraordinary thing is that there should so often be independent witness that these adventures actually took place.

There is, then, to his credit his achievement as a cartographer.

There is his achievement as a pioneer—for whether individual details are true or not, it is established beyond question that his leadership brought the colony through its difficulties to some degree of prosperity, which was immediately lost when he left it. There is his appreciation of the direction in which a real future for the colony lay. Many men still believed that only two things could save the colony, the discovery that Chesapeake Bay was the opening of a north-west passage to the Pacific, and the finding of a gold mine. Captain John Smith had no use for this view, but strove to make the colony a place in which men could live, not simply a step in the ascent from poverty to riches. There is to his credit also his skilled handling of the Indians; and even if his accounts of this represented simply what he thought ought to have happened, they would show real shrewdness. For him the savage was a child. A mixture of firmness and kindness was therefore needed. There is no trace of the desire to exploit Indians, as the native populations in the Spanish empire had been exploited. But there is the determination to show that the settlers could not be attacked with impunity, coupled with the resolve that punishment must not be sterner than necessary. Lastly, there is to his credit his work after his return home as a propagandist for American settlement. On any one of these achievements his fame might rest assured. And though his writings about himself are considerable, their tone is not boastful, and they are marked by touches of humour. Thus when he speaks of the quarrels on the outward voyage: 'Such factions here we had', he says, 'as commonly attend such voyages, that a pair of gallows was made: but Captain Smith for whom they were intended could not be persuaded to use them.' The strength of his purpose was always overriding. Already at that early stage he did what he wanted to do, in spite of Captain Newport, Bartholomew Gosnoll, Edward Wingfield, John Ratcliffe, John Martin, George Kendall and the rest of them. He was one of those people who prove to have been right, and thus he made enemies. But he made friends too. And wherever he went he could not help romantic things happening to him, till that moment when the bag of powder blew up and tore the flesh from his side, and he leaped into the sea to put out the flames on his clothes. After that, providence let him off romance for a time, though even yet for a few magic months she was to find her old form and provide him with some well authenticated adventures with pirates.

The lost colonists of 1587 were very much on Ralegh's mind in the years immediately following the second planting. But the efforts he had made to discover their whereabouts failed, and Ralegh's pre-occupations, first with the Spanish war, then with his own position in England, gradually banished the hope of tracing them. But the public had not forgotten them, and as the idea of a fresh attempt at colonisation gained a hearing (an idea for which a seaman named Bartholomew Gosnoll was mainly responsible) one of the parts cast for the proposed expedition was the finding of those men and women who nearly a generation before had left England for Virginia. Gold and the prospect of a new route to the Indies were also certainly important, and it is doubtful whether there were many who foresaw (as Smith certainly did) other possibilities for the venture. King James I, to whom Ralegh's rights had lapsed, issued Letters Patent authorising the formation of a board in London to govern the colony, and the appointment by it of a council to direct affairs on the spot. This council was to elect its own governor, and until the place chosen for planting had been found the names of the governors remained secret, even from themselves. Among the promoters were Sir Thomas Gates and Sir George Somers, afterwards to play an important part in its history; Hakluyt, who drafted instructions for the procedure to be followed on arrival; and a godson of Mary Tudor, Edward Maria Wingfield, who, unlike the three promoters already mentioned, sailed with the first expedition. The Letters Patent provided for two separate settlements, a southern and a northern, the latter to be allotted to a company of adventurers from the western cities, the former to London adventurers. The three ships were the 'Susan Constant', with seventy-one men aboard, the 'Godspeed' with fifty-two, and the 'Discovery', commanded by Captain Gosnoll himself, with twenty-one.

They had been directed by Hakluyt's instructions to look for some large inlet running westwards into the coast, which might be the mouth of a passage to the Pacific. A storm drove them to the mouth of Chesapeake Bay, and the opening reaches of what is now known as Hampton Roads seemed to stretch roughly in the direction that Hakluyt had required. It was determined, therefore, on 13 May 1607, that they should land, establish a fort (afterwards named Jamestown in honour of the King) and carry out the rest of the instructions drawn up in London. The box containing the names of the councillors was opened. Smith was found to be one. But owing to the incident of the gallows he was declared unsuitable, and sent off with a party under Captain Kendall and Captain Newport, to discover the upper reaches of the river. Six days' travel brought them to a point beyond which it was no longer navigable. While this expedition was in progress no precautions had been taken at the fort. An attack by Indians was made, and seventeen men were wounded, one lad being killed. This incident broke rudely in on the idyllic dream of that Virginian spring; and this, or the general situation, led to a demand that Smith should be allowed to take his place as a member of the council.

After a month Captain Newport returned to England, and his departure was followed in the settlement by a devastating outbreak of disease. While the ships were still there, there had been supplies of ordinary food available. With the cessation of these supplies, disease and death followed, and in the five months from May to September, fifty men were buried. Wingfield, who had been elected President, was deposed. Gosnoll was dead, and in Wingfield's place Ratcliffe was appointed Governor. It is not difficult to guess what had happened to Ralegh's colonists. This colony too would have disappeared if the Indians had not unaccountably begun to bring in supplies.

By the end of the summer Smith was playing an ever larger part in the colony's affairs. He saw the need for work, to build houses and to cultivate land, and he was one of those who did not mind how much trouble he took, and was eager to show by his example how work should be done. As supplies from the Indians began to fail again, he went down to Kecoughtan (near what is now Hampton) to bargain for more. After a show of violence, more were secured, and for some weeks the replenishing of supplies was his chief preoccupation. When he returned from one of these expeditions, ominous news met him. Some of the planters were intending to ship away back to England in the pinnace, and it was only by training the guns of the fort on her that he forced them to give up the plan. In the late autumn there was again plenty of food with the arrival of the waterfowl, and Smith was again sent off to discover the headwaters of the river to the west. In the course of this journey the most famous of his adventures happened.

Owing to the narrowness of the stream, he had moored his boat, and went on in a canoe, with two other Englishmen and two Indians. That afternoon as they rested, they were surprised at their campfire by two hundred Indians. Two of the Englishmen were killed outright. But Smith gave a good account of himself, killing three men, and was able to escape. In his haste to get back to his boat, he slipped into the mud of a small creek up to his waist. It was bitterly cold, with frost and snow, and he realised at once that there was nothing to do but surrender. His captors dragged him out of the mud, and it was then that the 'Cosmographicall lecture' was delivered that for the moment (helped out by the ivory compass) saved his life.

Thereupon he was conducted to a nearby village. It was a strange procession, led by men carrying the captured arms, and then 'three great lubbers' who conducted Smith himself. He had a guard of warriors, painted red over the heads and shoulders, with skins hanging as shields over their arms, and the dried skin of a bird with the wings spread as headdress. After a war dance in honour of the capture, he was led to a long hut, and brought food, enough for twenty men. Smith was suspicious. Cannibalism was practised in some of the islands, and he had an uneasy feeling that he was going to be fattened for the pot.

He was now given to understand that an assault on Jamestown was intended, and planned a characteristic device to impress his captors. Telling them that he wished to secure certain things from Jamestown, he wrote a note to this effect to his friends inside the town, sending it by Indian messengers. They dared not go in, but left the message in a conspicuous place. Returning a little later, they found what he had wished, and having no knowledge of the process of writing, were not a little impressed. Still, like the lecture, this was not in itself enough to save him, and after he had been led in a sort of triumphal progress through the territory of the neighbouring tribes, he was finally brought into the presence of the paramount chief, Powhatan. Powhatan was sitting on a seat like a bedstead, covered with furs, and at either hand sat a young girl. Along each side of the long hut was a row of men, and behind them rows of women, all gaily painted and decorated with feathers, down and beads. As he was led in there was a great shout, and a chieftain's wife brought him water to wash his hands, another a bunch of feathers to dry them. Then he was feasted; and then he noticed that there was a long consultation being held. At last two huge stones were brought and placed before Powhatan. Smith was seized by many hands and forced down on to them, while some lifted their clubs to beat out his brains.

So might have ended Captain John Smith, and with him the settlement in Virginia. But he was conscious that there was a hitch in the arrangements. Someone, a child, was talking rapidly; and suddenly she leaped forward and bent over him to save him. It was Pocahontas, Powhatan's favourite daughter. Like the princess in the fairy tale she begged off his life, and two days later a strange ceremony was held in the woods, which Smith took to indicate his adoption by Powhatan as his son. His first filial duty was to return to the fort with instructions to secure for Powhatan a present of two big guns—demi-culverin—and a grindstone. Once back at Jamestown with the Indians sent with him to bring back these presents, Smith satisfied them, and more than satisfied them, by firing the cannon into the woods. The stones with which they had been charged shattered the branches of a tree loaded with icicles, and the clatter and the roar were enough to discourage any further enthusiasm for cannon. But they took back instead trinkets and toys for Powhatan and his family, and something (we may hope) specially nice for Pocahontas. Less than ten years after this escape, a ceremony hardly less strange took place, when Pocahontas was introduced by her husband John Rolfe to the English court. Smith had written to the Queen of England asking her to show favour to this Indian princess who 'next under God was the instrument to preserve this colony from death, famine, and utter confusion'; and for a few brilliant months Pocahontas was the cynosure of King James' court. But the strange stiff clothes and the mists of London were too much for her, and she died of consumption at Tilbury, before she set sail back to that distant homeland.

After Smith's return to Jamestown, things went well for a time, for supplies of food were now readily brought in by the Indians as gifts. And it was at this time that the 'first supply' arrived. Two ships had been sent, but one of them was caught by a storm and driven far out of her course; and Captain Newport, in the other, arrived alone. Captain Newport was unaware how his stock had risen with Powhatan in his absence. Smith had been lecturing the Indians again. 'So he had inchanted those poore soules (being their Prisoner) in demonstrating unto them the roundnesse of the Worlde, the course of the Moone and Starres, the cause of the day and night, the largenesse of the Seas, the quality of our ships, shot and powder; the division of the World, with the diversitie of people, their complexions, customes and conditions. All which he fained to be under the command of Captaine Newport, whom he termed to them his

Father.' When Captain Newport realised his own importance, he began to offer exchanges of goods with Powhatan with a magnanimous generosity appropriate to his position that appalled Smith. Newport was seeking to please the insatiable savage, Smith to cause the savage to please him. And amid all these functions the 'first supply' outstayed its welcome. The sailors ate the food intended for the colonists, and it was three months before Newport left. He insisted on taking with him a cargo of 'certain yellow sand'. Gilded dirt, Smith called it, and it was in fact worthless. Shortly after Newport had left, his lost consort, the 'Phoenix', arrived. She had been driven to the West Indies and had refitted, and her captain had husbanded his stores so that he left with the colony provision for half a year.

At this point, trouble with the Indians, which Smith attributes to the too meticulous observance of instructions from London not to offend them, broke out again. Smith's policy, which he proceeded to put into operation, was a mild dose of terrorism, consisting of whipping and imprisonment. But he released his prisoners at Pocahontas' request. No Indian was killed; and with the air thus (as he claimed) cleared, the 'Phoenix' was loaded with cedar for her return voyage. Smith was able in the following months to explore the northern end of Chesapeake Bay, and to discover what he thought to be a mine of antimony. This exploration was virtually the only achievement of the colony in 1608, though a harvest was at last reaped; and in the autumn Smith was appointed, at last, President of the community of which he had been throughout the leading spirit.

A new supply was expected, and preparations were made for the reception, including the accommodation of more colonists. The supply arrived. But its accompaniments proved how little the adventurers in London understood what was going on. They had had two big ideas. One was to provide a barge in five pieces, which was to be carried over the mountains for the discovery of the South Seas—though the makers of the atlases were rightly showing the distance from the Atlantic to the Pacific in this latitude as several thousand miles. The other was to provide a basin, an ewer, an expensive bed and an even more expensive crown with which, so it was directed, King Powhatan should formally be crowned emperor. And they had provided no food for this new supply of planters. The President evidently thought the whole thing a mistake. Powhatan too regarded the prospect of coronation with deep misgiving. But orders from

London were orders from London. The bed being large and cumbersome had to be sent by water nearly a hundred miles, the journey by land being twelve miles or so. But at last it arrived. At last, by leaning hard on Powhatan's shoulders, they had induced him to stoop for the actual imposition of the crown. At last Captain Newport had exhausted the possibilities of prospecting for mines in the neighbourhood, and at last he was gone with a trial cargo of pitch, tar, and other such things; and the plantation could sit back and take stock. With the new supply, they were two hundred souls including some women. But with increased numbers the perennial danger of famine seemed nearer than ever. And there were new problems. Powhatan decided that he must have a house to go round his bed. Dutch artificers were sent to build it. But there were disaffected elements in the new supply, and this association of some of them with the Indian ruler opened up the possibility, soon to become a certainty, of treachery. By Christmas supplies of corn were a vital necessity, and Captain Smith went off once more to secure them. This time the effort nearly cost his own life and the lives of those with him. But by prompt action disaster was averted, and Powhatan, who had hoped to make an end of them, was convinced that he had no option but to produce the needed corn. During the President's absence things had gone from bad to worse in the settlement, metal objects being stolen by the traitors inside it to pass on to the Indians; and Smith might well have despaired.

But now that the food supply was secure for the winter, it was possible to get down to work. Houses were built and repaired, a blockhouse built on the isthmus to protect the settlement, fresh ground was broken for cultivation, and a well was sunk within the settlement. At last the settlement was developing its own economy, with a rapidly multiplying herd of pigs and stock of poultry. The frightful mortality of previous winters was reduced, and a cargo prepared for the next supply. When it arrived it was just such a rabble as the last had been. All was to do again. But Captain John Smith was not to do it, for it was then that the accident took place which lacerated his side and determined him to return to England. A record of his achievement, which derives from him, is included in Purchas' account; the harvest newly gathered, ten weeks' provisions in store, four hundred and ninety persons in the colony, the language and towns of the Indians known and explored, equipment and clothing provided, pigs, hens, goats and some sheep reared. His departure threw everything into confusion. Supplies were wasted in a few months. There was no leadership; and when Somers and Gates, who had been wrecked on the Bermudas, arrived, it was decided to abandon the settlement. 'But yet God would not so have it.' As they sailed down the river, Lord de la Warr moved into Chesapeake Bay with three ships, splendidly equipped, to take up the Governorship, to which he had been appointed by the London authorities. The settlers returned to Jamestown with him, and on 9 June 1610 the colony was reborn.

Captain John Smith never went back to Virginia, though he did a great work for the colony by his advocacy in England for it. He was not a sentimentalist. But as he looked back over the solid achievements of his life in Virginia, there was a streak of sentiment that ran through the memory of those rough years; and from his books we know that his mind went back again and again to Pocahontas. 'It is true, she was the very nonparell of his Kingdome, and at most not past thirteene or fourteene yeeres of age. Very oft she came to our Fort, with what shee could get for Captaine Smith, that ever loved and used all the Countrey well, but her especially hee ever much respected: and shee so well requited it, that when her father intended to have surprized him she by stealth in the darke night came through the wild Woods and told him of it.' She too is part of the shared inheritance of the English-speaking nations. For she trod not only the wild woods of Virginia, but, for a few fleeting weeks, the streets of London and the steps of Whitehall Palace; and in England she died. And on that slender thread had hung, for a single moment, the fate of Ralegh's new 'English nation'.

Notes

CHAPTER I

1. This suggestion was originally made in *The Times Literary Supplement* (2 Nov. 1935) in an article by H .S. Jevons. Professor Chambers suggests to me, however, that the accounts of Vespucci's second voyage (in which he mentions people who had all things in common and who had abundance of gold but utterly despised it) may be the source from which these ideas in *Utopia* are derived. If he had heard something of Peru, More's knowledge of a country still undiscovered is one instance of a feature that recurs time after time in the history of exploration; rumours of the truth current before the first explorers have set out to uncover it. Reports of the midnight sun and of frozen seas were evidently widespread long before the voyage of Pytheas of Marseilles or the other known northern explorers of classical antiquity.

2. It hardly occurred to most people at this time to draw a distinguishing line between fact and fiction. Thus Malory's book of the life, death and acts of King Arthur (generally known as the *Morte D'Arthur*), which was finished in 1469, is pure fiction, partly invented by himself, partly based on romantic French sources. But I find it hard to imagine, in reading it, that he did not believe most of it. It is one mark of the new age that the distinction begins to be drawn, and Caxton, in his preface to Malory, mentions (to dismiss) the completely sceptical view that Arthur never existed.

3. It is almost certainly to be identified with Watling Island. Throughout this section on Columbus I have depended largely on Mr Cecil Jane's book. Like almost every other book about Columbus, however, it contains some theories which have not won universal acceptance.

4. Dr Williamson, discussing the accuracy of instruments in use at this time in his book *The Voyage of the Cabots*, says that 'they gave results which erred by not more than two or three degrees at the most'. The error here is considerably greater and may be intentional. A similar error, but still further exaggerated, occurs in a chart actually made by one of Columbus' pilots, Juan de la Cosa, and Dr Williamson regards it there as intentional; cf. *op. cit.* p. 195. We may assume that in the 'letter', as set adrift, this inaccuracy did not occur.

5. It still appears in the atlases of Mercator (died 1594) and Ortelius (died 1598). Hakluyt included the story in his *Principal Navigations* in 1600.

[The development of geographical knowledge from medieval to Renaissance times can be illustrated well from maps, though in very few printed books, perhaps in none, is an example of the TO map to be found. The title-page of the Introduction to Apian's *Cosmography* (Landshut, c. 1523) has such a diagram however in a Renaissance form, with Africa rounded and shaped. A number of printed books have diagrammatic maps of the world divided into five zones, as described on p. 4, the torrid zone being 'inhabitabilis': such maps are to be found, for example, in editions of Macrobius' commentary on the *Somnium Scipionis*, and in editions of Sacro Bosco, *de Sphaera*. The British Museum set of postcards of early maps has some fine examples of medieval as well as of Renaissance maps. Ptolemy's world map (specimens of which are there illustrated) was used in many books besides actual editions of Ptolemy, e.g. in issues of the famous *Nuremberg Chronicle*, in the 1490's: these almost all show the version in which, in southern latitudes, Eastern Asia joins Africa, to enclose a vast landlocked sea in place of the Indian Ocean. From the time of the great Lafieri Ptolemy, with engraved maps, onwards (published in Florence in the 1470's) successive editions of Ptolemy had modern maps in increasing numbers included in them, in addition to the Ptolemaic maps.]

CHAPTER II

1. Willoughby's recorded observations are scanty, but they nevertheless provide adequate data for establishing what point he reached. The furthest east he touched was on 14 August when land was sighted in latitude 72°: and they turned back not later than 21 August, probably two or three days earlier. The Harbour 'Arzina' where Willoughby died is marked by Ortelius, and by Antony Jenkinson in his map of Russia (1562), as near the mouth of the White Sea. He reached there first on 14 September. It looks therefore as if the land sighted in latitude 72° on 21 August must have been Nova Zemlya. The island marked by Mercator on his map of the Arctic regions as 'Sir Hugo Willoughbie's land' neither exists, nor, if it did exist, would it fit in with Willoughby's record. He evidently missed the entrance to the White Sea on the outward and on the homeward journey. The harbour must have been on the Murman coast, but precisely where it was is not apparent. I find that this identification with Nova Zemlya has been made before.

2. Clement Adams in Hakluyt.

[The Source for Chapter II has been almost exclusively Hakluyt. Mercator's map of the North Polar Regions, reproduced as Pl. III, is of the greatest value for a study of these voyages. Also of value, especially as showing the penetration inland which resulted, is Antony Jenkinson's map of Russia, which was published in Ortelius' Atlas, and which I have frequently consulted. Another important map in the same atlas is the *Septentrionalium Regionum Descriptio*, extending about ten degrees to the east of the White Sea opening: and another the map of Asia (*Asiae Nova Descriptio*) which gives a map-maker's impression of the theory that there might be waterways from China into Northern Waters.]

CHAPTER III

1. Hawkins' letter to Queen Elizabeth announcing the disappearance of the two Portuguese is dated 16 September. He actually sailed on 2 October. I find it difficult to believe that in that fortnight the whole character of the expedition's equipment had been altered. The letter is quoted in full in Williamson, *Sir John Hawkins*, pp. 137–8.

2. This is not mentioned in the English account printed by Williamson as an appendix to his *Sir John Hawkins* (unless the mention occurred, as it may have done, at the top of f. 35 b). It is stated, however, in the Spanish report to which Dr Williamson alludes in his *Age of Drake* and there seems no good reason for doubting it.

3. I can find no evidence to support Froude's picture of the 'town' on the mainland. According to one account, some Spanish sailors had been in 'ambush'

on the mainland and come across in long boats during the fight. But this is the only mention of the mainland I have been able to find. At least it is certain that all the ships, English and Spanish alike, were off the island, not off the mainland.

4. John Chilton's account in Hakluyt says two miles. I have an eighteenth-century chart of Vera Cruz, which may show fairly accurately what this coast was like a century and a half before. The distance given there (in the text) is four or five 'cables' (a cable = 120 fathoms). Two-thirds of a sea mile is the distance from shore to shore according to the scale. This chart is reproduced, Pl. V.

5. Not Hawkins himself (as Hartop says). He left the 'Jesus' much later in the fight, as Hartop's own account shows.

6. One account says ten o'clock.

7. This point has some importance as evidence that the English had been moored to the southward of the Spanish ships, for the prevailing wind was from the north.

[For all that concerns Hawkins, Dr Williamson's *Sir John Hawkins* is the leading authority. Besides the accounts in Hakluyt, I have used other material made available for the first time in Dr Williamson's book. The MS. chart reproduced is more detailed, though unfortunately damaged, than another eighteenth-century plan in *A Description of the Spanish Islands and Settlements on the Coast of the West Indies...chiefly from original Drawings taken from the Spaniards in the Last War and Engraved by Thomas Jeffreys, London*, 1762; which has, however, also been useful. I have not yet been able to see any earlier map of St Juan de Ulua than these.]

CHAPTER IV

1. He may have been the author of an account of the third voyage, written in the cabin of the 'Jesus' from time to time as it proceeded, an account which has been several times quoted above; cf. Williamson, *op. cit.* p. 144.

2. Not apparently £40,000 as Froude said, followed by Sir Julian Corbett (*Drake and the Tudor Navy*). Dr Williamson doubts whether any payment was made, but the Spanish evidence that he quotes suggests strongly that it was: that it was 40,000 ducats, and that it was simply a slip of the pen that led Froude into the mistake. Hawkins' letter is quoted from Williamson, *op. cit.*

[Details of the Intrigue involving Mary Queen of Scots in Leader's *Mary Queen of Scots in Captivity*, and Hosack's *Mary Queen of Scots and her Accusers*, both sympathetic to Mary. Quotations in this chapter and Chapter VI are mainly from documents cited by one of these two. Owing to the war, it has not been possible to check these quotations or to give the original spelling. The work quoted on p. 59 is *The Copie of a Letter sent out of England to Don Bernadin Mendoza*...Imprinted at London by I. Vautrollier, for Richard Field, 1588. This is mentioned in the Navy Records Society's *Armada Papers*, but not reprinted there.]

CHAPTER V

1. Quoted from Taylor, *Tudor Geography*, p. 116.

2. From Port St Julian to Cape Virgins is approximately three hundred miles. They left harbour on the 17th (about noon: so Edward Cliffe in Hakluyt) and were opposite the straits on the 20th.

3. Hakluyt, 1600 edition, Vol. III, p. 734; 'From the Bay which he called the bay of the severing of friends.' This bay has not been before mentioned in the text. Immediately before this paragraph the ships are far out in the Pacific Ocean. Something has dropped out which recorded the loss of the 'Marigold' perhaps; and the confusion of the passage is at least evidence of the unwillingness of those who knew to clear up doubtful points. On any other supposition, Hakluyt's failure to publish a good account of the voyage is very hard to explain.

It is interesting to note that the story set about for the Spaniards' benefit was that Drake had spent two months ashore, refitting, in these islands; see Lopez Vaz in Hakluyt, p. 790.

4. A slightly different version from another source is given in Sir Richard Temple's edition of the *World Encompassed*, p. 225. The version in the text is from Hakluyt, *Relation of a voyage made by Nuno de Silva*.

5. Nuno de Silva says this was a device to increase speed, the ship being down by the bows. It is difficult to believe that he is right. Corbett's *Drake* gives a reference to Laughton in the *Dictionary of National Biography*; who suggests that the mistake is due to mistranslation.

[Hakluyt contains no adequate account of either of the voyages treated in this chapter. For the first an account which goes back ultimately to Drake himself was reprinted by Arber, and I have used this extensively. Its credibility is now generally accepted, having been questioned by Froude. For the voyage of circumnavigation, Sir Richard Temple's edition of the *World Encompassed* is indispensable, with its reprints of associated documents. The best West Indian maps to which I have had access are those mentioned in the note to Chapter III. World maps at this period are too large a subject to summarise. But for the Southern Continent cf. Wytfliet, *Descriptionis Ptolemaicae Augmentum*, Louvain, 1598, which has a fine map of the Southern continent and does not know of Cape Horn: cf. also Ortelius' maps for this. Some English maps about 1600 (e.g. the famous 'Molyneux' world map) recognise Drake's discovery of this Cape. A world map that shows satisfactorily Drake's idea of a route back to the Atlantic north of America is in the Basle Ptolemy of 1552. The Mercator world map which shows the imaginary location of Beach or Locach (see p. 71) was included in an edition of Strabo published in 1569. Ortelius' map of the East Indies shows well how Drake expected to find his way through to the South of Celebes. Ortelius knew nothing of the Gulf of Tomini into which Drake found he had sailed.]

CHAPTER VI

1. Shortened from the full text, given in Hakluyt. Here as elsewhere it must be remembered that Hakluyt 'edited' his material to some extent, without indicating the fact as a modern editor would do.

2. Compare for example the letter mentioned on p. 54 above, or one quoted by Froude, *English Seamen in the Sixteenth Century*, Chapter v.

3. Another instance is her decision, a decision which was purely and absolutely hers, not to marry Leicester.

4. Cf. the writer in *Bibl. Reg.* 7, c. xvl, a soldier who was on the 'Primrose'. Corbett says 1000, following Hakluyt's account, also by one of the soldiers of the expedition.

5. Not coronation, as the writer of the narrative in Hakluyt says, followed by Corbett. The Queen was crowned not in November, but in January.

6. Camden says that the letters were 'put in privily, and others received, through an hole in the wall, which was stopped with a loose stone'. He did not, however, have access, as we have, to Walsingham's correspondence. For the sections about Mary in this chapter, cf. the authorities quoted above for Chapter IV. They are the immediate sources of quotations.

7. *State Papers Domestic*, ccxiii, 28.

8. Marked 'S' on the plan reproduced (Pl. IX). No shoal is shown in this position by Borough. If this is where the 'Edward Bonaventure' went aground on the way to help him, he must presumably have been yet further out.

9. Borough in writing to the Lord Admiral a month later says 'we landed' at Lagos, but 'men were landed' at Sagres. It is possible that one phrase unconsciously indicates approval, the other not.

[The main quarry for this chapter has been the Navy Records Society's publication, *The Spanish War*, 1585–87, supplemented by Hakluyt. For sketch-maps of the greatest value (reproduced in Corbett's *Drake*), see the *Summarie and True Discourse of Sir Francis Drake's West Indian Voyage*. A comparison of the plan of Carthagena with later plans and charts (there were several published in England in 1741 to commemorate the attack on Carthagena then made) brings out some interesting facts about the origin of the *Summarie*. Drake does not appear, from what is said in the narratives, to have had detailed charts available when the attack was made. The engraved plan printed in the *Summarie* was evidently drawn only from a sketch, which gave a fairly adequate idea of the promontory stretching southwards and eastwards from Carthagena city, cutting off the outer from the inner harbour, and the outer harbour from the sea. This latter promontory was where the landing was made. The plan's notions of the eastern side of the harbour and of the environs of the city to east and north are misleading, and do not indicate that the city was impregnable in that direction, with water and marsh almost all round it eastwards and northwards except for the actual foreshore. The orientation of the plan is some 70° out of the true. It agrees with that of the narrative in the *Discourse*, but not with the facts. This plan is reproduced as Pl. VIII.

The plans in the *Summarie and True Discourse* are so well executed as engravings that a false idea of their accuracy may easily be suggested. They must be regarded in the light of sketch-maps, drawn not on the ground, but after the return to England, very useful to give a general notion of the attacks by land and indeed a valuable source of information about these attacks, but not necessarily trustworthy in the representation given of the lie of the land or of any individual details. There is very little attempt at scale drawing.]

CHAPTER VII

[The main source for this chapter is Hakluyt, and I have tried to harmonise as far as possible the accounts he gives. He reprints Hariot—without the illustrations or maps which are such an important part of the original. Ralegh's letter to Gilbert is quoted from Edward Thompson's *Sir Walter Ralegh*. The maps in Hariot's account were probably drawn by Hariot himself after White's sketches.]

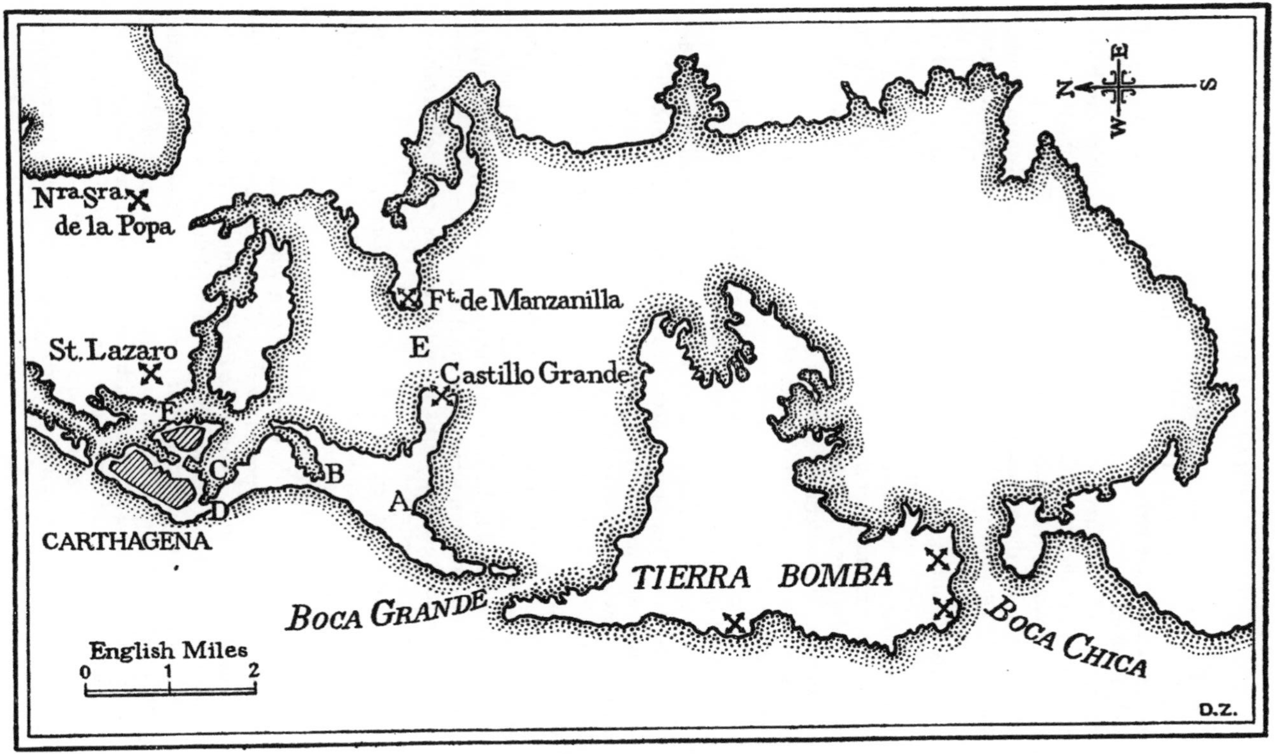

PLAN OF CARTHAGENA
for comparison with Plate VIII

CHAPTER VIII

1. Of the Royal Navy, there were twenty-six ships in the main fleet, ranging in size from Frobisher's ship the 'Triumph', to small pinnaces. Sixteen were of 250 tons or upwards. There were also eight or ten more ships built as ships of war but privately manned.

The effectiveness of these navy vessels and ships built as warships can be well shown by an analysis of the 'mentions in despatches' in Howard's official narrative. There are, on my reckoning, fifty such mentions. Only nine of these do not refer to ships of the navy. Of these nine, two 'mentions', both of Captain Fleming's ship, do not refer to fighting. The 'Delight', which is mentioned, though privately owned—she belonged to Wynter—may have been built for fighting. Three mentions go to Levanters, the 'Merchant Royal', the 'Centurion' and the 'Margaret and John', which, though merchant ships, were specially designed to give a good account of themselves in fighting. The 'Galleon Leicester' was evidently adapted for fighting, for she had been chosen to go on the West Indies' expedition. The 'Mayflower of London', mentioned for very valiant fighting, was a merchantman. That practically exhausts the list.

Though possibly an even smaller number of Spanish ships that fought in the Channel (disregarding, that is, the ten galleys which turned back) were built as war ships, they had been extensively fitted out as such and were included in a more elaborate squadronal organisation.

2. Sir Julian Corbett says that the crescent notion was started by Camden, writing fifteen years later. The Spanish fleet 'in a proportion of a half moon' is in fact mentioned in a letter written by Wynter to Walsingham on 1 August 1588. The formation is shown in the Adams chart drawn up within a year, and the first of the Howard tapestries, which must at least have been approved by Howard himself as plausible representations, shows this crescent formation. Incidentally the tapestries regularly show the position of the 'Ark Royal', Howard's flagship, by showing her flag, the Tudor Royal Standard. This detail would in itself suggest that the Lord Admiral had a hand in their planning. It may be noted that in the one incident in the campaign which does the Admiral little credit, his turning aside to attack the stranded galley at Calais, Howard's colours are not clearly shown in the engraving of the tapestry.

3. For Philip's instructions, cf. Sir Julian Corbett, *Drake*, Vol. II, p. 195. Contrast Laughton, *Defeat of Spanish Armada*, Vol. I, pp. xxxv–vi. Philip's plans were constantly changing.

4. The Adams chart shows all four of the English admirals being towed to the attack, led by Howard, who is on the starboard wing where Recalde's ship (with his flag) is shown in tow, and supported by the galleasses. Apart from Frobisher at the end of the port squadron, I count six English ships in all in tow. In the account given, it is assumed that this was the first phase of the action only: that the line of fire did not run north and south, but north-east and south-west, with the English trying to cover the Isle of Wight: and that in the latter part of the action, when the wind had risen, Drake's attack with the 'Nonpareil' and 'Mary Rose' was delivered in a north-easterly direction towards the Owers. The chief indications of this phase are in Spanish accounts, quoted by Corbett.

5. Sir Julian Corbett writes as if it were completely disorganised throughout

the day's fighting. This seems to me contrary to the evidence. For the beginning of the battle we have the testimony of the Adams chart, made in the following year. It shows the English fleet in no formation whatever, but the Armada in its usual excellent formation. It was this that prevented the actual losses of Spanish ships from being far higher in the course of the battle. For a probable testimony to this in the documents, cf. Wynter to Walsingham (in Laughton, *Spanish Armada*, Navy Records Society, Vol. II, pp. 10, 11): 'The fight continued from 9 of the clock until six of the clock at night, in the which time the Spanish army bare away NNE and N by E, as much as they could keeping company with one another. I assure your Lordship in very good order'—though the phrase may be sarcastic.

[For this chapter I used extensively the Armada papers published by the Navy Records Society, and Sir Julian Corbett's account in his *Sir Francis Drake*. Corbett reproduces John Adams' ten charts of the action against the Armada which were engraved for the *Expeditionis Hispanorum in Angliam vera descriptio* and are a contemporary authority. The text, and the above notes, show that I have used these charts for many details. About the turn of the century, tapestries were made, to Howard's order, which afterwards hung in the House of Lords (these were burnt in the disastrous fire in the nineteenth century). They are believed to have been designed by Cornelius Vroom. I have assumed that the designer was in touch with Howard and that it is fair to use the tapestries (which were fortunately finely engraved in 1739 by John Pine, and the designs of which have therefore survived) as corroborative evidence of Howard's impressions of the action. The 'Revenge' tapestry, reproduced as Pl. XII, gives an impression of what the tapestries must have looked like, though the border of the Armada Tapestries, uniform throughout, was more formal and it does not look as if they necessarily came from the same workshop.]

CHAPTER IX

1. 'Thule'—Iceland. 'The period of Cosmographie'—the full stop or furthest point of geographical knowledge.

2. The Royal Gold Cup in the British Museum. On Gondomar's death it passed into the possession of a Spanish convent, but came on the market nearly three hundred years later, and was brought back to England.

3. It is sometimes stated (e.g. in the *Dictionary of National Biography*, art. White) that Smith's map of Virginia is based on White's. Actually this is not so. The two maps cover entirely different areas.

[For Chapter IX I have used Professor Harlow's book, *Ralegh's Last Voyage*, in which the documents are reprinted; and for what I have written about Ralegh as a whole I am greatly indebted to his two introductions to the Ralegh books in that series. Some quotations have been borrowed from those introductions. Mr Edward Thompson's book has also been used, and Lady Ralegh's letter is quoted from that source. Ralph Fitch's journey is narrated in Hakluyt.

For Captain John Smith I have used almost exclusively the 1626 edition of Purchas, which includes the Map of Virginia (or rather of the Chesapeake region) drawn by Smith.]

INDEX

I. NAMES OF SHIPS

* Howard's 'White Lion', a smaller ship, is not mentioned in the text, but 'Lion' in the original documents often refers to her. She took part in the 1585 West Indies' voyage, the expedition to Cadiz of 1587, and the Armada fighting.

† Different ships having the same name.

II. GENERAL INDEX

CAMBRIDGE: PRINTED BY W. LEWIS, M.A., AT THE UNIVERSITY PRESS

For EU product safety concerns, contact us at Calle de José Abascal, 56–1°, 28003 Madrid, Spain or eugpsr@cambridge.org.

www.ingramcontent.com/pod-product-compliance
Ingram Content Group UK Ltd.
Pitfield, Milton Keynes, MK11 3LW, UK
UKHW010338140625
459647UK00010B/673

* 9 7 8 1 1 0 8 0 1 3 4 2 0 *